THE ILLUSTRATED DIRECTORY OF
MUSCLE CARS

**CHARTWELL
BOOKS, INC.**

Copyright © 2013 Pepperbox Press Ltd.

This edition published in 2013 by CHARTWELL BOOKS, INC.
A division of BOOK SALES, INC.
276 Fifth Avenue Suite 206
New York, New York 10001
USA

ISBN-13 978-0-7858-3030-6

Printed in China

Contents

Introduction

The American muscle car legend dates back to the 1940s, but the term itself only came into use in the early 1970s, just as the first generation of high-powered haulers were fading from the automotive scene. Some people say that General Motors launched the first muscle car engine, its overhead-valve V-8 of 1949. This would make the Oldsmobile Rocket 88 the first muscle car. It certainly was the essence of American muscle, a huge V-8 in a mid-sized body. Others give this honor to Chrysler's 300 Letter Series cars of 1955 or the Chevrolet Corvette of 1955. Production models became increasingly powerful as the 1950s wore on with the development of fuel-injection and supercharging. The muscle cars of these years were mostly developed in independent garages, but by the 1960s the automotive giants were adding their own beasts to the stable. By 1962 all of the main automakers were selling affordable muscle cars to the American public. At the beginning, these massive-engined monsters were a handful, but the manufacturers gradually refined their muscle cars into useable commuter cars.

By definition, a muscle car is a high-performance auto which combines power with excellent stopping and handling. This

▼ The Oldsmobile Rocket 88 of 1949 exemplified the muscle car formula of a huge V-8 in a mid-sized car body.

▶ America's Sports Car debuted in 1955. It was equipped with Ed Cole's V-8 powertrain.

heady cocktail resulted in some of the most iconic cars to come out of Detroit. Their monikers are legendary: the Boss Mustang, the Z/28 Camaro, the Trans Am Firebird, the 427 Ford, the Oldsmobile 4-2-2, the Road Runner, the Torino Cobra, the Hemi 'Cuda,

▲ A 1978 Camaro Z/28. The Camaro was launched in 1967 to compete for the Mustang market.

◀ Ford's Mustang debuted in 1964 inspired the "ponycar" tag. The car sold over one million units during its first eighteen months on the market.

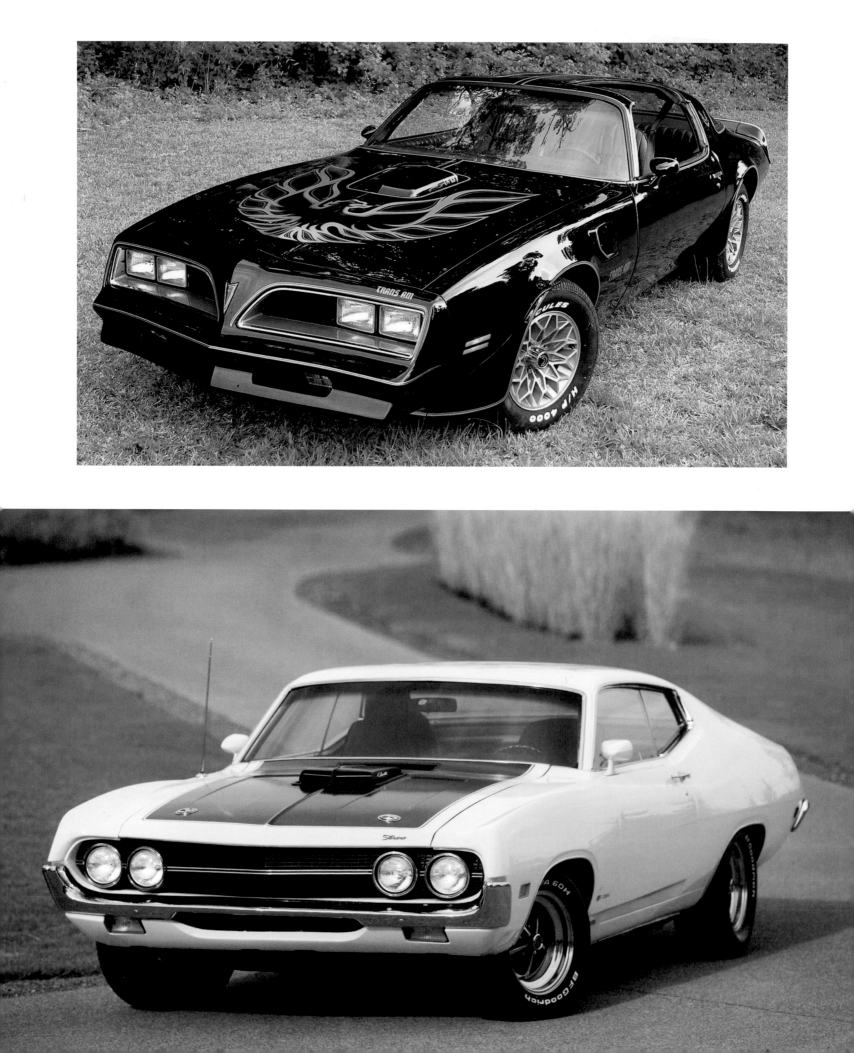

◀ The second generation of Pontiac's Firebird Trans Ams debuted in 1970. The car was fitted with the legendary 455, the biggest engine of the original muscle car era.

the SS 396 Chevelle, Buick's Gran Sport, and the Pontiac GTO. Each of these extraordinary cars was a milestone in muscle car development. The smaller ponycars of the sixties were also spawned by the American love of performance. The Mustang, Cougar, Camaro, 'Cuda, and Javelin brought muscle to the masses.

Muscle cars had a hugely beneficial effect on the entire American auto industry. Not only did these factory hot rods spawn many innovations and refinements (and continue to do so), but they also raised the profile of the domestic American motor car industry around the world. The development of the muscle car also generated positive competition between the major manufacturers that resulted in the magnificent machines of the 1970s.

Chevrolet's LS-6 454, the highest-rated ever engine at the time, was launched in 1970. Many muscle aficionados consider this powertrain to be the zenith of muscle car

◀ This Ford Torino Cobra 429 SCJ dates from 1970.

▲ A 1972 Plymouth Road Runner in vibrant Lemon Twist Yellow.

▲ This SS 396 Chevelle from 1969 is finished in Tuxedo Black with white SS stripes and a cordova top. The all-black interior is fitted with bucket seats.

◄ A red Pontiac GTO from 2006, fitted with 19-inch chrome-finished Foose Speed wheels.

power. The engine initiated ferocious competition between the other American car makers to produce their own red-hot powerhouses. This rivalry resulted in Buick's Stage 1 455, Chrysler's Hemi, Ford's 429 Cobra Jet, and Oldsmobile's W-30 4-4-2.

The fuel crisis of the early 1970s and Washington's emission control measures effectively killed off the first generation of American muscle. Pontiac's 1973 455 Super Duty Firebird was hot but looked old-fashioned in these more Puritan times. Only vintage muscle pounded the streets for the next fifteen years or so, but a new wave of modern muscle appeared in the late 1980s. These cars were even more powerful than their muscle ancestors, but they were leaner and meaner machines that handled and stopped better than their predecessors, were more practical and (thanks to electronic fuel delivery systems) much less thirsty. These engine-managed monsters are just as much fun to drive as the earlier cars, but much less scary. Heritage model names and letters have also made a welcome return to America's auto showrooms including GTO, Charger, Challenger, Z06, LS6, Mustang GT, Corvette, CTS, and Impala SS.

▲ A Buick Gran Sport 455 from Stage 1 from 1970. The car was equipped with GM's 400Cu V-8.

1933 Ford Deluxe Model 40-720 Coupe

Ford's first V-8 was introduced in 1932, the famous cast-iron flathead first
delivered 65 horsepower from 221-cid. The new V-8 was a great bargain
and had a top speed of 78 mph from 75 horsepower and caused a storm
of interest. Millions were drawn to its March unveiling but it was launched
too quickly for the engineers and without an ideal engine-testing program
because of the need to get the V-8 into the market as quickly as possible.
There were durability problems, such as cylinder head cracks and a rapid oil
burn off. In some cars, the engine mounts worked loose and ignition
problems came to light. Ford ended up having to replace thousands of
these, and the engine problems were reflected in lower sales for the year.
But Ford didn't allow themselves to be deflected by these teething
difficulties. They were soon resolved, and the V-8 gained a reputation as a
solid power unit that could that could withstand a considerable assault
from being driven hard and fast. Everything was sweet by 1933. The
generic Detroit style now consisted of streamlined models. Edsel Ford was
now the force behind the company's design, and came up with a balanced
new look for the 1933 Ford line-up that was very well received. The hood
extended back to the windshield and the sharp corner on the fender was
rounded off. The V-8 durability kept improving and the line was now

Engine:	eight-cylinder
Displacement:	221 cid
Horsepower:	75
Transmission:	Sliding gear
Compression Ratio:	6.3:1
Induction:	Mechanical, Detroit Lubricator Downdraft, single-barrel carburetor
Weight:	2538 lbs
Wheelbase:	112 inches
Base Price:	$540
Number produced:	15,894

1933 Ford Deluxe Model 40-720 Coupe

named the model 40. The speedy new V-8 was attracting many new enthusiasts, amongst them Public Enemy Number One, John Dillinger. Dillinger actually had the cheek to write to Henry Ford, praising the new engine.

The '33 wheelbase was 112 inches, now increased from the short 106.5-inch version. All models were delivered with black fenders and 17-inch wire spoke wheels. With

▲ With its small body and big V-8, some people consider the Ford Deluxe 40-720 to be the first muscle car.

improved reliability and aluminum cylinder heads, the engine now delivered a performance comparable with the detailing of the interior, which featured a new dash arrangement with the gauges arranged directly in front of the driver. Ford was finally getting in tune with its customers.

1950 Oldsmobile 'Rocket' Deluxe Holiday 88

Oldsmobile has the longest heritage of any U. S. auto manufacturer, its handbuilt, wooden carriage-style vehicles having arrived on America's roads in 1897. This Lansing, Michigan based division of General Motors was successful right from the start, and its Curved Dash was the most popular car manufactured in the US in the early part of the twentieth century. In the '50s, Olds was benefiting from the 'Futuramic' restyling of 1949 and technological advances of the '40s. The latter included Hydra-Matic transmission (the first version of which was actually introduced back in 1940) and the new highcompression overhead valve Rocket V-8 under the hood (first offered in '49).

This engine continued to roar around the racetracks in 1950, winning 10 out of 19 major NASCAR stock car races, handing the championship to driver Bill Rexford. Fitted to a Rocket 88, the engine broke a class speed record at Daytona, averaging 100.28 miles per hour, developing 263 lbs of torque per foot at 1800 rpm.

These assets contributed to Oldsmobile's sixth position in the league of motor manufacturing output for the year, of 408,060 cars. This was achieved under the management of General Manager S. E. Skinner.

The 88 series was Oldsmobile's mid-range line-up, with a total of seven body styles available. The 88 Holiday was introduced as a new hardtop body style to the junior series, and accounted for part of Oldsmobile's 8% share of the US hardtop market. Deluxe and standard trim versions were available.

The series was now in its second year, and continued to be one of the hottest performing ranges available. One-piece windscreens were added to the range in the middle of the year, as exemplified in our photographed car. The less expensive 76 series would be discontinued in 1951, and the 88 would become the standard Olds. The top-of-the-range 98 series was Olds first slab-sided car, and was larger and more luxurious, but less performance orientated than the slightly smaller 88s. Both series had the 'Rocket' V-8 engine, but the 98 had nearly 250 lbs more to haul, and a seven-inch longer chassis to move.

Engine:	Overhead valve vee-block,cast iron block
Displacement:	303.7 cid
Horsepower:	135 at 3600 rpm
Compression Ratio:	7.25:1
Number of Seats:	5
Weight:	3535lbs
Wheelbase:	119-1/2 inches
Base Price:	$2035
Number Produced:	12,682

▲ Many consider the 1950 'Rocket' 88 to be America's first post-war muscle car.

1952 Lincoln Capri Convertible

Like virtually every other US car manufacturer, Lincoln entered the post-war years by re-offering their pre-war models. However, they were still fantastically luxurious up-market cars and even in 1946, the top-of-the-range Continental model was selling for a staggering $4474.

But in 1952, Ford was the only one of the 'big three' car manufacturers to instigate a complete re-design of its entire model range, and Lincoln was a beneficiary of the 'All new for '52' look. For the first time at FoMoCo, both Lincoln and Mercury offered true pillarless hardtop models in their respective ranges. At Lincoln, this was the Capri two-door hardtop model. In fact, the entire '52 range shared the Ford corporate styling, and had a lean racy look.

The bumper and grille were integrated in the car bodies instead of being recessed. All the new Lincolns were fitted with Ford's first modern overhead valve, 5.2 litre V-8s. Hydra-Matic auto transmission was fitted as standard, and Ford is reputed to have fitted the first ball-joint front suspension to these Capri models. Their reputation for performance was reflected in the racing successes of the marque. Lincolns took first, second, third and fourth positions in the 1952 Pan American 2,000 mile Road Race in Mexico (although '53 cars were used). A 'maximum duty kit' was available as an optional extra for owners who wished to race their own cars. The watchword of the Lincoln range was that they were fine cars with outstanding performance. But although Lincoln was to retain its reputation for luxury and comfort, the Chrysler 300 letter cars were about to steal it's racing crown.

The 'Capri' badge was first used in 1950 as a limited edition version of a Continental, but became a product line in its own right as the new top Lincoln series for '52. The cars were well appointed, featuring fabric and leather upholstery. The gas tank filler was hidden behind the rear licence plate. The line remained virtually unchanged for a further three models years, until the heavy re-style of 1956. Cosmopolitan was the base line model for '52, though this being Lincoln, the cars were very well equipped and sold for well over $3,000.

Engine:	Overhead valve V-8, cast iron block
Displacement:	317.5 cid
Horsepower:	160 at 3900 rpm
Transmission:	Hydra-Matic automatic
Compression Ratio:	7.5:1
Number of Seats:	6
Weight:	4350 lbs
Base Price:	$3665
Number Produced:	1,191

▲   The Lincoln Capri Convertible was equipped with a huge 5.2 liter V-8 in a small two-door car – a classic muscle car configuration.

1955 Chevrolet Bel Air

In economic terms, 1955 was a boom year. It saw the opening of the first McDonald's drive-in restaurant and Disneyland California. Rock and Roll was now in its infancy, and Bill Haley and the Comets topped the charts with 'Rock Around the Clock'. The automotive industry experienced a record production year - 7,920,186 units being churned out by Detroit. Chevrolet was still outperforming Ford by over a quarter of a million cars, selling over 1.7 million with the advertising slogan 'The Hot One!' The average car now cost $2,300, with average pay running at $3851 per annum, so instalment buying is becoming more and more common for the average family.

The Chevy cars of '55 are some of the most popular restoration projects in the world – the combination of great 'fifties styling and the superb new V-8 engine. They were difficult to improve upon.

Engine:	V-8 overhead valve, cast iron block
Displacement:	265 cid
Horsepower:	162 at 4400 rpm
Transmission:	three-speed manual with column mounted gearshift standard, over-drive available as an option. Power-glide two-speed automatic transmission available as an option at $178 extra, optional V-8 'power-pack' also available with dual ex-haust
Compression:	8.0:1
Induction:	Rochester two-barrel carburetor two-barrel Model 7008006
Number of Seats:	5
Wheelbase Length:	115 inches
Price:	$2305
Number Produced:	(V-8 and 6-cylinder Convertibles) 41,292

The Bel Air was the company's top series, and standard equipment was generous and interiors comfortable and stylish. The exterior styling was also sharpened up, and the chrome accents were far more subtle. But the most important change by far was the introduction of the V-8 engine to the series. Although all the models in the Bel Air range were still available in the six-cylinder engine type, the V-8 was so fundamental a change that It was classed as a separate series rather than an option. In fact, this remained the case for at least some of the model shapes until the Bel Airs were eventually phased out.

▲ With its massive engine, the 1955 Chevrolet Bel Air was launched as "The Hot One."

1955 Chevrolet Corvette Roadster

Engine:	(Most popular for this model year) V-
8 Overhead valve.	Cast iron block
Displacement:	265 cid
Horsepower:	195 at 6000 rpm
Compression:	8.0:1
Body Style:	Two-door convertible roadster
Weight:	2705 lbs
Price:	$2934
Number Produced:	700

Car sales for the decade peaked in 1955 with record-breaking sales of seven-million plus. The frantic GM/Ford price war of 1953-54 had resulted in the mortal wounding of several surviving independent manufacturers, and the market was polarising in the hands of the three great companies – GM, Ford and Chevrolet. Throughout these years, Detroit was in a 'horse-power race' to rival the technological Cold War between the East and West.

At Corvette, the big news for 1955 was the introduction of the V-8 engine in nearly all of the cars produced in that year. An enlarged golden 'V' embellishing the Chevrolet logo on the front fender was a quick way to identify cars fitted with the new engine, and a 12-volt electrical system. The earlier cars had had a six-cylinder engine and six-volt electrical system. In this transitional period, Chevrolet used three engine number suffixes to denote the three types of car available - YG for the six-cylinder engines, FG for V-8 and automatic transmission models and GR for V-8 cars with manual transmissions. Ironically, although the six-cylinder engine was offered as standard, with the V-8 as an extra (costing $135), only six non V-8s were sold.

The V-8 'Vettes could go from 0-100 miles per hour in 24.7 seconds.

The car retained its original styling for '55, and the distinctive Corvette grille was now established as an identification trademark of the car's design – the thirteen chrome 'teeth' were originally designed to carry the Chevrolet family identity. The very first '53 models had had only three, which had led to concerns that the fibreglass bodywork was unprotected against parking knocks.

Various (rather basic) options were available for the car at extra cost – signal seeking AM radio at $145.15, windshield washer at $11.85, heater at $91.40 and parking brake alarm at $5.65.

However, the continuing low volume of sales – just 700 for 1955 meant that, yet again, Chevrolet came close to dropping the model from the range.

So ironic, in view of its continuing success to this day, when so many better selling contemporary cars are remembered only in the archives.

◀ '55 Corvettes were available in a range of colours including Gypsy Red with a beige top.

1955 Chrysler C-300 Coupe

Don't laugh, but this big beautiful luxury cruiser just may have been America's first muscle car. Born almost 10 years before Pontiac introduced its GTO, the first of Chrysler's famed "letter-cars" appeared in January 1955 and instantly wowed the world with it fabulous combination of serious speed and posh prestige.

Styling chief Virgil Exner had already spent a hundred million bucks remaking the corporation's 1955 models when chief engineer Robert MacGregor Rodger came up with the letter-car idea. Exner liked Rodger's idea, as did Chrysler division manager Ed Quinn, who gave the go-ahead as long as costs were kept down. The buck was then passed on to Cliff Voss, head of the Chrysler Imperial design studio, who, along with Rodger and production chief Tom Piorier, managed to pull off the feat in classic fashion.

Combining some lavish Imperial features with the hot 331 cubic-inch "hemi" V-8, Chrysler's first letter car was named for its output rating of 300 horsepower. Officially the car was labeled the "C-300," undoubtedly in honor of Briggs Cunningham's various hemi-powered LeMans racers of

Wheelbase:	126 inches
Weight:	4,005 pounds
Base price:	$4,360
Engine:	300-horsepower 331-cid Firepower "Hemi" OHV V-8
Induction:	two Carter four-barrel carburetors
Transmission:	two-speed Powerflite automatic
Suspension:	independent A-arms w/coil springs in front, live axle with leaf springs in back
Brakes:	four-wheel hydraulic drums
Performance:	0-60 in 9.5 seconds, quarter-mile in 17.6 seconds at 82 mph
Production:	1,725, including exports.

1951-54, all of which were identified by an appropriate "C" prefix. When a second letter-series Chrysler showed up in 1956 it was tagged the "300B," and thus began a progression that followed in alphabetical order for each year to follow. With the exception of omitting the letter "I," supposedly to avoid confusion with the Roman numeral "I," Chrysler's letter car legacy carried on through 11 model runs, ending in 1965 with the 300L.

Based on a New Yorker hardtop bodyshell, the 1955 C-300 mounted an attractive egg-crate Imperial grille and understated Windsor bodyside trim. Inside was a padded dashboard, a 150-mph speedometer, and tan leather appointments. Rodger's contribution was the 300-horse hemi with its twin Carter four-barrel carbs, high-lift cam, solid lifters, 8.5:1 compression and dual low-restriction exhausts.

Built as "a sports touring car designed to bring Chrysler the benefit of a high-performance reputation," the C-300 did not disappoint. Even as big and heavy as it was, it could still run almost as fast as Chevrolet's new V-8 Corvette. According to Mechanix Illustrated scribe Tom McCahill, the '55 C-300 was "the most powerful sedan in the world, and the fastest, teamed up with rock-crushing suspension and a competition engine capable

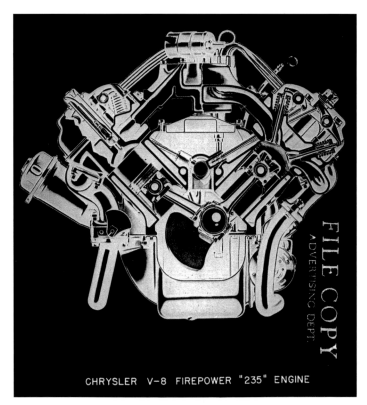

CHRYSLER V-8 FIREPOWER "235" ENGINE

▲ Chrysler's C-300 established all-new precedents for performance and prestige.

◄ In 1954, the Firepower hemi V-8 produced 235 horsepower, 55 ponies more than it had delivered when introduced in 1951.

of yanking Bob Fulton's steamboat over the George Washington Bridge." With that established, McCahill continued on, explaining that "this is definitely not the car for Henrietta Blushbottom, your maiden schoolmarm aunt, to use for hustling up popsicles. This is a hard-boiled, magnificent piece of semi-competition transportation, built for the real automotive connoisseur."

Semi-competition? Chrysler's first 300 went right to the track with ease, first setting a flying-mile speed record of 127.58 mph on the beach at Daytona. Next came complete domination of NASCAR and AAA stock-car racing in 1955 thanks to the factory-sponsored efforts of Carl Kiekhaefer's Mercury Outboards racing team. On the NASCAR circuit, Tim Flock won 13 consecutive Grand National races at the wheel of his Kiekhaefer 300 on the way to copping the season title.

▶ A 150-mph speedometer was standard.

▼ Tim Flock's C-300 in action on Daytona's old beach/road course. Flock and his Chrysler were runaway NASCAR champs in 1955.

▼ Chrysler's first "letter-car" took its name (left) from its output rating: 300 horsepower

MILESTONE FACTS

- The "C" in "C-300" probably was an honorary reference to legendary international racer Briggs Cunningham, who had used Chrysler hemi-head V-8s in various competition cars during the early Fifties.

- The name "300" came from the car's unprecedented power output. Save for a few very rare, very expensive Duesenberg's built before World War II, the '55 C-300 was America's first car to come standard with 300 horsepower.

- Chrysler's letter-series models were built for 11 years. Following the C-300 of 1955 came the 300B in 1956, the 300C in 1957, the 300D in 1958, and so on up to the 300L in 1965.

- The letter "I" was skipped in 1964 to avoid confusion with the Roman numeral "I."

- All Chrysler 300 models built in 1955 were two-door coupes fitted with Powerflite automatic transmissions; a convertible version was introduced in 1957.

- Only three color choices were available for the C-300 in 1955: Tango Red, Chrysler Platinum White and black.

- Power brakes, leather upholstery, a custom steering wheel and full wheelcovers were standard. Dazzling wire wheels and power steering were optional, as was a power seat.

▲ Flashy deluxe wheelcovers were standard on the C-300. Dazzling wire wheels were optional.

▶ Unique door handles represented just one of many elegant touches on the car later called the "beautiful brute."

Another Kiefhaefer Chrysler, driven by Frank Mundy, won the AAA crown. In all, Chrysler 300s won 37 stock car races in 1955. Another 22 NASCAR wins followed for the 300B in 1956 as Buck Baker's Kiekhaefer Chrysler took the championship. The dominating Kiefkhaefer team was then broken up in December 1956.

Chrysler's beautiful brute kept on rolling strong even after it retired from racing. After becoming America's first car to offer more than one horsepower per cubic inch (by way of the optional 355-horse 354 hemi) in 1956, the 300 remained among Detroit's most powerful offerings. Optional output in 1957 hit 390 horsepower; it reached the 400 mark in 1960. But with the Sixties came the modern muscle car wave, led by the GTO. The 300 letter cars became dinosaurs once speed-sensitive Americans began flocking to this new breed of mid-sized performance machines. Although sales were brisk for the 300K and 300L in 1964 and '65, the decision was still made to honorably end the legacy on a high note before the handwriting on the wall became any more obvious.

By then, Chrysler officials already knew that most American would soon be forgetting which car truly originated the muscle car craze. No, baby-boomers, it wasn't the GTO.

▼ Chrysler 300 tailfins were modest in 1955. They would soar in 1957.

1956 DeSoto FireFlite Two-door Convertible

In a year when general manufacturing production was eased, DeSoto moved up to number 11 in the output league table, but the company's sales fell yet again to 109,442 cars. A refined Fireflite convertible was introduced to the market in 1956. To re-inforce the more widespread use of the V- 8, the new perforated mesh grille with a large central 'V' dominating the front aspect of the car.

The taillight clusters were redesigned, but color sweep two-tone remained a feature (although the shape of the panels was redesigned). The headlamps still had chrome plated headlamp hoods.

Mechanically, all Fireflite models were now fitted with PowerFlite automatic transmission as standard. This was now controlled by push-button gear selection.

On January 11 1956, DeSoto announced that a Fireflite convertible with heavy-duty underpinnings, but standard engine, would act as a pace car at the Indianapolis 500 and that a limited 'Pacesetter' convertible would be available to the public. These cars had the same special features and a heavy complement of power accessories but were not lettered like the authentic pace car shown in the photograph.

The gold and white trim of this limited edition car was commemorated in the slightly later 'Adventurer', an exclusive sub-series of the Fireflite range launched to compete with the Chrysler 300-B, Dodge D-500 and Plymouth Fury. The convertible pace car carried a premium of $110 over the regular convertible model in the Fireflite range, but no separate production total was released.

▶ The 1956 DeSoto FireFlite was used as the pace car at the Indianapolis 500 race of May 30, 1956. The car was equipped with a 330cu V-8 engine.

Engine:	V-8 overhead valve, cast iron block
Displacement:	330.4 cid
Horsepower:	255 at 4400 rpm
Compression	Ratio: 8.5:1
Weight:	4070 lbs
Wheelbase:	126 inches
Base Price:	$3565
Nos. Produced (All Fireflite Convertibles)	: 1485

1956 Dodge D-500 V-8 Two-door Custom Royal/Lancer Hardtop

Dodge began a major restyling project in 1956, with back fenders sprouting fins, and technologically, a push-button PowerFlite automatic transmission was introduced to both Dodge and Chrysler models. The D-500 model was launched as a flag-waving performance car for the Royal range.

But the re-style did nothing to improve sales, which actually tumbled by 22.4% to just over 200,000 units, and gave the company a market share of exactly 3.7%. M.C. Patterson became the President of the Dodge division in 1956, with a brief to improve its performance.

The 1956 Custom Royal was Dodge's top-of-the-range and most prestigious line, with the most intense trim options. They had everything the Royal models did and more – hooded and painted headlight housings, and extra grooved taillight assemblies. Several special models were introduced as part of the Custom Royal two-door hardtop Lancer line-up for the year, including the Golden Lancer and the rather bizarre Dodge La Femme. The first American car specifically introduced to appeal to women buyers, the 1956 La Femme appeared in a sickly livery of two-tone

Engine:	D-500 V-8 overhead valve, hemispherical combustion chambers, cast iron block
Displacement:	315 cid
Horsepower:	260 at 4400 rpm
Compression Ratio:	9.25:1
Induction:	Carter four-barrel Type WCFB
Weight: (Two-door Lancer Hardtop)	3505 lbs
Wheelbase:	120 inches
Base Price:	$2658
Number Produced:	40,100

lavender, and gold-flecked interior. It also had a patronising array of matching feminine accoutrements such as a cap, a pair of boots, an umbrella, a shoulder bag and floral upholstery fabric… sales were reassuringly miniscule. The almost equally tasteful Golden Lancer has a Sapphire white body, with a Gallant Saddle Gold exterior and interior trim.

At the other end of the Custom Royal market, the D-500 (complete with hemi V-8) was introduced to demonstrate the performance

capabilities of the marque. These were underlined by the Dodge performance at the year's NASCAR races, where they won eleven victories. A Dodge Custom Royal fourdoor sedan was driven 31,224 miles in 14 days, and set 306 speed records at the Bonneville Salt Flats in Utah. Dodge was thus saved from a potentially embarrassing year.

▲   The D-500 was equipped with the big Hemi V-8 and was the highest-performing Dodge of 1956.

1956 Plymouth Fury Hardtop

Plymouth was number four in the production league in 1956, very slightly behind Buick in the number three position, with an output of 571,634 vehicles.

Introduced in 1956 with a 240-horsepower 303 V-8, the Fury had sharply peaked tail fins, a Cadillac-like logo and special side trim. It was a great example of Plymouths 'All new Aerodynamic' styling for the year, which was instigated as part of Virgil Exner's 1955 Chrysler-wide 'Forward Look' re-style. The front and rear windshields were wraparounds, and the side windows were pillarless.

The Fury was introduced to heat up Plymouth's performance image, for '56 was a seminal, powerorientated, year for the entire US automotive industry. Effectively, it was the Division's first muscle car. Plymouth chose to introduce the production version of the car with a 240-horsepower 303 V-8, a polyspheric head engine, rather than the 'hemi' used by the other Chrysler divisions.

At the Daytona Beach February Speed Week, the Plymouth Fury FX, driven by Phil Walters beat even the Chrysler 300 'B', by achieving a record pace of over 149 miles per hour. This made it the fastest Plymouth every built. Evidently, this was not a source of unalloyed joy to the board at Chrysler, who had hoped the 'B' would be totally invincible by allcomers, including their own. As well as being truly quick, the Fury also handled well, with its body lowered an inch from the other Belvedere models.

▼ The 1956 Fury was heated-up with the big Fury V-8.

Engine:	Overhead valve Fury V-8
Displacement:	303 cid
Horsepower:	240 at 4800 rpm
Transmission:	Three-speed manual with optional overdrive and automatic
Compression Ratio:	9.25:1
Body Style:	Two-door Sports Coupe
Number of Seats:	6
Weight:	3650 lbs
Wheelbase:	115 inches (overall length 204.8 inches)
Base Price:	$2807
Number Produced:	4485

1957 Chrysler 300-C Two-door Convertible

The 300C was the third (following on from the C-300 and 300-B), and first convertible generation of the Chrysler 300 series. The model continued to fly the flag as the fastest production car in America. A completely new direction in styling, 'The Forward Look' had been applied to the 1957 300s by Exner and the Chrysler design team. The main features of the new body style were the elegant tailfins and masculine grille. The cars were restrained compared to the flamboyance of several contemporary models (the Chevy Bel Air Convertible, and Plymouth Fury are just two examples), but won the company several design awards. The cars were also built with a new torsion bar front suspension, replacing coil springs, that was to be used by Chrysler well into the 1980s.

Motor Trend Magazine awarded the model 'Car of the Year', mainly for its excellent handling and engineering.

The Firepower hemi was again fitted to the car, but this would be its penultimate year in the model, the Golden Lion V-8 would be used from 1958.

1957 Chrysler 300-C Two-door Convertible

Although considered part of the New Yorker series by Chrysler, the 300s were really a world away from even their production stable mates for power and handling. They were also much more simply trimmed, with a just a single sidespear running along the rear the rear quarter panels on both sides of the car. The wheels, at 14 inches, were smaller than the previous model, and typical of the wheel size of contemporary US cars. Two model shapes were now available, a revised two-door hardtop, and the new two-door convertible. The hardtop sold 1918 cars to the convertible's 484, but was $430 less expensive.

Engine:	V-8, overhead valve with hemi-spherical combustion chambers
Displacement:	392 cid
Horsepower:	375 at 5200 rpm
Transmission:	TorqueFlite
Compression ratio:	9.25:1
Number of Seats:	6
Weight:	4390 lbs
Wheelbase Length:	126 inches (overall length 219.2 inches)
Base Price:	$5359
Number Produced:	484 Convertibles

▼ This ragtop muscle car is loaded with Chrysler's Hemi V-8.

1957 Corvette

The Corvette styling for '56, '57 and '58 remained pretty well unchanged except for modest tweaking of the chrome between model years. But the new 283 V-8s under the hood offered one horsepower per cubic inch with Chevy's new 'Ramjet' fuel injection. As the adverts of the time proclaimed, 'For the first time in automotive history – one horsepower for every cubic inch.' Of course, this wasn't actually true, the Chrysler 300 series was the first American car in this field.

The spirit of the car also remained unchanged, it was designed as a fun and economical sports car for young people, and remains so to this day. The original car was built in fiberglass to lower the initial production cost.

Amongst the standard features fitted to the car in this model year were dual exhaust pipes, all-vinyl bucket seats, three-spoke competition style steering wheel and carpeting. Seven optional colours were available, Onyx black, Polo white, Aztec copper, Artic blue, Cascade green, silver or, the colour of our photographed car – Venetian red. In two-tone cars, the 'cove' in the side panels could be picked out in white, silver or beige.

Engine:	v-8 overhead valve, cast iron block. Fuel injection available as an option.
Displacement:	283 cid
Horsepower:	220 at 4800 rpm
Transmission:	Three-speed manual floor shift, or four-speed manual floor shift or Powerglide as optional extras
Compression Ratio:	9.50:1
Induction:	Carter four-barrel Model 3744925
Weight:	2730 lbs
Wheelbase:	102 inches (overall length 168 inches)
Base Price:	$3,465
Number Produced:	6,339

For a model that Chevy only retained to compete with Ford's Thunderbird, Corvette sales were virtually doubled from 1956, and continued to climb for the rest of the '50s.

Interesting option included a detachable hardtop ($215), Whitewall tires ($32), Hydraulic power top ($99), automatic transmission ($175), three versions of the fuel-injected engine were available (the most expensive of which could from 0-60 mph in 5.7 seconds, and achieve a top speed of 132 mph) and heavy-duty racing suspension ($725). In fact, only 1040 of the 1957 'Vettes were manufactured with fuel injection.

▲ This fabulous Venetian red 'Vette has the cheeky grille of the early models.

1957 Dodge D-500 Convertible

The year 1957 saw the introduction of Virgil Exner's second generation 'Forward Look' applied to all the Chrysler products, including Dodge. The Dodge brand of the styling was denoted as 'Swept-Wing Styling' – and it was.

The Dodge tailfins made the cars look as though they could take off, and with the D-500 super package, they virtually could. This supercharged version of their Hemi V-8 developed up to 340 horsepower, which put the car into some very good Chrysler company.

Body-wise, the cars were longer, lower and wider than any previous Dodge, and the wheelbase was longer than anything the company had built since 1933. The change over to fourteen-inch wheels helped to lower the silhouette of the car, and the torsion bar suspension (introduced over at Chrysler) was also new. The grille featured a gull-wing shaped bar that surrounded a huge Dodge crest. All the 1957 models had a single chrome bar along the body, and chrome trim under the rear fins. But the new styling could not disguise some quality control problems that were to dog the company and hinder sales for a couple of years.

In fact, the D-500 was actually designed as a high-performance engine that could be used in all the 1957 series, but the specifications given are for the engine fitted to two versions of the Custom Royal series (the two-door sedan and the two-door convertible) – but the model shown in the photograph is a Coronet (two-door Lancer convertible) fitted with the D-500. The Coronet was now the base Dodge model, and sales of this series made up over 160,000 of the sales figures for the year.

As a company, Dodge was performing much better, climbing to seventh in the league of sales, and produced nearly 290,000 cars in the year. Over 96% of the 1957 cars were automatics, and 93.4% were fitted with a V-8.

▶ Cool ragtop, hot Hemi. The car's looks reflect the second generation of the Chrysler Group's "Forward Look" styling.

Engine:	D-500 V-8 overhead valve, cast iron block, hemispherical heads
Displacement:	354 cid
Horsepower:	340 at 5200 rpm
Compression Ratio:	10.0:1
Induction:	Carter four-barrel Type WCFB
Body Style:	Two-door Convertible
Number of Seats:	6
Weight:	3975 lbs
Wheelbase:	122 inches
Base Price:	$3635
Number Produced:	6,960 Two-door Convertibles across all ranges

1957 Ford Thunderbird

Ford had first introduced the Thunderbird two-seater 'personal' car in 1955 to counter Chevrolet's 1953-introduced Corvette. At almost exactly the same base price as its more established rival, the T-bird hugely outsold the 'Vette in its first year. Buyers loved the sleek good looks of the car, and the practical lift-off hardtop. 16,155 examples were sold in the car's first model year, as opposed to a slightly pathetic 700 Corvette roadsters.

By 1957, the Thunderbird was still well ahead in the sales race, (21,380 to 9,168) although the Corvette was considerably more expensive by this model year, and followed the general trend as Fords outsold Chevys for the first time in a good while. The Thunderbird was also available as the more powerful option by the time the new 1957 model was introduced in October 1956. Whilst Chevy offered 283 horsepower via its optional Ramjet fuel injector (one horsepower per cubic inch) Ford was offering a far more massive power option. The supercharged Thunderbird Special Supercharge V-8 belted out 340 horsepower at 5300 rpm in the NASCAR version of the car. Both Thunderbirds and Corvettes were available with a single body option in 1957, the standard two-door convertible.

Thunderbirds had been heavily re-styled for the 1957 model year, as were all the cars in this decisive year in Ford's history. The redesign included a revised body shape, including huge tailfins (or 'high-canted fender blades') and the abolition of the externally mounted spare wheel. Interior changes included a new instrument panel and 'Lifeguard Design' safety features (including a padded dashboard and dished steering wheel). Six engine options were available for the T-bird, a six-cylinder version (serial number code 'A') and five increasingly powerful V-8s (serial number codes 'B', 'C', 'D', 'E' and 'F'). All kinds of optional refinements were available at extra cost – everything from power windows to white sidewall tires.

Despite its success, 1957 turned out to be the final year for the two-seater version of the Thunderbird. 1958 witnessed the introduction of the luxury fourpassenger 'Square Birds'. A ragtop version was also launched. Effectively, this took Thunderbirds out of the American sports car market, and Corvette inherited the two-seater roadster market.

1957 Ford Thunderbird

Engine:	Standard V-8. Overhead valve
Displacement:	272 cid
Horsepower:	190 at 4500 rpm
Compression Ratio:	8.6:1
Wheelbase:	102 inches (181.4 inches overall)
Base Price:	$3408
Number Produced:	21,380

▲ This J-2-equipped Starfire was all muscle with its big-block, triple carb, Rocket V-8.

1957 Oldsmobile Starfire Convertible

Oldsmobile introduced three restyled model ranges for 1957 in November '56. The entire Eighty-eight entry series was named 'Golden Rocket' in honor of the up-coming 50th anniversary. Eighty-eights were the base models and Super Eighty-eights were the mid-range models for the year. Starfire Ninety-eights were the four-model top range. Standard equipment on the senior lineup included all the Eight-eight features, plus electric windows, special emblems, power steering, power brakes and Jetaway Hyda-Matic transmission. Interior trim included cloth, morocceen and leather.

The 'Starfire' name went back to a two-seater concept car that Oldsmobile toured with the GM Motorama Car Show back in '53, named in honor of the Lockheed F-94B Starfire jet fighter. This particular version had a bright turquoise fiberglass body, and turquoise-and-white leather interior. Although this original concept never found its way into production, the Oldsmobile continued to search for a car of this type, to give Ford's 'personal luxury car', the Thunderbird, some direct competition. But the Starfire model introduced in '57 was a car of a completely different stamp, being a full-sized luxury convertible. The name subsequently became synonymous with big, flashy, sporty cars, and it wasn't until 1961 that the Oldsmobile Division considered reconfiguring the car to be a serious rival to the (now four-seat) T-bird.

However, even in '57, the Starfire was available with a range of J-2 performance options. This technology had been designed to re-assert Oldsmobile's power superiority over Chevy and their small-block V-8. The top J-2 option (the triple-carb Rocket with 300 horsepower) wasn't recommended for road cars, but Lee and Richard Petty drove the multi-carbureted engines to NASCAR success, until the racing authorities banned this type of induction. Olds subsequently pulled out of factory-backed racing.

With J. F. Wolfram as Divisional CEO, Oldsmobile was the fifth best performing automobile manufacturer in 1957, gaining a 6.2% share of the US market. The company was now solidly positioned as the sales leader in medium-priced cars.

Their concept cars continued to tour with the GM Motorama car show. This year, their big idea was the Mona Lisa, a Starfire Holiday Coupe.

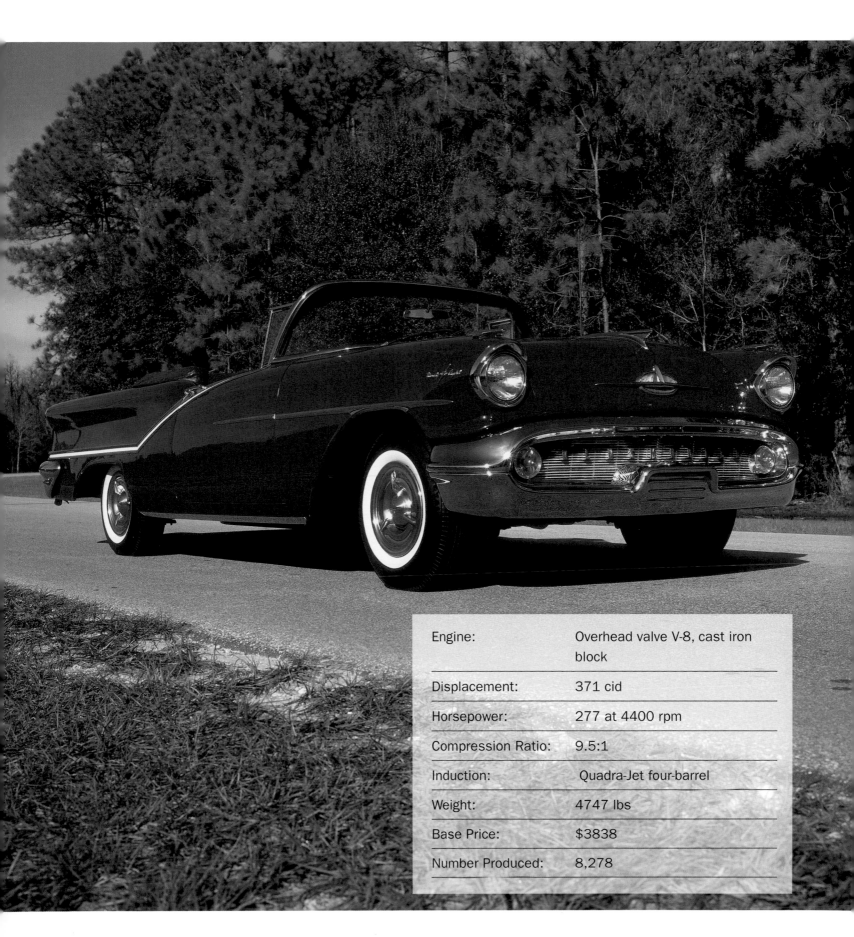

Engine:	Overhead valve V-8, cast iron block
Displacement:	371 cid
Horsepower:	277 at 4400 rpm
Compression Ratio:	9.5:1
Induction:	Quadra-Jet four-barrel
Weight:	4747 lbs
Base Price:	$3838
Number Produced:	8,278

▲ This J-2-eqipped Starfire was all muscle with its big-block, triple carb, Rocket V-8.

1957 Pontiac Bonneville Convertible

Big things were happening at Pontiac in 1957. Semon E. 'Bunkie' Knudsen became Pontiac's new general manager in '56, the son of former GM President William S. Knudsen, he became the youngest general manager at GM at the ripe old age of 43. The change marked the quiet insurgence of Pontiac into the youth car market. Knudsen hired Pete Estes (who became Chief Engineer at Pontiac in '57) and John DeLorean to head up the design and engineering teams, together with a series of huge performance advances, their work was to positively shape Pontiac cars for years to come. The Strato-Streak V-8 was launched in 1955, it was lighter than the GM Straight 8, and cheaper to manufacture than the Oldsmobile Rocket V-8.

There was a huge emphasis at Pontiac on research and development, and a constant striving for engineering advances. The company funded an influential 'Product Engineering' department.

During this period, they experimented with four-speed floor-shift, rear-mounted transaxles and supercharging.

A unique, limited edition Custom Bonneville Convertible was released in January 1957. It was Pontiac's first Bonneville. The car was in the Custom Star Chief sub-series (series 28) in which there were four body styles. The cars were released on a one-to-a-dealer basis, and availability was very limited – only 630 production examples were built, plus two prototypes. The car was only available with a convertible top and the Bonneville V-8, an enlarged Strato-Streak, which developed an estimated 315 horsepower at 4800 rpm. The cars were also fitted with a Rochester mechanical fuel injection system. A NASCAR certified triple-carb option was also available.

The Bonnies were hugely accessorized, and were fitted with air suspension, power seats, power brakes, power windows, power steering, leather upholstery and Hydra-Matic drive. The only options were air conditioning, and 'continental' externally mounted tires.

Engine:	Overhead valve V-8, cast iron block
Displacement:	347 cid
Horsepower:	(estimated) 315 at 4800 rpm
Transmission:	Strato-Flight Hydra-Matic
Compression Ratio:	10.25:1
Induction:	Rochester mechanical fuel injection
Number of Seats:	6
Weight:	4285 lbs
Wheelbase:	124 inches
Base Price:	$5782

▼ This stunning Kenya Ivory and Fontaine Blue painted Bonneville Convertible is one of only a hundred surviving examples of the model.

1958 Plymouth Fury

Plymouth had made it back to third position in the producers' league in 1957, and retained this place in '58 with just over a 30% share of the market.

The 1958 Fury was a Belvedere sub-series containing only the high performance sports coupe.

First introduced as a midyear model back in '56, the Fury was designed to heat up Plymouth's new performance-orientated image, equipped with a 240 horsepower V-8, and special gold-anodized side trim (this trim persisted into the '58 range). Like the rest of the Plymouth line, the Fury hardtop emerged from the 1957 styling bigger, bolder and better-handling than the first model, complete with a 290-horse V-8. The '58 Fury was a limited edition two-door hardtop with Fury rear fender, nameplates, bumper wing guards, padded interior, and front and rear foam seats. It was effectively a revised and super-charged Belvedere. Just as is '57, the Belvederes remained the top Plymouth range, Plazas were

▲ The '58 Fury was available in a single two-door Hardtop coupe, in Buckskin Beige with gold trim.

the base models, whilst the Savoys comprised the medium-priced series.

The '58 Furys were now powered by an overhead valve Fury V-8, and an optional Bendix fuel injection (EFI) system was also available for the big-block Golden Commando V-8, but these were later recalled and reconverted. These Golden Commando 'big block' wedge head V-8s were capable of 0-60 miles per hour in 7.7 seconds and could run the quarter-mile in 16.1 seconds.

The '58 model Fury is the car immortalized by Stephen King in his book Christine, but there are several inconsistencies with reality. In the King's book (as in John Carpenter's 1983 film version), Christine is red and white, but the real model was only available in buckskin

beige with gold trim. In the book, King refers to the car as having four doors, but the '58 models were only available in the singe two-door version. He also mentions that car as having hydramatic transmission with a transmission lever, but the car actually had TorqueFlite, push-button transmission.

Plus, the real life Furys did not kill people that insulted their owners!

Engine:	Fury v-8 overhead valve
Displacement:	317.6 cid
Horsepower:	225 at 4400 rpm
Transmission:	Three-speed manual with Torqueflite automatic optional
Compression Ratio:	9.25:1
Body Style:	Two-door Hardtop Coupe
Weight:	3510 lbs
Wheelbase:	118 inches (206 inches overall)
Base Price:	$3032
Number Produced:	5,303

1959 Plymouth Sport Fury

Plymouth sales leapt a full 11.6 per cent in their 30th anniversary model year of 1959, holding third position in the industry sales charts. Although its actual share of the market was reduced – overall production was raised by over 30 per cent. The unsuccessful fuel injection option was deleted from the list of available options. General Manager Harry E. Cheesbrough marked the production of the company's eleven-millionth car.

All Plymouths were heavily re-styled for 1959, gaining huge tailfins and a tire bulge on the trunk lid. Technologically, not much had changed for the 1957-58 models, though.

Furys became a separate series in the 1959 production year, rather strangely grouped together with the Sport Suburban station wagons. They were marketed as higher-level Plymouth offerings and came only with V-8 attachments. The cars were equipped with all the Belvedere options, plus several unique to the new series, such as a deluxe steering wheel with horn ring, lockable glove box, cigar lighter and disc wheel covers.

A Fury four-door hardtop was converted into the latest in a series of Chrysler turbine-engined cars, making a 576-mile cross-country reliability run.

Sport Fury was the highest Plymouth range of all, and was designated as their only 'premium' series. It was a hybrid luxury/performance model. Two body styles were manufactured, a sports coupe and a convertible, available only with 'Sport Fury' or 'Golden Commando' V-8 power. The Sport Fury V-8 developed 260 horsepower at 4400 rpm, as opposed to the 230 generated by the regular V-8. Golden Commando 395 V-8 produced 305 horsepower at 4600 rpm. The huge torque generated by Golden Commando necessitated a beefed-up transmission.

Standard equipment for the model included everything the Fury had, plus swivel front seats, sport deck lid tire cover and custom padded steering wheel.

Engine:	Sport Fury V-8, overhead valve
Displacement:	317.6 cid
Horsepower:	260 at 4400 rpm
Transmission:	three-speed manual transmission, with PowerFlite automatic as an option (Golden Commando V-8 as standard)
Compression Ratio:	9.0:1
Weight:	3670 lbs
Wheelbase:	118 inches
Base Price:	$3125
Number Produced:	5,990

▲ The Sport Fury Convertible was new for '59, with huge tailfins to emphasise its improved performance.

1960 Dodge Dart D-500

Dodge introduced a new crest in 1960, but more importantly, the structure of their entire model range was revised with new model names and target markets. In addition to the full-size Doge models, Chrysler also introduced the new 'downsized' Dart series, with a shorter, 118-inch wheelbase.

The newly introduced low-priced Dart was Dodge's big seller for 1960, and doubled their sales for the year (367,804 as opposed for 156,385). Dodge ran the model head-to-head with Plymouth, and almost achieved their rival's output for the year, hindered as their opponents were by their rather old-fashioned 'jukebox on wheels' styling. The Darts were built on the same wheelbase length as the Plymouth models.

Dodge's basic rationale in entering the Darts onto the market had been to compete directly with the 'big three' manufacturers (Ford, GM and Chrysler).

The Dart was also the forerunner to their compact models of 1961. The Seneca was the entry-level model, and boasted Chrysler's new overhead valve 'Slant Six' engine, which was destined to be a corporate mainstay for three decades.

The other Dart engine option was the 'A' block, small series V-8.

The Darts had a unitised body/chassis that was designed to give the car greater rigidity. Body styling remained recognizably Dodge, but the Darts were slightly more subdued in their trim than the other Dodge models. The

Engine:	V-8
Displacement:	381 cid
Horsepower:	310 at 4800 rpm
Compression Ratio:	10.0:1
Wheelbase:	118 inches
Base Price:	$2607 (plus $418 for D-500)
Number Produced: (all Darts)	306,603

▲ D-500 was a performance option available for all three levels of Dart trim.

side styling was simple with a single horizontal chrome strip, beginning at the front wheel well and ending at the rear bumper. The headlight 'eyebrows' disappeared, to be replaced by chrome bezels. The taillights were also surrounded by chromed bezels. Dodge also offered an unprecedented, long line of luxury extras, including air conditioning.

The Darts were tiered in three levels of trim. The Seneca was the base model, the Pioneer intermediate, and the Pheonix the top-of-the-range. All three tiers were available with the D-500 performance option, a 361 or 383-cid

V-8 engine with cross-ram induction and dual four-barrel carburettors giving a supercharged effect. 1960 was the epitome of it's power, the engine was detuned in '61. A D-500 modified Dart Pheonix, driven by Norm Thatcher set three world records at Bonneville in the 'B' class races for supercharged gas coupes. The supercharged 383-cid V-8 equipped Dart achieved a top speed of 191.8 mph.

1960 Plymouth Sonoramic Commando

By the mid-fifties, Plymouth had an excellent reputation as a very reliable family car was long and well established. But this was becoming fairly ordinary, so the car-buying public began to look for new selling points from the auto industry, technical advances and styling changes.

Plymouth entered a difficult decade for the company in 1960. Their sales plummeted during the sixties, with only brief recoveries. The rather ugly tailfins of the 1960 Savoy, Belvedere, Fury and Suburban Plymouth models ensured that they were rather coolly received by the market. But things didn't improve with the introduction of the compact models in '62, which the buying public shunned in favor of larger Ford and Chevy models.

However, 1960 was a significant year for Plymouth in several regards. It was the final model year for the famous, unattractive 'fins' (or stabilizers as they were called in the sales literature. The cars were also the first manufactured with the 'unibody' construction. This offered weight and material savings over the then conventional body-on-frame construction. It also stiffened the body.

This is a practically universal construction method used to this day.

Technically, 1960 also saw the introduction of two legendary engines. The slant six, and the Sonoramic Commando V-8, complete with the cross-ram induction intake manifold, the Plymouth version was available on the 383 and 361-cid 'B' engines. These were first introduced as race tune engines for use in the NASCAR series, then as 'Street Hemi' production options. The package also included heavy-duty suspension and oversized brackets. Richard Petty raced these to three Plymouth victories at the NHRA Nationals in Detroit. His winning time for the quarter mile was 14.51 seconds at 87.82 mph.

Our photographed car is the two-door Belvedere hardtop sedan, which was also available with the slant six-cylinder engine and the standard Plymouth V-8.

The Sonoramic Commando option added a further $389 to the base price of the model, plus a further $211 for the necessary Torqueflite

transmission. The passenger car Belvederes had the model script on the rather bizarre front fender 'coves' and three shield medallions on the tailfins.

▲   The Belvedere is ornamented with the 'Sonoramic Commando Power' badge on the front fender – or, as they were called in the '60s, 'scare emblems'. The badge continued to be used in '61.

Engine:	Sonoramic Commando V-8
Displacement:	383-cid
Horsepower:	330 at 5000 rpm
Transmission:	Torqueflite
Induction:	Dual four-barrel carburetor
Weight:	3505 lbs
Wheelbase:	118 inches
Base Price:	$2545
Number Produced:	14,085

1960 Pontiac Ventura

Engine: V-8,	overhead valve, cast iron block
Displacement:	389 cid
Horsepower:	283 at 4400 rpm
Transmission:	Hydra-Matic
Compression Ratio:	10.25:1
Body Style:	Two-door Hardtop
Weight:	3865 lbs
Wheelbase:	122 inches
Base Price:	$2971
Number Produced:	27,577

Starting with the 1959 models, the image of a sporty, youthful car with appeal across the spectrum of car buyers emerged at Pontiac, in sharp contract to its previous 'dull but reliable' image. This resulted in a six-year period in which the company's output was dominated by low-slung, 'Wide-Track' full-size performance cars that performed well in the sales league, and on the track.

Pontiac's major styling changes for the 1960 line included undivided horizontal bar grilles, straight full-length side trim moldings, and a new deck lid that seemed to almost rest on the fenders. The base Catalina models, of which there were seven, had plain beltline moldings. Standard features included turn signals, an oil filter and five tubeless tires. Ironically, the divided grille that had been evident in 1959 was to return and become a trademark of the division. The Catalina range was Pontiac's sales leader for 1960. The new cars were introduced to the public on October 1 1959.

The Ventura model range cars were effectively custom-level Catalinas.

They were offered in two options – a four-door Vista Hardtop and a two-door hardtop, both models sold fairly equal numbers, which totalled 56,277.

Venturas shared the short wheelbase of the Catalina models. They also had plain belt moldings. Venturas had all the Catalina features, plus custom steering wheel, electric clock, deluxe wheel discs, full carpeting, triple-tone Morrokide seats, right-hand ashtrays and special décor molding.

Nearly all of the cars were fitted with Hydramatic automatic, only 2,381 were built with synchromesh gears.

Pontiac produced 396,716 cars in 1960, to reach fifth position in the automakers' sales league. This gave them a 6.6 per cent share of the market.

1960 was also the year when Pontiac began to assert itself in the NASCAR racing series, of which they won four. Jim Wangers also drove a 1960 Pontiac to the NHRA 'Top Eliminator' title. Mickey Thompson, on the other hand, fitted four Pontiac engines in his Challenger I World Land Speed Record car and drove it at 363.67 mph... How things had changed.

◀   This two-door hardtop Ventura features the single-year undivided grille theme.

1961 Chevrolet SS 409

Chevrolet was the first to offer real horsepower to the masses in 1955. Then the guys who brought you "The Hot One" followed that up six years later with its fabled "409," the potent powerplant that overnight had everyone singing its praises. Most notable were the lyrics released by "The Beach Boys" in May 1962.

"She's real fine, my four-or-nine," began Brian Wilson's epic tune, which would be remembered long after the engine itself faded away into the automotive archives.

The 409 tale dates back to 1958 when Chevrolet introduced its 348-cubic-inch V-8, often called a "W-head" because of the pattern made by its alternating valve positions. Look down on top of a 348 cylinder head and the valves traced out a "W"—or an "M" depending on your relative position. Many today still think the 409 was simply a bored-and-stroked 348, but the leap from one to the other wasn't anywhere near that easy.

First and foremost, boring out the 348 block was not suggested—there wasn't enough cast-iron in place between the water jacket and cylinders. Engineers had to recast the block to increase the bore, then they stretched the stroke to

▲ The Impala two-door coupe body was, as some would argue, at it's best in the 1961 car. Later models somehow lacked the simplicity and charm of the original.

produce the displacement that fit so well in Wilson's song.

From there, modifications were plenty, so much so that swapping parts between the 348 and 409 was basically out of the question. New forged aluminum pistons featured centered wrist pins and symmetrical valve reliefs milled straight across the piston top in pairs. Their 348 counterparts had offset wrist pins and one large intake relief, one smaller exhaust relief, meaning two opposite sets of four pistons were required. All 409 pistons interchanged regardless of which cylinder bank they belonged to.

Wheelbase:	119 inches
Weight:	3,737 pounds
Original price:	$3,500, approximately
Engine:	409 cubic-inch "W-head" V-8
Induction:	single Carter four-barrel carburetor
Compression:	11.25:1
Horsepower:	360 at 5,800 rpm
Torque:	409 at 3,600 rpm
Transmission:	Muncie four-speed manual
Suspension:	independent A-arms w/coil springs in front; four-link live axle with coil springs in back
Brakes:	four-wheel drums
Performance:	14.2 seconds at 98.14 mph in the quarter-mile, according to Motor Trend
Production:	453 Impala Super Sports with both engines, 348 and 409—409 V-8 production is listed at 142 with no breakdown given as to model (some went into Bel Airs, Biscaynes, etc.)

Improved components for the 409 included a beefed-up forged steel crank; shortened, reinforced connecting rods; and more durable aluminum bearings. Heads were also specially cast to accept larger diameter pushrods and machined on top for heavier valve springs.

▼ Chevy's sport coupe body with its large rear window was the perfect base for the 1961 Super Sport.

The 409's solid-lifter cam was also much more aggressive than its 348 cousin.

Happily feeding hefty gulps of fuel/air mixture was a large Carter AFB four-barrel carburetor on an aluminum intake, equipment that flowed every bit as strongly as the triple-carb setup used by the top-shelf 348s. A Delco-Remy ignition featuring a dual-breaker, centrifugal-advance distributor sparked that

▶ Chevy's first SS model represented the best combination of performance and pizzazz ever seen by Average Joe Carbuyer.

▼ Wildly upholstered bucket seats showed up on a 1961 Impala showcar. All 1961 Super Sports came with a front bench.

mixture, and spent gases were hauled away by low-restriction iron manifolds. Output was 360 horsepower.

A mandatory supporting cast for the 409 included a 3.36:1 rear axle and a four-speed manual transmission. Powerglide and air condition-ing reportedly were not available, but power steering and brakes were, as was an all-important positraction differential. Over-the-counter optional rear gears (running as low as 4.56:1) were also offered.

Most interesting on the options list was the

▲ Special SS badging appeared on the deck lid.

Super Sport kit. Introduced shortly after the 409 appeared, the SS equipment was born basically to showcase the king of the W-heads. Included was an awfully nice collection of imagery and performance equipment.

On the outside, tri-blade spinner wheelcovers caught the eye, and the attraction was further enhanced inside with a padded dashboard and a Corvette-type grab bar atop the glove box opening. A 7000-rpm tachometer, mounted on the steering column, was standard, as was an exclusive dress-up floor plate for four-speed Super Sports. "SS"

▶ Four-speed Super Sports were treated to a bright floor-shifter surround.

▼ A 7000-rpm column-mounted tachometer (above) was standard on all SS models, whether automatic or manual-equipped.

▲ Spinner hubcaps were also standard.

identification inside and out completed the show. But there was more.

Underneath, Limited Production Optiona (LPO) number 1108, the police handling package, added a stiffer sway bar up front, sintered-metallic brake linings, and heavy-duty springs and shocks all around. Power steering and brakes and 8.00x14 narrow-band whitewall tires were included, too.

MILESTONE FACTS

• Chevrolet built the 409 up through 1965 before it was superseded by Chevrolet's all-new Mk IV big-block V-8 displacing 396 cubic inches.

• Brochures claimed the Super Sport Kit could be ordered on any model in 1961, including four-doors. No such applications, however, are known.

• The Impala SS legacy ran strong until 1969. It was later reborn in 1994, this time based on the four-door Caprice platform.

• The 409 V-8 was a derivation of the 348, which explains why more than one wag over the years has labeled the former a "truck engine." The latter, when introduced in 1958, was indeed targeted for Chevrolet's truck line, though it also appeared as the top-performance engine option for the passenger-car line until 1961.

• A 409-horsepower 409 V-8 option was introduced very late in the 1961 model run.

• Only Chevy's baddest big-blocks, the 348 and 409, were offered for the Impala SS in 1961. In 1962, Super Sport buyers could also pick the 235-cid six-cylinder and 283 and 327 small-blocks.

• Output for the 409 V-8 topped out at 425 horsepower in 1963.

• From 1961 to '63, the Impala SS was an options package. Then the full-sized Super Sport gained individual model-line status in 1964. Total production that year soared to 185,325.

▲ ◀ The SS 409 body was updated in 1962 with a new side profile and grille plus, of course, a new badge

Overall, the 409 SS Impala looked and played the part of a truly hot car as well as anything Detroit had to offer in 1961. Rest to 60 mph took only seven seconds or so, and the metallic brakes were an able match for that power. Meanwhile, the police chassis did a nice job of apprehending body roll and keeping the 3,700-pond Super Sport dirty-side down. Wrapping things up was an image that screamed "cool" every bit as loud as the

exhaust notes backing up "The Beach Boys" on their big 1962 hit.

The 1961 Impala SS kicked off Chevrolet's legendary SS legacy, a bloodline that would eventually branch out to practically anything on four wheels wearing a Bow-Tie badge. And although the 409, like its 348 forefather, would soon itself become an antique, for a few short years it was the machine many performance buyers were saving their pennies and dimes for.

To some nostalgic baby-boomers, she's still real fine.

▶ The car was restyled again in 1963 with changes to the front end, a new sleeker side profile with a lower rubbing strip and faired-in rear wheels. The rear end also received a makeover with restyled lights and a new aluminum surround panel.

▲ ▶ This is the dashboard in a 1962 car. The same year the rear end was extensively restyled with new light clusters and a tooled aluminum surround.

1961 Chevrolet SS 409

1961 Dodge Polara D-500

The 'new for '61' Dodges didn't sell at all well. Their styling was controversial, and some dealers even rejected the division's offerings for the new model year. Sales went down to just over a quarter of a million cars, falling away by over 100,000 units from the previous year and Dodge dropped three places in the league of auto producers to ninth position.

The downsized Darts remained as Dodge's bestseller for '61, when a heavy facelift made the car look more like the company's senior models. Their rather bizarre 'reverse slant' tailfins were a dubious Dodge idea that appeared for this year only. Dodge also introduced the compact Lancer in a three-level model range in '61.

The Polara (RD1) was now the only full-sized Dodge series on offer, with the classic 122-inch wheelbase. Six models were offered in this complete range.

This senior line assumed a Dart look-alike appearance with an identical grille, though its taillights were deeply recessed. These were contained in the wraparound sweep of the tailfins, and looked like nothing less than jet plane exhausts. The model trim featured chrome moldings around the front windshield and rear window and a split chrome side strip with a contrasting aluminum insert. An odd 'Flight Sweep' trunk lid wheel cover was also optional.

The standard engine fitted to the line was the 265 horsepower 361-cid V-8, with an optional 383-cid version. The D-500 V-8 and Ram-Induction D-500 V-8s were also available as optional extras for the Polara. Both featured an unusual intake system with two Carter AFB four-barrel carburettors mounted on a 30- inch long intake manifold. The carburettor mounted on the right (over the valve cover) actually fed the left bank of the engine and vice-versa. The extremely long manifolds produced incredible low-end torque. This was known as the 'Sonoramic' long ram engine.

Polaras have a great following today, they look like the essence of '60s space travel on wheels, with their bizarre styling and sputnik-like ornaments.

1961 Dodge Polara D-500

The equipment nomenclature of the line thoroughly reinforced this impression, with its 'MirrOMatic' rear-view mirror, 'Satellite' revolving clock, 'Tower Bank' front seats and 'Astrophonic' radio.

▼ The Kelsey Hayes wire wheels and whitewall tires set off the sporting good looks of this D-500 equipped convertible.

Engine:	V-8 overhead valve, cast iron block
Displacement:	383 cid
Horsepower:	325 at 4800 rpm
Compression Ratio:	10.0:1
Weight:	3765 lbs
Wheelbase:	122 inches
Base Price:	$3252
Number Produced:	14,032 built in 1961

1961 Ford Galaxie Sunliner

It was a battle for the ages, Ford vs. Chevy; the former poised to finally catch the latter in Detroit's sales race after following for far too long. The year was 1957, and horsepower was a prime selling point. Chevrolet's "Hot One," the high-winding, overhead-valve small-block V-8 introduced to raves in 1955, was getting hotter by the year.

New for '57 was optional fuel-injection, which could boost output for the newly enlarged 283-cube small-block all the way up to 283 horses. Ford engineers, meanwhile, were bolting dual-carb setups and even Paxton superchargers onto their 312 cubic-inch Y-block V-8. Both companies had

▶ The Sunliner was the sporty version of Ford's Galaxie. The car won an award from the International Fashion Authority for its "functional expression of classic beauty." It was a typical product of Detroit in the 1960s.

NASCAR tracks in mind when they developed these parts as Detroit's automakers were now well aware of the promotional value of a race-winning reputation.

But hold your horses... In June the Automobile Manufacturers Association enacted its "ban" on factory racing involvement, supposedly to help demonstrate Detroit's new awareness of automotive safety issues. Actually, the AMA edict was probably more of a ploy used by its chairman, Red

Wheelbase:	209.9 inches
Weight:	3,694 pounds
Base Price:	$2,847 (for V-8 Sunliner convertible)
Engine:	390 cubic-inch FE-series V-8
Compression:	10.6:1
Induction:	three Holley two-barrel carburetors on an aluminum intake manifold
Horsepower:	401 at 6,000 rpm
Torque:	430 at 3,500 rpm
Transmission:	column-shifted Borg-Warner T-85 three-speed manual
Suspension:	independent A-arms w/coil springs in front; live axle with leaf springs in back; springs, brakes and shocks were all special heavy-duty pieces
Brakes:	heavy-duty four-wheel drums

▲ The skinny treads used in the early Sixties didn't stand a chance against Ford's 401-horse triple-carb V-8.

Curtice, to undercut Ford's efforts to one-up Chevrolet. Curtice was also president of General Motors. A mere coincidence? We think not. Whatever the case, Ford followed the AMA ban to the letter, while cheaters like Chevrolet and Pontiac continued promoting (albeit somewhat clandestinely) their performance programs like nothing had changed.

Dearborn-bred performance then suffered for two years before the Blue-Oval boys finally decided to get back in the race late in 1959. First came the 360-horse 352-cid Interceptor Special FE-series V-8—Ford's first modern musclebound mill—as an option for 1960 models. That was followed up by an even

▲ A column-shifted three-speed manual gearbox was standard behind the 390-6V big-block V-8 in 1961.

▼ Adding three Holley two-barrel carbs to Ford's 390-cid FE-series V-8 in 1961 upped the output ante from 375 horses to 401.

larger FE, the 390, in 1961. Fed by single a four-barrel carburetor, the top-dog 390 that year was rated at 375 horsepower. All that oomph translated into 158.8 mph on Ford's test track in Romeo, Michigan, and a flying-mile speed record of 159.320 mph at Daytona Beach down Florida way.

But that wasn't all... "In 1960, Ford answered the complaints of dyed-in-the-wool enthusiasts who were tired of watching the competition disappear in the distance by introducing a 352-inch, 360-horsed high-performance V-8," wrote Hot Rod's Ray Brock. "For 1961, they stepped up the tempo with a 390-inch V-8 rated at 375 horsepower. Now here a few months later is another shot in the arm for Ford owners."

That poke in the shoulder was Ford's "6V induction system," the "6V" referring to the six throats of this new option's three Holley

▲ Sunliner convertibles in 1961 were treated to Ford's top-shelf Galaxie-line trim treatment, which included stone shields behind each rear wheel.

▼ The Starliner coupe and Sunliner convertible were the flagships of the Galaxie series in 1961. Each received appropriate fender badges.

70

two-barrel carburetors, which dropped right down in place of the 375-horse 390's single-carb intake. Available only as a dealer-installed option, the 6V setup was reportedly delivered to your friendly neighborhood Ford store boxed up in the trunk of said 375-horse car. The switch was then made right before a buyer's eyes and bingo, an instant boost to 401 horsepower. Price for the 6V option was $260.

Among the first to take advantage of this deal was drag racer Les Ritchey. He took the three Holleys out of his '61 Ford's trunk and went racing at the 1961 NHRA Winternationals, managing a best run of 13.33 seconds at 105.50 mph at the wheel of his 401-horse Ford. Mean indeed for a two-ton brute.

Ford's hottest 390 V-8s were offered beneath the hoods of all 1961 models save station wagons—thus the 401-horse Sunliner convertible shown here. Introduced midyear in 1961 as well was Ford's first modern four-on-the-floor, a Borg-Warner T-10 four-speed manual transmission. This Sunliner, however, features the more typical T-85 three-speed, which was "standard" behind the 375- and 401-horse 390 V-8s. Like the triple-carb option, the T-10 four-speed was a dealer-installed option only.

Typical foundation fortification came along with any 1961 Ford fitted with either the 375- or 401-horse 390 (both engines used the same ordering code, "Z"), beginning with typically beefed springs and shock absorbers. Also

included were bigger brakes with three-inch wide shoes, an oversized three-inch diameter driveshaft incorporating tougher U-joints, high-speed Firestone nylon tires on 15-inch wheels, and a four-pinion differential.

In 1962, both the triple-carb intake and four-speed stick went from dealer-installed items to true factory-delivered options. New that year too was an even larger FE, the 406, which then morphed the following year into the famed 427... That, however, is another story.

MILESTONE FACTS

- When the AMA "anti-racing" edict was enacted in the summer of 1957, Ford overnight cancelled its high-performance options, including its supercharged 312 V-8.

- In April 1959, Ford finally announced it would be offering high-performance options again with hopes of making up lost ground to Chevrolet and Pontiac.

- Engineers in 1961 bored and stroked the existing 352 cubic-inch FE-series big-block, resulting in the 390 V-8.

- Ford used the "4V" label to describe their four-barrel V-8s, the "V" being short for venturi. The company's triple two-barrel induction setup then logically became the "6V."

- The 390-6V V-8 was Ford's first engine to surpass 400 advertised horsepower.

- Lee Iacocca took over as Ford general manager in November 1960.

- Advertisements called the 1961 Fords "The Lively Ones."

- Ford named its 401-horsepower triple-carb V-8 the "Thunderbird Special." Its official engine code was "Z."

1961 Pontiac Catalina Super Duty 389

Bunkie Knudsen moved to Chevrolet in 1961, and Estes took over at Pontiac. Under his able management, the division continued to grow both in sales volume, and performance reputation. The Tempest, a radical new compact model introduced in 1961, projected the company to number three in the autoproducers' league with its great success. Traditionally, this was a hot spot for competing manufacturers, but Pontiac managed to dominate this rung on the ladder for most of the decade.

The Super Duty performance cars ended Pontiac's formerly staid image forever, preparing the ground for the GTO models that came later in the sixties. Jim Wangers, winner of the 1960 'Top Eliminator' title, was a Pontiac promotions guy who drag- raced the company cars in his spare time. He and group of keen young Pontiac engineers were instrumental in bringing the Super Duty race-car options together. By their very nature the Super Duty Pontiacs were limited-production special options. The Catalinas were most often fitted out with the racing package, being the smallest and lightest cars full-size cars in the Pontiac stable.

The 1961 version used the 389 cid (6.1 liter) Super Duty engine, and took Pontiac to success in 21 of 52 NASCAR Grand National stock car races. But the omnipresent threat of the big Chevy 409 engine meant that engine power was increased to 421 cid (6.3 liters) in 1962, becoming the ultimate Super Duty engine option. It was strengthened with forged pistons and four-bolt main-bearing caps.

Engine:	Super Duty V-8
Displacement:	389 cid
Horsepower:	348 at 4800 rpm
Compression Ratio:	10.75:1
Wheelbase:	119 inches
Base Price:	$2766
Number Produced:	14,524

The strength was no more than the engine required, as it developed a reputed output greater than 500 horsepower. In 1963, the engineers added a McKellar solid-lifter camshaft with dual-valve springs and transistorised ignition. This brought the rating right up to 550 horsepower. To maximise the effect of this huge power output, the cars were radically lightened, with reduced-weight front ends, aluminium bumper brackets, trunk lids and radiator supports. Even the glass windows could be changed to plexiglass as a dealer-fitted option. Most radical of all were

▲ This simple Catalina belies the power under the hood.

the so-called 'Swiss Cheese Catalinas' with holes drilled into their chassis. This option reduced the weight of the car to an extraordinarily low 3325 lbs (considering the weight of the extra go-goodies). A Swiss Cheese Super Duty car with full providence would now be worth in excess of $100,000. So the Super Dutys reached the epitome of their developmental success, just in time for GM to impose a factory-sponsored racing ban.

1962 Dodge Polara 413 Max Wedge

Things remained depressed at Dodge in '62, but general production remained at a similarly low level, and the company stayed at ninth in the auto producers' league. C.E. Briggs was the general manager of the division.

But there were chinks of light in the company year, perhaps the brightest was the development of the 'Max Wedge' performance engine. This was actually street slang for Dodge's Ramcharger 413 V-8. 'Max' for maximum performance and 'Wedge' for its shape. The Max Wedge was introduced in '62 as Dodge's answer to the Chevy 409 and Pontiac's 421 Super Duty engines. All of these were now in cut-throat competition on the super-stock race circuit. Chrysler was the last of the 'big three' to join up, but with Tom Hoover now in charge of the competition performance program, they didn't lag behind for long. The first thing Hoover did was to turn his attention to the newly revamped Dart/Polara models. The Polara 500 was the top trim level production Dodge for 1962. It shared body and chassis components with the

Dart series, and was built on the same 116-inch wheelbase.

Hoover also used the division's existing 413-cid V-8 as the basis for a completely revamped super-stock competition powerhouse. Longer exhaust valves were fitted, and a forged steel crankshaft. Magnafluxed forged steel rods, lightweight forged aluminium pistons and redesigned cylinder heads were also added to reduce weight and increase output. Unfortunately, it

Wheelbase:	116 inches
Weight:	3,500 pounds
Engine:	413 cubic-inch "Ramcharger 413" V-8
Horsepower:	410 with 11:1 compression; 420 with 13.5:1
Induction:	two Carter AFB (aluminum four-barrel) carburetors on an aluminum cross-ram manifold
Transmission:	Borg-Warner T-85 three-speed manual
Suspension:	independent A-arms w/coil springs in front; live axle with leaf springs in back
Brakes:	four-wheel drums
Performance:	13.44 seconds at 109.76 mph for the quarter-mile (Motor Trend, August 1962)
Production:	300, estimated for both Dodge and Plymouth models

▼ This Polara is unusually high in trim to be fitted with the Max Wedge, most other examples were basic sedans.

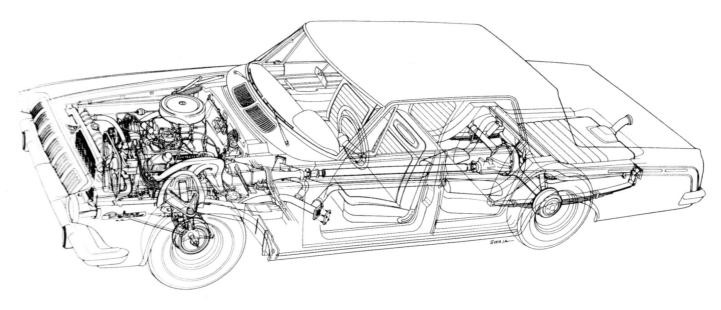

▲ Race-ready Max Wedge Mopars could break into the quarter-mile's 12-second bracket with ease.

▼ Wild free-flowing exhaust manifolds with special cutouts were Max Wedge features in 1962 and '63.

proved impossible to install oil seals, so the engine proved to be a terrible oil burner. Induction was provided by a unique cross-ram aluminum intake with twin Carter carburettors positioned diagonally. Cast iron manifolds were adjusted to provide open operation in race situations. Reviewer Roger Huntington heralded the manifolds as a work of art.

The Ramcharger 413 was available in two forms, one rated at 410 horsepower, the other at 420. Transmission was provided by either a

▼ A Borg-Warner three-speed manual or a Torqueflite automatic handled the horses handed off by a 1962 Max Wedge V-8.

◢ Full-dress Polara trim (below) and snazzy interior appointments were not common to Dodge's Max Wedge. Most were bare-bones sedans.

MILESTONE FACTS

- The term "Max Wedge" was street slang that applied to both Dodge and Plymouth models fitted with Chrysler Corporation's hot 413 super-stock V-8.

- Dodge's Ramcharger 413 was available in two forms in 1962, one rated at 410 horsepower, the other at 420. Compression was 11:1 for the former, a molecule-mashing 13.5:1 for the latter.

- Motor Trend magazine's Roger Huntington called the Max Wedge's exhaust manifolds "a work of art—far and away the most efficient [system] ever put on an American car."

- Behind the Max Wedge 413 V-8 in 1962 was either a heavy-duty Borg-Warner T-85 three-speed manual with a 10.5-inch clutch or the impressive A-727 Torqueflite three-speed automatic.

- Thanks to the durable Torqueflite, Max Wedge Dodges quickly became the runaway favorite in drag racings's Super Stock/Automatic classes.

- Additional Max Wedge Dodge features in 1962 included a heavy-duty driveshaft; beefy brakes, shocks and six-leaf rear springs, all taken from the police car parts shelf.

- Dodge's 420-horse 413 V-8 came with specific instructions in 1962: "A final word of warning, the 13.5:1 engine must never be run at top speeds for more than 15 seconds at a time."

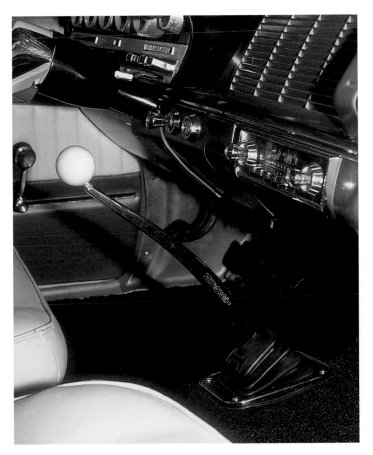

heavy-duty Borg-Warner manual gearbox, or a Torqueflite three-speed automatic. Beefed-up braking and suspension were also fitted to the beast. Parts for the latter were borrowed from Dodge's super-tough police car models.

The Max Wedge was also designed for street use, and Motor Trend Magazine's road test of August '62 produced a top speed of almost 110 mph. In fact, the Polar 413 actually became the first production stock car with a factory option engine to break the quarter-mile-in-12-seconds barrier.

▲ Max Wedge displacement went from 413 cubic inches to 426 in 1963.

▼ "Max Wedge" was actually street slang for Dodge and Plymouth's special 413 V-8. In Dodge terms, the official name was "Ramcharger 413."

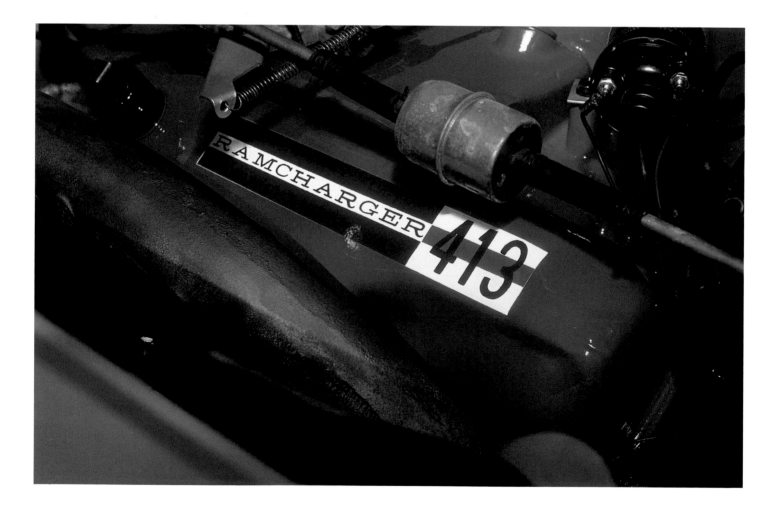

▲ The Max Wedge was launched in April 1962. It was well publicized.

▼ The 1962 Max Wedge shared the same body as the Dodge Dart.

1962 Oldsmobile Starfire

Oldsmobile were at number five in the automakers' league for 1962, on a production of 428,853 units. Oldsmobile was somewhat upstaged in the performance arena of the late '50s by the introduction of the Chrysler Hemi and high-winging Chevrolet V-8, but continued to manufacture solid, popular and comfortable cars. The company also re-asserted itself in the high performance stakes with its introduction of the tri-carb-based J-2 option that was offered on most models.

Like so many other US automakers, the early sixties Oldsmobile models looked as though they had just landed from outer space. Mid-1961 saw the introduction of the Starfire convertible that started the swing to big sporty cars. The car was fitted with standard 'buckety' front seats, and hard-to-see tachometer. The car was equipped with abundant bright trim, this had been limited in the other GM ranges for '61, but was more in evidence at Oldsmobile.

Starfire became a separate range for '62, after the positive reception to the initial model in the previous year. The Holiday hardtop coupe was added to the big bucket-seat ragtop, and immediately outsold it, virtually five to one. The two cars were Oldsmobile's attempt to corner a greater share of the personal/luxury car market. To compete with the other cars in this

Engine:	V-8
Displacement:	394-cid
Horsepower:	345 at 4600 rpm
Transmission:	Hydra-Matic automatic
Compression Ratio:	10.50:1
Induction:	Rochester 4GC four-barrel
Body Style:	Two-door Convertible
Weight:	4488lbs
Wheelbase:	123 inches
Base Price:	$4744
Number Produced:	7149

market, they were deliberately well-equipped with all the hardware of the less expensive Olds models, plus sports console, Hydra-Matic automatic with console shifter, power brakes, power steering, brushed aluminum side trim, a dual exhaust with fiberglass packed mufflers and leather upholstery.

▲ This Convertible Starfire sold roughly the same number as the original '61 model.

The big technological news at Olds for '62 was the introduction of America's first production turbocharged V-8 engine. It was launched in mid-season as the 'Turbo Rocket', and fitted to the new Jetfire coupe. Featuring 'fluid injection', the 215-cid engine-block pumped out 215 horsepower, and had lively acceleration. But initially, the engine had some reliability problems that somewhat curtailed sales.

1962 Pontiac 421 SD

No one, off the beach or otherwise, ever sang a note about this car, perhaps because saving pennies and dimes in this case would've got you nowhere fast. The engine along cost around $1,300, a bunch of bucks today, a small fortune 40 years back. But its sky-high price notwithstanding, nothing beat a Super Duty Pontiac in 1962. Nothing, not even a 409.

Designed to do battle on dragstrips and stock-car tracks, Pontiac's 421 Super Duty Catalina was never meant for polite society, which makes comparison between toned-down super-stock rivals from Ford and Chevrolet akin to squaring off apples and oranges. Like those Max Wedge Mopars also introduced in 1962, the 421 SD Catalina was an all-out factory super stock, plain and simple. Base 406 Fords and 409 Chevys in 1962 could've been driven on the street with relative ease; anyone who tried to tame a 421 Super Duty that year was in for a tough time. "These

cars are not intended for general passenger car use," read a corporate disclaimer, "and they are not supplied by Pontiac Motor Division for such purposes."

Super Duty roots run back to December 1959 with the introduction of various high-performance parts intended to put Pontiac out in front on NASCAR tracks. Rated at 363 horsepower, the 389 cubic-inch Super Duty V-8 proved its worth at Daytona in February 1960 when Fireball Roberts' Pontiac lapped

▼   The 421 Super Duty was Pontiac's offering to the sport drag racing fraternity of the 1960s. Their most potent option was the Catalina Super Stock package.

Wheelbase:	120 inches
Curb weight:	3,800 pounds
Original price:	$4,400
Engine:	421 cubic-inch Super Duty V-8
Horsepower:	405 at 5,600 rpm
Torque:	425 at 4,400 rpm
Compression:	11:1
Induction:	two Carter AFB four-barrel carburetors
Transmission:	Borg-Warner T-10 four-speed manual
Suspension:	independent A-arms w/coil springs in front; live axle with leaf springs in back
Brakes:	drums at all four wheels

the superspeedway at a then-incredible 155 mph. Output for the 389 SD was upped to 368 horses in 1961, helping Pontiac pull off a 1-2-3 finish at Daytona. In all, Super Duty Pontiacs copped 30 of 52 NASCAR races that year.

After a bore job in late 1961, the 421-cube Super Duty picked right up where the 389 variety left off. Motor Trend's Roger Huntington went for a ride in one with Pontiac ad-man Jim Wangers in January 1962, and he couldn't say enough about the car's outrageous performance: "Wangers got into that big Poncho, and we went. Low gear was a rubber-burning fishtail. A snap shift to 2nd

at 5500 rpm and 60 mph came up in a bit over five seconds. Second and 3rd gears almost tore my head off. Then across the finish line in high at 5300—stopping the watch at 13.9 ad 107 mph. Acceleration figures like these are not uncommon in Super/Stock classes on our dragstrips. But when you can turn them with a car just the way you buy it, you have something to scream about."

Purpose built from air cleaner to oil pan as a certified super-stock screamer, the 421 Super Duty featured a beefy four-bolt block with a forged steel crank and 11:1 compression Mickey Thompson forged aluminum pistons.

An aggressive #10 "McKellar" cam (named after Pontiac's fast-thinking engineer Malcolm McKellar) activated big valves (1.92-inch intake, 1.76 exhaust) through solid lifters and 1.65:1 rockers. Two big Carter AFB carbs, with a total flow of 1000 cfm, sat atop an aluminum intake. And spent gases were hauled away by a pair of intriguing cast-iron, individual-runner "long branch" headers incorporating convenient cutouts for wide-open running.

Additional track-ready Super Duty fare included various lightweight body parts. Steel could've been traded for weight-saving aluminum for the hood, front bumper, fenders, inner fenders and radiator brackets. Pontiac was the first to offer weight-saving components for its factory super-stocks, but by the end of 1962 all of Detroit was in the aluminum (or fiberglass) game.

Exotic optional aluminum exhaust manifolds helped trim the fat, too, as did a special frame that featured perimeter rails that were cut out to transform rectangular tubes into channel. A customer also could have specified the deletion of insulation and sound deadener, but only a handful did. Other options included a Safe-T-Track differential with a wide range of gear ratios, bullet-proof axles, beefier brakes with larger 15-inch wheels, stiffer springs and shocks, front and rear sway bars, and all of Pontiac's popular style and

MILESTONE FACTS

- Pontiac built 200 405-horse 421 Super Duty V-8s in 1962 to satisfy new NHRA drag racing rules specifying that a factory could only legalize a particular engine for its dragstrips by selling it in "regular-production" form to the public. Of these SD engines, at least 179 made into 1962 Pontiac models.

- Among the 421 Super Duty V-8's race-ready standard features were deep-grooved pulleys and a high-volume oil pump. A deep-sump eight-quart oil pan was optional.

- A column-shifted Borg-Warner T-85 three-speed manual was standard behind the 421 Super Duty V-8. A T-10 four-speed was optional

- Surprisingly, 16 421 Super Duty V-8s were installed in luxury-minded Grand Prix coupes in 1962.

- Super Duty Pontiacs were built again early in 1963 before General Motors executives ordered all of its divisions to cease their involvement in racing projects.

- Super Duty exhaust manifolds, known as "long branch" headers, featured individual runners that led to two openings, one the flowed into an exhaust pipe, another that could be opened up for non-restrictive operation. These cast-iron manifolds were also available in lightweight aluminum form.

- Heavy-duty 11-inch finned aluminum front brake drums were optional for the Super Duty Catalina, as were 4.30:1 rear gears.

- Catalinas typically rolled on 14-inch wheels in 1962. Adding the heavy-duty brake package to a Super Duty model brought along bigger 15-inch wheels.

◀ Pontiac's 421 Super Duty of 1961 was designed specifically for the drag strip.

appearance packages, such as the attractive eight-lug rims and sporty Venture trim group with its tri-tone "Morrokide" upholstery. Though dressing up a Super Duty wasn't the idea, at least 16 customers in 1962 thought it might be cool to combine the savage Super Duty V-8 with the sensual Grand Prix coupe, in its first year as one of Detroit's sexiest luxo-cruisers.

Nearly all other Super Duty cars, however, went right to the track, where they dominated NASCAR racing yet again in 1962. And those that did find their way onto the street had

◀ A Hurst-shifted four-speed transmission was optional for the '62 Super Duty.

▼ That snazzy tri-tone interior was included as part of Pontiac's optional Ventura trim package. Most Super Duty models in 1962 featured plain-Jane appointments.

many a foolish stoplight challenger singing the blues. As Roger Huntington explained further after his wild ride, "I must say, [the] 421 Pontiac is a terrific piece of automobile. I'm still shaking."

▲ 1963's Super Duty engine.

▶ Heavy duty brake drums finned for cooling were also optional.

▼ Each Super Duty exhaust manifold featured a covered cutout opening—unbolting that cover allowed unrestricted, cupboard-rattling operation.

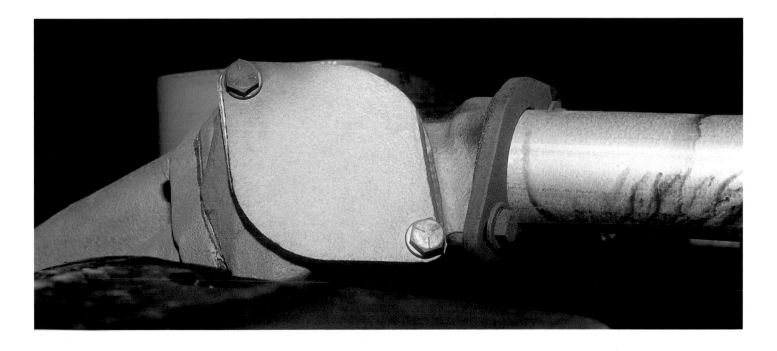

1963 Chevrolet Corvette Sting Ray Z06 Fastback Coupe

The 1963 Corvette turned out to one of the greatest ever, a brilliant synthesis of styling and performance. The cars were called 'Sting Rays' to emphasise that they were different to all the Corvettes that had gone before. The Sting Ray was the joint concept of design guru Bill Mitchell, and engineering genius Zora Duntov. Duntov had been a racing driver, and was very aware of the handling and performance of the car, while Mitchell wanted to inject the glamor of the European sports cars into Corvette. The contemporary Jaguars in particular are credited with influencing the sinuous, cat-like lines of the car. He himself drove an E-Type.

The Corvette received a major restyle in 1963, for the first time since its introduction ten years earlier. Two models were available for the first time. The traditional convertible, and the first Corvette coupe, introduced for the first time in this model year. This 'boattail' fastback would be the only Corvette ever to have the unique 'split' rear window, now highly coveted by classic car collectors. It gave the car the appearance of a kind of fish spine running the entire length of the car. Apart from this unusual feature, the rear deck view resembled that of the '62 body, but the rest of the car was unrecognisable from its predecessors. The headlights were hidden in an electronically operated panel. This was not a gimmick, but a serious attempt to improve the aerodynamics of the car. Corvette and Jaguar were two of the few marques to have grasped this concept in the early '60s. Corvette was the first manufacturer to introduce hidden headlights since the DeSoto of 1942. The recessed fake hood louvers were of the more superficial styling type, however.

Mechanically, this was the year when Duntov introduced the famous ladder-frame chassis and suspension layout. The center of gravity for the car was lowered from nineteen to sixteen and a half inches (so that ground clearance was reduced to only five inches) and weight was evenly distributed between the front and rear axles. This gave the car both excellent road holding and ride quality. The interior had circular gauges with black faces. Windshield washers, carpeting, an outside rearview mirror, dual

1963 Chevrolet Corvette Sting Ray Z06 Fastback Coupe

exhaust, tachometer, electric clock, heater and defroster, cigarette lighter, and safety belts were all fitted as standard.

The Sting Rays also hugely improved Corvette's performance in the market place,

and the car sold over 22,000 units in the first year of this model.

▼ This Silver Blue Sting Ray was one of seven colours offered – the others were black, white, silver, Daytona Blue, red, and tan.

Engine:	V-8 overhead valve, cast iron block
Displacement:	327 cid
Horsepower:	250 at 4400 rpm
Compression Ratio:	10.5:1
Base Price:	$4257
Number Produced:	10,594

1963 Chevrolet Impala SS

Chevrolet launched their widest ever range in 1963, and sold three out of every ten cars in America, over 2,300,3000 units (including Corvette and Corvair). This output was 700,000 cars more than that of closest rival, Ford. Bunkie Knudsen was still at the helm of the division. This was a vintage year for factory drag racing options, and the Chevelle launch year. At the other end of the model range, the full-size Impala was the 'upper crust' Chevy model. It was the only '63 model to receive new sheetmetal, and looked elegant and uncluttered. Impala had started life in the late fifties as a model in the Bel Air series, and soon became instantly recognisable by their triple taillight treatment. A large range of options were available for the car, including the RPO Z11 race ready package.

Impala was Chevy's largest seller, and their plushest car had most of the equipment standard on lower lines. They also had bright aluminium front seat end panels, patterned cloth and leather grained vinyl upholstery in color-coordinated materials over thick foam seat cushions. A sport-style steering wheel was fitted, and other extras included an electric clock, parking brake warning lamp, and dashboard face panels in textured bright metal. The Super Sport (RPO Z03) trim was up-rated for '63, with the addition of special chrome spinner hubs, extra emblems, matching cove inserts, bucket seats and a locking storage compartment (when the transmission was upgraded to four-speed or Powerglide automatic). Super Sports also had the option to fit the Turbo-Fire 409-cid V-8, and most of these fitted in '63 were installed on this model. This was just one of six V-

Engine:	(Base V-8) Overhead valve
Displacement:	283 cid
Horsepower:	195 at 4800 rpm
Compression Ratio:	9.25:1
Wheelbase:	119 inches
Base Price:	$2774
Number Produced:	399,224

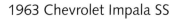

8 options that were available, producing between 250 and 430 horsepower, all the way from mild to wild. The biggest engine was available only with the Z11 package, and was the prototype for the spectacularly successful 396-cid V-8 of 1965.

Motor Trend Magazine road tested two Impala SS sport coupes with V-8 engines at both ends of the mild and wild scale – the 250 horsepower 327 and the newly introduced

340 horsepower 409. Both cars were installed with Powerglide automatic, power steering and power brakes. The tester found the automatic gears tricky on both cars, and slow to shift, but liked their performance in the acceleration tests. Of course, the 409-cid engine was much quicker, covering a quarter mile in 15.9 seconds, reaching 88 mph.

▲ This Impala two-door Hardtop Sport Coupe could be fitted with any one of six Chevy V-8s.

1963 Ford Galaxie 500 427

Ford completely revised their full-size car range for the fifth year in a row. As in the previous year, the base model cars were devoid of any sculptural lines except for the beltline feature line. Each model name was carried in script on the fender immediately behind the front wheel opening. Once again, the taillights were large round units mounted at the top of the rear fenders with a stamped aluminium panel being used on the Galaxie 500 series.

There are several Galaxies model years that describe the top range as '500s'. The number does not stand for 500 horsepower or 500 cubic inch displacement. The leading rumour for the origination of the notation is the 500 miles as in the 500-mile stock car races in which the Galaxie models competed.

The '63 Galaxie was a classic from the first day it rolled off the showroom floor, the car's distinctive lines and styling are timeless and are now among the most collected Fords of any era.

The Galaxie 500 series was the top trim level for the model in this year. The series contained sedans, hardtops and convertibles. The model was slightly more elaborately trimmed that the simply-styled base-model Galaxies, having an attractive full length upper and lower body side molding, and trimmed with chromed 'A' pillar and window moldings. There were also two horizontal chrome strips on the side of the car. Between the two chrome pieces, just in front of the taillights were six cast 'hash marks'. The 500 XL models were available as two- and four-door hardtops, convertible and midyear fastback model. The fastback featured a sporty new roofline with no post and Starliner type looks. The standard equipment on these cars was a deluxe offering with standard bucket seats and console, spinner wheelcovers, wall to wall carpeting, courtesy lights and contoured deluxe seat upholstery.

The 427-cid big-block V-8 was the most powerful engine option for the year. The high-performance race with other US manufacturers was in full swing by now, and this was the most powerful engine in Ford's entire history. It fully reflected FoMoCo's determination to sell more cars via racing successes. Two versions of the engine were introduced, a single four-barrel version at 410 horsepower and a dual four-barrel carburettor at an astounding 425

Engine:	Thunderbird High-performance V-8
Displacement:	427 cid
Horsepower:	425 at 6000 rpm
Compression Ratio:	11.5:1
Base Price:	$3268
Number Produced:	33,870

horsepower. Transmission types were the SynchroSmooth manual column shift, a four-on-the-floor manual, Ford-O-Matic Drive automatic and Cruise-O-Matic three speed automatic.

▲ Options for the '63 Galaxie included power front seats, power windows/steering/brakes, padded dash/visors and Select Aire Conditioner.

1963 Ford Thunderbird 'M-Code' Sports Roadster

The Thunderbird was Ford's answer to the Chevrolet Corvette and debuted onto the market in 1955. It started out as a two-seat personal car, but was re-built as a four-seat model in 1958. This was the last time it would appear as a true two-seat car until 2002, but the Sports Roadster of 1962/63 was a partial return to two-seat styling. It seemed the perfect answer to the nostalgia felt for the original T-birds. The model was an attempt to revive the sporty appearance of the original 'personal' cars. It featured a fibreglass tonneau package (designed by Bud Kaufman), which covered the back seat of the car to give a two-seat appearance. The tonneau covered the twin front headrests and was 'flowed' from these to the back of the car to make the styling more aerodynamic. The convertible top could operate with the tonneau in position. The introduction of the Sports Roadster meant that the car buyer could purchase a sporty two-passenger convertible and four-passenger car in one and the same car.

For its second and final model year, the car received new doors and front fenders, and a bodyside crease. The Sports Roadster was fitted with a dash-mounted grab bar for the passenger, and four dazzling Kelsey-Hayes wire wheels. The rear fender skirts were deleted to allow clearance for the knock-off wheel centers. For performance fans, Ford offered a special 'M-code' 390-cid FE V-8 rated engine, rated at 340 brake horsepower. It was equipped with three Holley two-barrel carburettors and an aluminum manifold to keep the carbs level and at the same height. The 'M-code' option was rare, and only 145 Thunderbirds were ever built with this engine, including thirty-seven '63 Sports Roadsters.

Although the idea for the Sports Roadster was intriguing (it is usually attributed to Lee Iacocca), a combination of the model's high price and difficult tonneau-installation limited its sales. The price was so high, that the buyer could have a Cadillac Convertible for only $162 more. The Kelsey-Hayes wire wheels have also been blamed for the demise of the car, not only because they added expense (a whopping $372.30), but because they were blamed for causing wheel failure, extremely dangerous at speed.

Engine:	'M-code' Thunderbird Special Six-Barrel V-8
Displacement:	390-cid
Horsepower:	340 at 5000 rpm
Compression Ratio:	10.5:1
Base Price:	$5563
Number Produced:	37

The best-known customer of the Sports Roadster, Elvis Presley, had a blow out accident at high speed that immediately hit the headlines. Ford discontinued the model in '63.

▲ This 1963 'M-Code' Sports Roadster is a very rare model, one of just 37 built.

1963 Mercury S-55

Mercury cars had first been introduced in 1939 as intermediate models, priced between Ford and Lincoln. The joint Lincoln-Mercury division was founded by Ford in 1945, and so it wasn't until the 1949 models appeared that Mercurys were able to shed their image as glorified Fords (at least for the moment). The youth-appeal of the cars was hugely improved when James Dean drove a Mercury in the cult movie Rebel Without a Cause. However, Fords and Mercurys shared body shells throughout the fifties, and early 60s so it was difficult for the marque to define itself. Later advertising also stressed the classy heritage of their stable-mate Lincolns.

Basic Monterey styling for the year was reminiscent of the 1961 models, with six taillights located in the rear deck panel, and a concave vertical bar grille housed four chrome-trimmed headlights. The Monterey Custom was the intermediate model for the year, and had additional chroming and standard features.

The 1963 Mercury Monterey S-55 was the top of the Mercury model line for this year, and was offered in four body styles – the two-door convertible, two-door Marauder Fastback Coupe, four-door Breezeway Hardtop sedan and the two-door Breezeway Hardtop. The unique and practical Breezeway roof, first offered in 1957 on the Turnpike Cruiser and reintroduced in this model year, featured a roll-down back window. The standard engine for the line was the Marauder Super 390-cid V-8, with four-barrel carburetor, but the Marauder 390 V-8 with two-barrel carburetor was available as a no-cost option. The Marauder Fastbacks were true muscle cars that were raced to victory in the 1963 NASCAR series, with 427-cid V-8s. They had been designed with aerodynamics and

Engine:	V-8 overhead valve, cast iron block
Displacement:	390-cid
Horsepower:	250 at 4400 rpm
Compression Ratio:	8.9:1
Number Produced:	1203

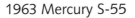

speed in mind. Transmission options for the production models were three or four-speed manual or Multi-Drive Merc-O-Matic automatic. S-55s were identified by marque insignia in front of the rear fender, chrome bars and special wheel covers.

The Mercury advertising slogan for '63 was 'Shift to the Real Performer! Go Mercury!' The S-55 was a real sizzler that delivered the luxury of the Monterey Custom series plus sports car features – individually adjustable bucket seats, bright-metal floor console with shift lever and storage compartment. Red and white courtesy lights were positioned inside the doors. When the doors were opened the interiors were revealed as deeply luxurious, complete with vinyl upholstery, front and rear armrests and a padded dashboard.

▲   This S-55 hardtop looks cool in two-tone.

1963 Studebaker Avanti

Studebaker had introduced the Lark in 1958, and the car proved to be a big success. However, the board could not agree on how to spend the profits. President Harold Churchill wanted to invest in the future, using the money to keep Studebaker at the forefront of small car development. But the remainder of the directors wanted to diversify. The disagreement led to Churchill's early replacement by Sherwood Egbert in '61. It was under his direction that the company launched the Gran Turismo Hawk and Avanti models.

The Avanti was Studebaker's almost unique fiberglass-bodied sport coupe, and was the first completely new-bodied model that the company had introduced since 1953. It was built on a modified Lark Daytona convertible chassis. In 1961, Egbert commissioned Raymond Loewy to design the car. Egbert flew himself to Palm Springs to meet the celebrity industrial designer. The car was a triumph, with smooth lines, an under-the-bumper radiator air intake and wedge-shaped design the model hallmarks. All '63 Avantis had round headlight enclosures. Avanti interiors were equipped with four aircraft-inspired seats. Two power units were available for the car, the Avanti R1 V-8 that developed 240 horsepower, or the Avanti Supercharge R2 V-8, capable of 289 horsepower. The latter was a $210 option.

Daniel Jedlicka wrote an Esquire article about the car (after the demise of Studebaker) in 1969, called 'Instant Classics'. In it, he wrote of the Avanti 'Raymond Loewy styled it and liked it even better than his slick '53 Studebaker coupe. Ian Fleming bought one. The roof was trimmed with a steel boxlike frame attached to a hefty roll bar and windshield support. There were aircraft type rocker switches mounted in the roof, a Paxton supercharge V-8 and a fibreglass body with tremendous impact resistance. It hit 170 mph at Bonneville'. It was all true.

Despite the success and acclaim generated by the Avanti, Studebaker's position continued to be precarious, and the company lost money. Egbert stepped down from his position in '63, due to failing health. Production was now centralized at the Hamilton, Ontario plant in Canada. The writing was on the wall for the Avanti, and production was discontinued in December '63.

Engine:	Avanti Supercharged R2 V-8
Displacement:	289-cid
Horsepower:	289
Compression Ratio:	9.0:1
Weight:	3148 lbs
Wheelbase:	109 inches
Base Price:	$4445
Number Produced:	3834

▲ The Loewy-styled Avanti soon achieved iconic status.

1964 Mercury Comet Caliente

Mercury celebrated its Silver Anniversary in 1964, and was at number nine in the auto producers' league with an output of 298,609 cars. The Comet models were produced by Mercury between 1960 and 1967. The original Comet series was based on the Ford Falcon platform of 1960. The sister cars shared many technical features, but the Comet had its own distinct bodylines, exterior ornamentation and interior trim. The first convertible Comet was introduced in the '63 line-up.

The Mercury Comets were extensively re-styled for 1964, with a Lincoln-Continental-style grille. The same theme was repeated on the rear deck panel. A wraparound trim piece was seen on the tips of the front fenders.

Three thin, vertical trim slashes were on the sides of the front fenders. The signal lights remained embedded in the front bumper. Overall, the new squared-off bodyline, slightly longer than the earlier models, made the cars far more futuristic looking.

The 1964 range introduced new names to the Comet line-up, the Comet 202, Comet 404 and Caliente: three distinctive packages with the same bodylines and drivetrain components. The Caliente was the sports model Comet, with bucket seats. Six-cylinder and V-8 engines were available for the model, as were manual and automatic transmission options. The Cyclone was the ultimate Comet package with the V-8 engine as standard equipment and 6000rpm factory dashboard tachometer.

'Every bit as hot as it looks!' was how the sales literature described the Caliente series. The model trim consisted of a wide, full-length molding on its sides and a nameplate on the lower front fenders. The interior of the car was embellished with a padded instrument panel with walnut grain trim and deeploop carpeting as luxury standard features. Caliente hardtops and convertibles were available only in solid colors. A third model, a four-door sedan was also on offer.

A team of customized Calientes, equipped with 289 cid/271 horsepower V-8s joined the Mercury muscle car club by travelling for over 100,000 miles at average speeds of over a hundred miles per hour.

Engine: Six-cylinder, overhead valve

Displacement: 170 cid

Horsepower: 101 at 4400 rpm

Compression Ratio: 8.7:1

Body Style: Two-door Convertible

Wheelbase: 114 inches

Base Price: $2636

Number Produced: 9039

▲ The Caliente was the sports package Comet for 1964. This was the second year for a convertible Comet.

1964 Oldsmobile F-85 Cutlass 4-4-2

The F-85, launched in 1961, was the smallest Oldsmobile model in decades. It was a compact companion to the full-size Super 88 Holiday model, and strongly resembled this car. The four-door model, the coupe and the four-door wagons were sold in the $2300-$2900 range. F-85 output totalled 76,394 for this model year. The F-85s rode on a 112 inch wheelbase.

Sportiest of the new F-85 range was the mid-year, Deluxe-trim, bucket-seat pillared coupe called the Cutlass. This progenitor of a well-regarded Oldsmobile model name was priced at $2621 attracted 9935 sales. The car came with only one engine option – the 155 horsepower aluminum V-8.

Convertibles were added to the compact F-85 range in '62, in both base and bucket-seat Cutlass trim. The Cutlass model sold 9893. In 1963, Oldsmobile retained the trim options of the F-85s, but gave the car more of a big-car appearance, as the buyers had requested. The new Cutlass Sports Coupe hardtop was the bestselling model in the range, attracting 29,269 buyers with an attractive base price of $2592. All F-85 models were equipped with a 215-cid aluminum V-8 engine, rated with either 155 or 215 horsepower.

The F-85 went from a compact model to mid-size 'senior compacts' for '64, by adopting a handsome new 'A-body' platform, shared with several GM stablemates – the Buick Special and Skylark, the Pontiac Tempest and Le Mans and the new Chevy from Chevelle. It was completely redesigned, and gained a full eleven inches in length (just three inches on the wheelbase). The Sporty Cutlass now became a separate three-model series, which included a two-door coupe, two-door Holiday hardtop and two-

Engine:	V-8, overhead valve, cast-iron block
Displacement:	330-cid
Horsepower:	210 at 4400 rpm
Compression Ratio:	9.0:1
Number Produced:	36,153

door convertible. The $2784 Holiday hardtop coupe was the bestselling model in the range, with sales of 36,153. Cutlasses also now came with a new cast-iron 'Rocket' 330-cid V-8 making 290 horsepower. The aluminium block was a thing of the past.

1964 was also the introductory year for the 4-4-2 equipment package, at an extra price of $136, RPO code B09. This translated as four-barrel, four-speed and dual exhaust. Other equipment included a heavy-duty suspension, dualsnorkel air cleaner, oversized redline tires and special badges. The cars were also fitted with a heater/defroster, self-adjusting brakes, oil filter, front stabilizer and dual sun visors. Deluxe models also boasted a Deluxe steering wheel, padded dashboard and carpets. Interiors were vinyl or cloth.

The F-85 models were built in six Oldsmobile plants at Lansing, Atlanta, Kansas City, Linden, Southgate and Arlington.

▲ This F-85 Cutlass Holiday hardtop was the best-selling model in the range.

1964 Pontiac GTO

America's first modern muscle car, Pontiac's GTO, didn't become the performance segment's solid sales leader by being the fastest car on the road. The "Goat" emerged as an overnight marvel in 1964 because it represented an unprecedented combination of high performance and low cost that left even General Motors' conservative upper crust wondering where the hell all this fast-thinking was heading, as well as where it had come from.

Pontiac general manager Pete Estes had managed to sneak the supposedly taboo GTO past unwary corporate killjoys before they had a chance to do that voodoo that they did so well. Complaining company execs then shut up in a hurry after this hard charger hit the ground running in October 1963 and proceeded to take Detroit by storm.

The whole idea was so simple: take a lightweight car, drop in a big-block engine, bolt on a bit of heavy-duty hardware, and wrap it all up with a price tag readily within the reach of the baby boomer youth market then coming of age—presto, instant winner. Not only was that youth market just growing ripe for the picking at the time, but GM then was also

preparing to unveil the right car for the job, the A-body intermediate.

A-bodies picked up where GM's so-called "senior compacts" left off, retaining the latter's existing nameplates while they were at it. Buick's Special, Oldsmobile's F-85 and Pontiac's Tempest were boosted up a notch into the new mid-sized ranks, where they were joined by Chevrolet's all-new Chevelle. Much bigger than a compact yet still smaller than the full-sized liners, these mid-sized models were relatively roomy yet comparatively light and agile. Most importantly, they could handle some serious V-8 power, something their forerunners couldn't.

John DeLorean and fellow

Wheelbase:	115 inches
Weight:	3,360 pounds
Original price:	$3,400
Engine:	389 cubic-inch Tri-Power V-8
Induction:	three Rochester two-barrel carburetors
Compression:	10.75:1
Horsepower:	348 at 4,900 rpm
Torque:	428 at 3,600 rpm
Transmission:	Hurst-shifted four-speed manual
Suspension:	independent A-arms w/coil springs in front; live axle with coil springs in back
Brakes:	drums front and rear
Performance:	14.30 seconds on the quarter-mile, according to Popular Hot Rodding
Production (with Tri-Power 389):	8,245 all models

engineer Bill Collins at Pontiac had experimented with a big-block V-8 Tempest in 1963, but the unit-body/rear-transaxle layout wasn't exactly designed with high performance in mind. That all changed,

▲ ▼ Pontiac's GTO hit the ground running in 1964 and remained Detroit's best-selling muscle car up through 1968.

however, once the redesigned '64 Tempest came along with its full-perimeter frame and conventional solid rear axle.

Never one to overlook a chance to speed

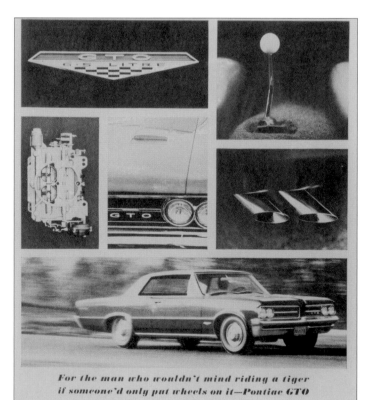

For the man who wouldn't mind riding a tiger if someone'd only put wheels on it—Pontiac GTO

▲ Stainless-steel Custom wheelcovers were optional for Pontiac's first GTO, as were bright exhaust tips.

things up, Pontiac's ever-present advertising wizard, Jim Wangers, was already at work with DeLorean on a trend-setting performance package before the ink even dried on the A-body's blueprints. DeLorean had the engineering groundwork laid, while Wangers had his finger on the pulse of an excitable market poised to pounce on his powerful proposition. All that remained was to sell the idea of a big-block intermediate to GM's top brass, a task that wouldn't be easy considering the corporation's anti-performance stance, as well as its 330 cubic-inch maximum displacement limit for its new mid-sized models.

Well aware of these roadblocks, Wangers and DeLorean made an end run. New models required corporate approval, but option packages didn't. They decided to quietly

MILESTONE FACTS

- The original GTO package initially was offered for the LeMans sports coupe and convertible. A hardtop then joined the mix soon after introduction.

- According to Car and Driver's David E. Davis in 1964, the new GTO "does what so many others only talk about—it really does combine brute, blasting performance with balance and stability of a superior nature."

- In 1964 and '65, the GTO came by way of an options group. In 1966 it was became transformed into its own individual model line.

- Car and Driver shocked its readers in 1964 with a road test that claimed the new GTO could run from rest to 100 mph in only 11.8 seconds. What the report didn't necessarily detail was their test car's many modifictions, made by the guys at Royal Pontiac in Royal Oak, Michigan.

- The GTO's nicknames included "Goat," "The Tiger," and "The Great One."

- Total GTO production in 1964 was 32,450, including 6,644 convertibles

- GTO sales in 1975 soared beyond 75,000.

- Pontiac set the single-season muscle car sales high with 96,946 GTOs unleashed in 1966.

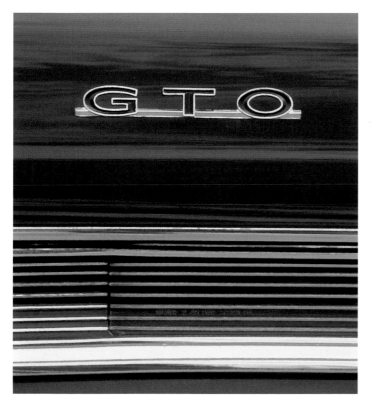

◀ ▼ The GTO legacy survived until 1974 then was revived 30 years later. Polite dress-up features included "GTO" identification, a blacked-out grille and twin dummy hood scoops.

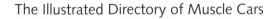

▲ When topped with Pontiac's famed "Tri Power" triple-carburetor option, the GTO's 389 cubic-inch V-8 produced 348 horsepower.

create a 389 option for the Tempest and worry about the consequences later. Of course, the plan would've never worked without Estes' support. But he loved the idea and went nose-to-nose with GM's disagreeable ivory tower execs to insure its success.

Credit for the name went to DeLorean, who unabashedly "borrowed" GTO from Enzo Ferrari. While purists cringed, the American public ate it up. Pontiac sales manager Frank Bridge predicted 1964 sales, at best, would reach 5,000. By the time the tire smoke

◄ The gauge cluster of the 1964 Pontiac GTO.

◀ The power plant of a 1964 Pontiac GTO.

▲ The sumptuous interior of a 1964 Pontiac GTO.

▼ A fine example of the convertible Pontiac GTO Excellent of 1968. This was the second best-ever sales year for the GTO.

cleared, 32,450 Goats had rolled out the door. Even more could've been sold had the production line been able to keep up with demand.

Officially released on October 1, 1963, Pontiac's GTO debuted as an option package for the deluxe Tempest model, the LeMans. Coded W62, the option group included a 325-horse 389 V-8 wearing pair of high-compression heads borrowed from the 389's big brother, the 421. Stiffer suspension and a three-speed manual were also part of the deal. Popular options included a Muncie four-speed and an even hotter 348-horse 389 topped by three Rochester two-barrel carbs, Pontiac's famed "Tri-Power" setup.

▲ The vertically-stacked headlights of the 1965 Pontiac GTO, showing the recessed grille.

◀ The 1965 Pontiac GTO shifter.

▼ Buyer's loved the 1966 GTO's all-new styling which had evolved into a curvier Coke-bottle shape. It was equipped with a bow-tie shaped split grille and stacked headlights.

▲ The 1972 Pontiac GTO was equipped with the big-block V-8.

▼ A front angle shot of the re-styled 1965 Pontiac GTO hardtop. The new car was 3.1 inches longer than the 1964 model and was a hundred pounds heavier. Although the interior dimensions were the same, the dashboard was also re-designed.

Pontiac's first GTO surely would have stood as the star of Detroit's 1964 show had not Ford chosen the same year to introduce its Mustang, a mass-market marvel if there ever was one. Nonetheless, Estes and crew weren't disappointed in the least; they had made their mark with the GTO, the car that first broke the rules then made new ones for the rest of Detroit to follow. That reality alone should be enough to allow Pontiac to take credit for the muscle car's conception.

Anyone out there want to argue?

1964-½ Ford Mustang 260

The big news at Ford for 1964 was the introduction of the Mustang in April. As this was late in the model year, the cars are often known as '64-1/2s'. Lee Iacocca is attributed with its introduction, despite the reluctance of the Ford top brass. The Ford Studio team presented the original design in response to a brief set out by Iacocca. The cars were Ford's response to the improving economy of the early '60s, when consumers were looking for smaller cars complete with luxury and good performance. The car was designed with such clean, attractive lines that it was awarded the Tiffany Award for Excellence in American Design, the only car ever to be so honored. It was the right car at the right time, and went on to have spectacular success, selling over half a million examples in its first year of production. A million were sold in the first two years. An unbroken record to this day. This unprecedented achievement can be attributed to its clever combination of desirable features and striking design aimed at a large segment of the buying public. Not only did the Mustang spawn an entire class of family sports car, but an entire cohort of youthful Americans became known as the Mustang generation. In some regards, this is misleading, as it was the fact that the car appealed to such a large cross-section of age groups, which was the crux of its desirability.

The car was received with such a wave of universal enthusiasm that demand outstripped production for almost a year. Its combination of comfort, convenience, luxury and economy engendered a pride of ownership unmatched in this price bracket. Although the Mustang was the very first of the 'pony' muscle cars, it was first designed and marketed to be a low cost 'personal luxury' sports car. The initial production did not have serious performance engines. The base engine option was the six-cylinder 170-cid, developing a rather weak 101 horsepower. The base V-8 displaced 260 cid and developed 164 horsepower. The top V-8 option, the Challenger High-Performance (Hi-Po) engine was introduced in June '64. This powerplant developed a punchy 271 horsepower, and came with a special handling package, including fourteen-inch red line tires. Only 7273 Hi-Po Mustangs were built.

1964 Ford Mustang 260

The original Mustang would diversify into an enormous range of variants, factory special editions, performance options and custom-built models. The streets of America were soon full of them.

▼ This Skylight Blue Mustang is equipped with the base V-8 option.

Engine: V-8, overhead valve, cast iron block

Displacement: 260 cid

Horsepower: 164 at 4400 rpm

Compression Ratio: 8.8:1

Wheelbase: 108 inches

Base Price: $2368

Number Produced: 97,705

1965 Buick Skylark Gran Sport

American car sales accelerated dramatically in the mid-sixties, partly encouraged by the launch of a host of tasty models by the big automakers and by the growth of the economy. Multi-car households were greatly on the rise, and the industry sold more than nine million cars for the first time in 1965. On the flip side of the market, some old names were on the way out, including Studebaker and Packard.

Buick slipped past both Dodge and Oldsmobile in 1965 to climb to fourth position in the automakers' league of production, with an output of 653,838 units. The 'Father of the Skylark', Edward T. Rollert moved to GM head office, and a new Buick General Manager, Robert L. Kessler, was appointed.

The son of the Skylark, on the other hand, took poll position as the epitome of the '65 Buick range. The Gran Sport was the top optional package for both three Skylark models (the two-door coupe, sport coupe and convertible) and the senior Riviera model ranges. The Riviera version was advertised as an 'Iron Fist in a Velvet Glove', the Skylark GS (a midyear introduction) as a 'Howitzer with windshield wipers'. Both cars were fitted with the Wildcat 401-cid V-8 engine 'Buick engineering wraps their potent 401 powerplant and super quick Turbine trans with a reinforced Skylark shell' proclaimed a contemporary article in Hot Rod Magazine. 'The Buick Gran Sport evolves as one of the hottest of factory-produced street/strip hybrids.' Indeed, many people view this model as Buick's first serious attempt to enter the muscle car market, although it also had a reputation for luxury and refinement. The 1965 Skylarks were plush with cloth and vinyl (or leather-grained vinyl) with bucket seats optional. Outside, the cars were adorned with unique coved styling on the exterior. This intermediate Buick range was very much aimed at the new market, which demanded both 'young' styling and high performance.

From a performance point of view, the engines produced 325 horsepower, with the addition of heavy-duty cross-flow radiators and dual exhaust manifolds with oversized pipes.

▶ A red-filled Gran Sport badge on the grille of this 1965 Skylark Sport Coupe identifies the car with this elite Buick series.

1965 Buick Skylark Gran Sport

Engine:	Wildcat V-8
Displacement:	401 cid
Horsepower:	325 at 4400 rpm
Transmission:	Turbine drive automatic
Compression Ratio:	10.25:1
Induction:	Carter AFB four-barrel
Body Style:	Two-door Sport Coupe
Wheelbase:	115 inches
Base Price:	$2622
Number Produced: (for Skylark model)	4501

1965 Chevrolet Chevelle Malibu SS Z16

Chevrolet had launched the Chevelle/Malibu range in 1964, anticipating a general improvement in the market for cars priced and sized below fullsized models – senior compacts. The car was placed between the compact Chevy II and the regular full-sized models, and was designed to take the same market share that the classic mid-size Chevys of the mid fifties had done.

Projected demand was so high that Chevy even opened a new factory in Fremont, California. The model was quite square in it styling, but had curved side window glass and a 'wide' look that gave the range a distinctive new look.

Eleven models were available in two basic lines called Chevelle 300 and Chevelle Malibu, with a convertible as an exclusive upper level offering. A Super Sport option was also released. The car had SS insignia, and bucket front seats were popular options.

For their second year, the Chevelles were mildly restyled. The nose was 'veed' slightly outwards and a new grille came in. At the rear, Chevy gave the line new taillights. The Chevelle Malibu SS 396 (RPO Z16) was the top-of-the-range car. It was aimed at a young, muscle car-obsessed market. Z16s were blacktop-bruising powerhouses, accurately described as 'one of the wildest pieces of equipment on wheels'. They were introduced as a special midyear package, and featured the 396- cid V-8 with dual exhaust and chrome accents.

Mechanically, the cars were constructed on the stronger convertible frame, and fitted with special shocks and a brawny sports suspension with front and rear sway bars. Heavy duty cooling was also installed. The cars were also fitted with hydraulic power-assisted steering for more responsive handling, and power brakes. Fifteen-inch wide simulated mag style wheel covers were included in the package, and enhanced with Firestone gold line tires. Despite this, considering the power and cost of the upgrade to the Z16s ($1500), they were quite discreetly styled, and it was tricky to instantly differentiate them from the other Chevelles. The interiors also had an SS-396 emblem on the dashboard, and were equipped with a 160 mph speedometer and an AM/FM stereo multiplex radio.

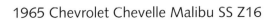

Only 201 cars equipped in this way were built in '65: 200 hardtops and one super-rare convertible. Surviving Z16s are revered today as one of the most rare and powerful muscle cars ever produced.

▲ This Z16 looks good in Regal Red. The car was also available in Tuxedo Black and Crocus Yellow.

Engine:	V-8
Displacement:	396 cid
Horsepower:	375 at 5600 rpm
Wheelbase:	115 inches
Base Price:	$4091
Number Produced:	200 hardtops, one convertible

1965 Chevrolet Corvette Roadster

The Year 1964 has seen the birth of the 'sporty compact' Ford Mustang, but as the advertising slogan of 1965 proclaimed, 'Corvette is America's one true sports car'. Even so, these first 'pony cars' had more 'youth appeal' than any other car on the road at this time with the exception of the Corvette. The Sting Rays were now offered in two body styles, five engines and three transmissions, so the car came in a good many configurations. These ranged from the plush for the 'boulevardier' to the seriously sporty for the 'aficionado' and several in-between options. The car itself was getting increasingly sophisticated in both appearance and driving enjoyment.

Every Corvette now came with four-wheel disc brakes (although drums were available as a minus cost option), fully independent suspension, retractable highlights and a bucket-seated interior. The big mechanical change for '65 was the introduction of a big block V-8. This was the height of the muscle car era in America and performance (together with 'think young' styling) was the driving force behind the phenomenal success of Detroit in this period. Introduced midyear, the engine that was to become known as the Turbo Jet came with up to 427 horsepower. In fact, it was so big that an impressive power bulge appeared on the hood lid. This 'W' engine had been used for five years already in Chevy saloons, and on the NASCAR circuits in '63. For some strange reason, Chevy had decreed that medium-sized cars like the Corvette should not have engines with a higher displacement than 400 cid, so the engine was sleeved down to 396. To handle the power of the Turbo Jet, the Borg-Warner gearbox was replaced by a home grown GM model.

Manufactured at Muncie, Indiana, it became known as the 'Muncie Box'. A beefed up clutch and cooling system were also added. Duntov had to rebalance the car due to the increased engine weight, but managed to do so with characteristic precision.

The car itself had cleaned up looks, with very limited ornament. The look was more uncompromising and rather less sinuous than the early models, more piscine than panther, perhaps. The front fender vents certainly had a

Engine:	(standard) V-8, overhead valve
Displacement:	327 cid
Horsepower:	250 at 4400 rpm
Compression Ratio:	10.5:1
Wheelbase:	98 inches (175.2 overall)
Base Price:	$3212
Number Produced:	15,377 convertibles

look of shark gills, and would become a mainstay of Corvette design. This all led to Corvette seats reaching another new high of 23,562 cars.

▲ This yellow convertible with goldwall tires has a detachable hardtop (optional at $236.75). Other colours available were black, white, red, blue, green, silver, and maroon.

1965 Ford AC Cobra 289

Racing driver Carroll Shelby had been warned by his doctor to stop racing in the early '60s, due to a bad heart. Forced to abandon active race participation, he conceived a dream to build a sports car, the fastest car in world production, which would 'blow Ferrari's ass off'. This was to be a car that combined European styling with American power. Shelby visited the AC factory in Thames Ditton, England and had the idea to power their Ace twintube aluminum chassis sportscar with a Ford Fairlane powerplant, rather than the Bristol six-cylinder two-litre engine they were using at the time. He returned to the US and arranged for two of these to be shipped to AC. As luck would have it, Ford had also been toying with the idea of getting into high performance racing machines and were very open to Shelby's suggestion.

Billy Krause raced the prototype of this hybrid, the CSX2002 at Riverside, California. The car was running away with the competition until a broken rear hub stopped it in its tracks.

The first true Cobra 289 was completed in '62, and had its first victory at Riverside in January '63, driven by Dave MacDonald. The car also competed at Nassau, Daytona, Sebring and LeMans. One of two Cobra 289s, driven by Ninian Sanderson and Peter Bolton came seventh. The 289 was based on an earlier Cobra, the 260, and offered even more power than the original. It used a revised Ford V-8, but retained the original steering arrangement and miniscule coachwork. An evolved version of the car was renamed the AC 289. This version featured

Engine:	Overhead valve V-8, cast iron block
Displacement:	289 cid
Horsepower:	271 at 5800 rpm
Compression Ratio:	10.1:1
Base Price:	$5995
Number Produced: (in total)	505

1965 Ford AC Cobra 289

▲   The Cobra name instantly conjures image of high
performance cars and pure bred racing machines.

rack-and-pinion steering and flared wheel arches.

The first Cobra 427-engined prototype appeared in October '63, and had developed into the Cobra Daytona Coupe by '64. LeMans of that year produced a fourth place for the car. Shelby and Ford now cooperated to substantially redesign the car, and produced a revised 427 in a bid to win the elusive GT championship. A win at Reims in France on July 4 1965 clinched this championship for the Cobra Ford team. Sadly, 427 production finished in 1966. The final 289s left the factory in '68.

▼ An original Ford Cobra 289cid engine. These were fitted in the Shelby Cobras between 1963 and 1965.

▶ This Cobra has a factory-fitted hood scoop.

◢ The more powerful "big block" Cobra 427 was introduced in 1965. This instrumental cluster is from a 427. The car was equipped with a seven liter V-8 engine.

1965 Ford AC Cobra 289

Today, the Cobra 289 tends to live in the shadow of the big block Cobra 427, which enthusiasts tend to view as the ultimate Cobra. Even so, all surviving Cobras are highly collectible, and command very high prices. They are now one of the most copied cars in the world, and many replica Cobras are produced in kit form.

▲ The Shelby Cobra was born in 1962 when Carroll Shelby made a deal with AC to drop a modified Ford V-8 into their chassis.

◀ The iconic Cobra logo.

1965 Ford AC Cobra 289

▲ The 1985 AC Cobra Autokraft Mark IV was equipped with a 302 Ford V-8.

▼ The elegant dash of a 1963 Shelby Cobra 289 Roadster Le Mans.

▲ The later 1965 Cobras were produced with the 427 engine. Caroll Shelby produced three-hundred of these. This is a CSX3016.

▼ Race driver Dick Roe's first competed in his Tousley Ford Cobra 289 in 1966.

▶ The steering wheel boss of the AC Cobra CSX 2142.

▶ AC decided to manufacture its 2010 Mark IV at Gullwing in Germany. The car was equipped with a 6.2 liter V-8.

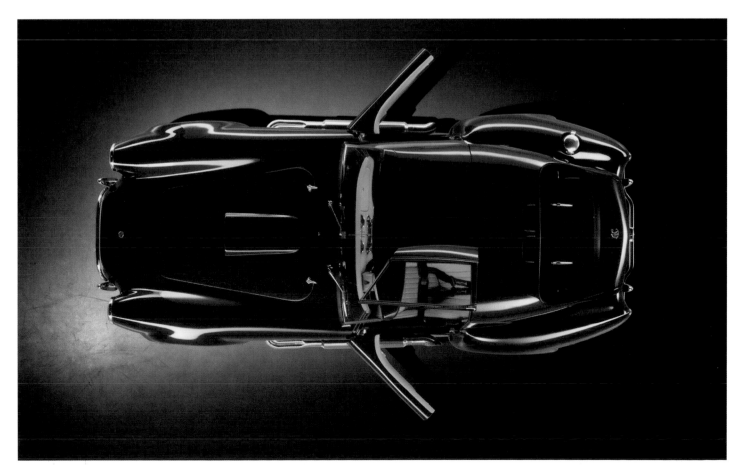

▲   The later AC 427 engine block was fitted from late 1965 onwards.

◥   A 1964 289 Shelby Cobra.

▶   The cockpit of a 1965 Shelby Cobra 289.

1965 Ford AC Cobra 289

1965 Pontiac Catalina Convertible

Stacked headlights continued on Pontiac's all new big '65 models, as did the performance oriented '2+2' package option. 2+2 was only available for the big Catalina convertible and the semi-fastback Sport Coupe hardtop. The package had first been introduced to the Catalina range in 1964, and was the first such performance option to be offered by Pontiac on the full-size models. The 2+2-adapted cars were marketed as a sort of giant five-seat luxury sports car with a long list of technical and luxury choices '...as fine as you want – or as fierce'.

The top '64 engine option was a 370 horsepower version of the 410-cid V-8, which came fitted with Tri Power (three two-barrel carburetors). However, the weight of the car topped 4,000lbs, which tended to slow things down, somewhat.

Power for the 2+2 option was up-rated in the following model year, but when comparing even the revised performance of the package with the GTO option, it has to be said that even this sporty package wasn't quite as spectacular in these bigger cars as it had been on the smaller GTO models. Even so, the '65 2+2 option cars came fully loaded with a 338 horsepower, a four-barrel 421-cid V-8 fitted as standard that developed 338 horsepower at 4600rmp. Hardtops fitted with this engine could achieve 0-60 mph in 7.4 seconds, and the quarter mile in 15.8. This engine option was available for an extra price of $108 - $174 on other Pontiac models. The 2+2 421 was offered in three different strengths, including a top-rated 421, capable of 370 horsepower equipped with Tri Power as in '64. With this version fitted, the cars could achieve 0-60 mph in just over seven seconds (7.2) and the quarter mile in 15.5. Hydra-Matic automatic transmission came fitted as standard with the package.

The basic problem remained the weight/power ratio. The entire Pontiac range became bigger and wider for 1965, wheelbases lengthened to 121 and 124 inches, and the Wide Track chassis was wider than ever. The 2+2 Catalinas were muscle cars, but only just. Other styling changes for the '65 Catalina models included twin air-slot grilles, V-shaped hoods with a prominent center bulge, curved side-glass and symmetrical 'Venturi' contours with fin-shaped creases along the lower body. Coupes and convertibles with the 2+2 package

were trimmed with '421' engine badges on the front fenders, 2+2 numbering on the rear fenders and deck lid, and simulated louvers behind the front wheel cut-outs.

▲ The 2+2 Catalinas were muscle cars, but only just. Hindered by their weight/power ratio, they were no contest for the GTOs.

Engine:	V-8
Displacement:	421-cid
Horsepower:	338 at 4600rpm
Compression Ratio:	10.5:1
Weight:	3795lbs
Wheelbase:	121 inches
Base Price: (Catalina Convertible)	$3103

1966 Ford Fairlane 427

The Ford Fairlane model range was manufactured by FoMoCo from 1955 through to 1969. The original body design was the full sized Ford body. This body started out as a family vehicle, and evolved into many different models and body styles. The exterior paint and trim options were virtually endless, with a rainbow of paint colors and massive variety of cloth trim for inside.

From 1960-62 the Fairlanes began to decrease in size and the car went from a large to mid-sized model. The first sports coupe model was introduced in 1962, which continued until 1965. These models were bigger than the Falcons, but smaller than the Galaxies and offered the best of both worlds with solid performance and great economy.

In 1966, Ford restyled all the full-sized cars for this model year, including the Fairlane. The model was getting larger again, but still not a full-size Ford. The mid-sized Fairlanes were all new for this model year, wearing swoopier GM-type styling on slightly larger dimensions, though the body weight remained pretty much the same. The new dual stacked headlamp design was popular from the start. The model now boasted many available options and performance goodies to include 427 dual-carburetor engine setups, four-speed manual transmission, bucket seats and a console. A '66 Fairlane built specifically for the dragstrip was produced with a fiberglass hood. Fifty-seven of these were built with stripped down race specifications, and equipped with 427-cid race engines. However, the great majority of 1966 Fairlaines were actually fitted with a standard 200-cid six-cylinder engine, and a 200-horsepower 289-cid as the base option V-8.

This model year also introduced the Fairlane convertible, which was available in GT, GTA, 500XL and 500 models. The GT and GTA models were offered with more of the performance accessories and were most commonly built with 390-cid big block engines and luxury interiors complete with bucket seats and consoles. The GTA was a 'GT' with an 'A' automatic transmission, GTs were fitted with four-on-the-floor manual transmission. Disc brakes weren't introduced until the following year.

▶ The 427-cid V-8 was the performance option. This car has the optional 'Ram Air' hood scoop.

1966 Ford Fairlane 427

Engine:	Single Overhead Camshaft 8V V-8
Displacement:	427 cid
Horsepower:	657 at 7500 rpm
Transmission:	Four-speed manual
Compression Ratio:	12.1:1
Induction:	Two Holley four-barrel
Body Style:	Two-door Hardtop Coupe
Wheelbase:	116 inches
Base Price:	$2649

1966 Ford Galaxie 500 7-Liter Series Convertible

Ford finally made it to number one in the production league table for 1966, under the leadership of Donald N. Frey. FoMoCo continued its policy of major annual re-styling for several model lines. While 1965 and 1966 full-sized Fords bear a resemblance to each other, they are quite different cars. The hood is the only interchangeable exterior body component. The '66 models featured more rounded lines than the previous year, though the feature lines were in exactly the same positions.

Galaxie was the intermediate Ford trim for 1966, and offered a full range of seven different series containing nineteen different models. The series were the LTD, the Galaxie 500XL, the Galaxie 500 –Litre, the Galaxie 500 and Custom 500, and the lower trim levels also existed as a parallel V-8 format. Hardtops, sedan and convertible Galaxies were on offer. The model became known for both its clean lines and performance options.

The LTD had a rather different look with a distinctive trim, ornamentation and interior trim. The 500 XL was the ultimate Galaxie in '66 with deep foam contoured bucket seats, full-length console, wall-to-wall carpeting, padded dashboard and visors and special 500 XL exterior ornamentation. Ford also offered an impressive eight different engine choices, all the way from a standard economy six-cylinder to the 'side oiler' 427-cid engine with dual carburetion and 425 horsepower. FoMoCo also introduced a new 428 cubic inch Thunderbird V-8 that was standard equipment on the Galaxie 7-Litre model.

Engine:	Thunderbird Special V-8
Displacement:	428 cid
Horsepower:	345 at 4600 rpm
Transmission:	Cruise-O-Matic automatic
Compression Ratio:	10.5:1
Number Produced:	2368

The 7-Litre was the high performance version of the Galaxie 500 XL, equipped with Cruise-O-Matic transmission. The four-speed manual was also available as a no-cost option for those who chose the even sportier driving characteristics it imparted. The cars also had low restriction dual exhausts, a non-silenced air cleaner system and power disc brakes. The model also had a Sport steering wheel, of simulated English walnut. The Galaxie exterior was available in fifteen Super Diamond Lustre enamels, in twenty-three two-tone combinations. Vinyl-covered roofs were also on offer. Inside the cars, forty-two different upholstery choices were available. The '66s had several power options, for steering, windows and seats together with optional disc brakes and air conditioning.

▲ The Galaxie 500 7-Liter model was available as either a Fastback Coupe, or this Convertible.

1966 Ford GT40

Ford was at number one in the 1966 league of autoproducers. This was in part to their successful introduction of production performance cars like the Torino, Mustang and Thunderbird. These were both inspired, and initiated by technological advances learned at the classic American races and at Le Mans. As far back as 1962, Henry Ford II had decided that Ford should participate in the International Competition field.

The prototype Mark II GT40s made their first appearance at the 1965 LeMans, featuring a NASCAR approved 427 cid V-8. Unfortunately, the cars were obliged to retire with transmission problems. Ford and racing partner Shelby American spent the rest of '65 developing the Mark II for the 1966 endurance-racing season. They refined the big block 427, reducing the engine weight by fifty pounds by using aluminium heads with smaller valves and other modifications. Shelby American did most of the work on the chassis and suspension, reinforcing and revising these where necessary. The GT40 body consisted of a semi-monocoque construction of 0.61mm steel, hinged front and rear panel sections and doors of reinforced fibreglass.

Their work was fully justified. The cars not only took 1-2-3-5 at the first 24- hour Daytona Continental race, but 1-2-3 at the '66 LeMans. In fact, the GT40 was the first American car to win this prestigious race. The winning car was driven by Bruce McLaren and Chris Amon, and set a new average race speed of 125.4 mph. It had a top speed of 205 mph. This is where the GT40 earned its reputation as a 'Ferrari eater', proving more than a match for the P3.

Despite failing to win at Monza and the Nurnburgring 1000km race in Germany, Ford took the constructors' championship for prototype and series production cars. This resulted in the GT40 Mark II becoming the vehicle that showed the world that heavier, larger displacement cars could deliver spectacular performance. It was a victory for American talent, and gained a reputation for the GT40 as the being the best supercar of the era. As well as the fifty-plus cars that FIA rules insisted upon, Ford also had to produce at least 1,000 units of the car for public sale to qualify for competition in the production car series. These were known as the GT40 Mark III cars. Several changes had to be made to ensure that the car complied with safety regulations. The engine was changed to the 289-cid used on Shelby 350 Mustangs, but the clutch and transmission were identical to the race set-up.

Engine:	V-8
Displacement:	427 cid
Horsepower:	485 at 6200 rpm
Weight:	2450 lbs
Wheelbase:	95 inches

▲ The 1966 GT40 appeared as the race-ready Mark II
and the production Mark III model.

1966 Oldsmobile 4-4-2 W-30

Oldsmobile entered the supercar sweepstakes in April '64 with a selfexplanatory

name four-four-two – four-barrel carburettor, four-on-the-floor transmission and dual exhausts. The name remained the same for fifteen years, even though the transmission was also made available as both three-speed synchomesh and automatic over this period.

In 1966, Oldsmobile introduced the W-30 option, which later became known as 'Outside Air Induction'. This fantastic package became Olds hottest muscle car equipment. The package consisted of a RPO list of extras, designed to boost the 4-4-2s to be suitable for super-stock drag racing. The package consisted of a 400-cid L69 big-block V-8. This 360 horsepower engine had been introduced in the November of the previous year. It was equipped with three Rochester two-barrel carburetors, designed to keep the air/fuel mixture cooler and denser, to increase the available power. The engine option was not limited to the W-30 models, however, they were also fitted to 2,129 production models, including the F-85 Cutlasses.

The W-30 equipment also included ram-air ductwork that rammed cool air into the Rochester via two authentic large plastic scoops, which were situated in two openings of the front bumper, reserved for the turn signals in ordinary production cars. The hoses took up so much room under the hood that the battery was re-located to the trunk at the back of the car, which had the additional benefit of loading some weight onto the rear wheels. Other '66 W-30 equipment included a four-bladed fan with no

Engine:	L69 V-8
Displacement:	400-cid
Horsepower:	360 at 5000 rpm
Body Style:	Two-door Coupe
Wheelbase:	115 inches
Number Produced:	54

clutch, heavy-duty three-core radiator, close-ratio manual transmission and a hydraulic, high-lift, longduartion camshaft. Despite all this heavy gear, no output rating change was listed for the W-30-equipped Oldsmobile.

Only 54 of these W-30 cars were built in 1966. The cars were not actively promoted at all. As soon as they were, production jumped to a far healthier 502 cars in '67. Some equipment changes were made, including replacing the carburetor system with a single four-barrel unit. This was due to a GM edict banning multiple-carb setups. An optional automatic transmission was offered.

The W-30 was most popular in 1970 when 3,100 W-30 equipped cars hit the streets. Oldsmobile continued to offer the package until 1980, but it was substantially diluted by this time.

▼ This W-30 equipped 4-4-2 clearly shows the simulated hood louvers.

1966 Plymouth Belvedere

Plymouth was now at number four in the auto producers' league, but on a reduced production output of 678,514 cars. There were quite of lot of interesting developments at Plymouth for '66 - mostly positive. The revived fullsize Fury was re-introduced to the range, with mild styling tweaks (including vertically stacked headlights). The 'glassback' Barracuda continued to make a valiant attempt to take pony car sales away from Ford's Mustang (without a great deal of success, it has to be said). The Fury VIP model was added to the Plymouth range to give the Ford LTD and Chevy Caprice a run for their money in the luxury hardtop coupe market. The car came with a 230 horsepower 318-cid V-8 as standard, but engine options went all the way up to a 365 horsepower 440-cid V-8. Like Dodge, Plymouth also offered a muscular Street Hemi on selected models, including the top-of-the-line Satellite Belvederes.

The 1966 Belvederes received a major restyling. The new car had a square body, and slab-like fenders. A full-length sculptural depression panel relieved this. The large front wheel opening now curved up to this panel. In profile, the edge of the front fender thrust forward into a wide V-shaped form. The sedan models had a square-angular roof with thick rear pillars. Hardtops retained the cantilevered roof treatment with a thicker base, and this treatment was echoed at the rear of the station wagon models. As in the previous model year, Belvederes were offered in a three-tier model range, the Is, IIs and Satellites.

Belvedere Is (three models) had thin, straight moldings along the lower feature line, a heater and defroster, front seat belts, an oil filter and five blackwall tires. Belvedere II models (of which there were five), were adorned with a wide full-length chrome spear placed above the bodyside centreline.

Inside the cars, there was upgraded upholstery and carpeting. Satellites, as usual, had less side trim than the other models, but came with a fancy trunk treatment, rocker panel moldings, bucket seats and console, wheel covers and vinyl trim. As in '65, there were two models – the two-door hardtop coupe and two-door convertible.

Engine:	Street Hemi V-8, overhead valve with hemispherical combustion chambers
Displacement:	426-cid
Horsepower:	425 at 5600 rpm
Compression Ratio:	10.25:1
Body Style:	Two-door Convertible
Weight:	3320 lbs
Wheelbase:	116 inches
Base Price:	$2910
Number Produced:	2,759

▲ This two-door Convertible Belvedere Satellite is fitted with the Street Hemi engine option.

1966 Pontiac GTO

Back in 1964, Pontiac had succeeded in launching its first GTO option model by skirting GM head office policy do drop its most popular engine, the 389-cid V-8 into medium-sized Tempest bodies in true hot rod fashion. GTO actually stood for Gran Turismo Omologato, which was mean to imply that, like the Ferrari GTO, the car had been homologated for racing. The tag was actually quite controversial in some quarters, but as they say, there's no such thing as bad publicity. 1965 had seen a major restyle on the Le Mans/GTO and in 1966 the GTO became a series in its own right, with distinctive trim on the new Tempest sheet metal, unique grille and GTO nameplates and lettering. The GTOs were available in three body styles: a two-door (semi-fastback) hardtop, a two-door coupe and a two-door convertible.

Fully equipped, the '66 GTOs could achieve 0-60 miles an hour in 6.8 seconds. The base GTO engine was rated at 335 horsepower, whilst the most powerful option available in this model year was the 389-cid V-8 with Tri Power carburetion, rated at 360 horsepower. A convertible with this option was timed at 15.5 seconds over the quarter mile (at 93 mph). But this was to be the final year for the Tri Power set-up, as GM instigated a ban on multiple-carburetion for all models, with the single exception of the Corvette. The GTOs were also equipped with dual exhaust, plus heavy-duty shocks, springs and stabilizer bar.

Whatever the model mix, the GTOs were the undisputed kings of the muscle car market in 1966, selling more units than any of its competitors (ignoring the pony cars). This was quite an achievement considering that the market was now crowded with copycat quick-car contenders. Ford had fitted a 390-cid V-8 to the Fairlane GT and GTA models, while Mercury had metamorphosed the Comet into a veritable Cyclone. Both of these cars could also be ordered with a 427-cid (seven liter) option, and Chrysler's 426-cid Hemi was just about the hit the scene. The GM cars were at a great disadvantage from the high-handed head office decrees that stated that the intermediate cars could not be fitted with engines larger than 400-cid. This time, this edict actually stuck. But this did nothing to dent GTO sales (a huge

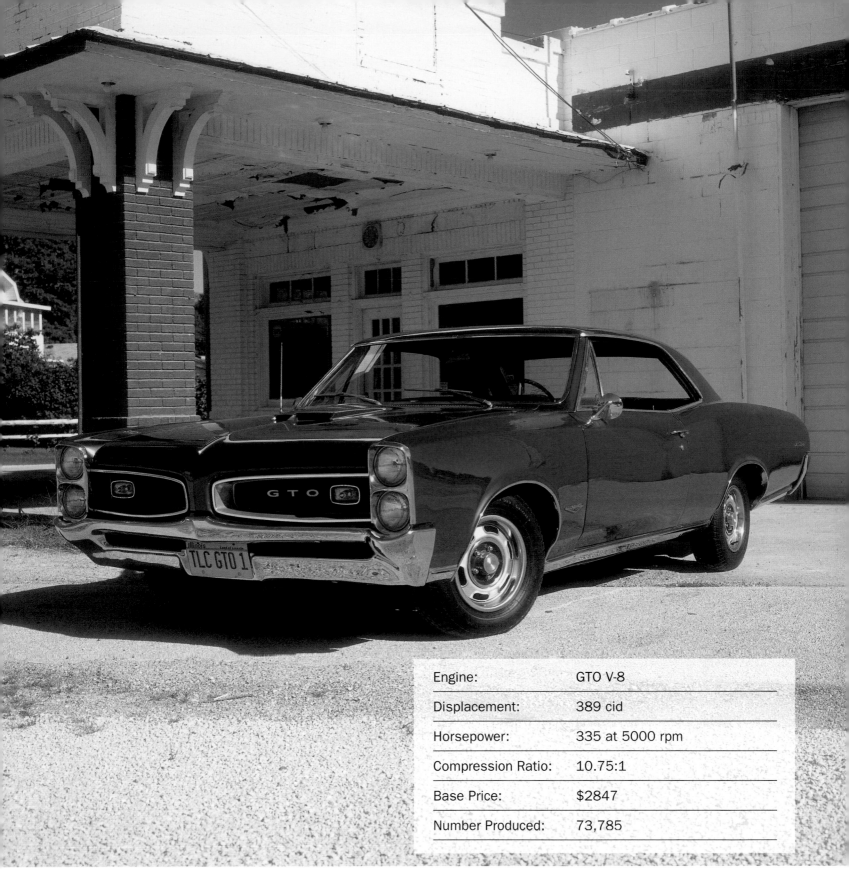

Engine:	GTO V-8
Displacement:	389 cid
Horsepower:	335 at 5000 rpm
Compression Ratio:	10.75:1
Base Price:	$2847
Number Produced:	73,785

96,946 units for the '66 model year) which were positively affected by the new Coke-bottle styling. The powertrain options were also improved, with the addition of a Ram Air option for the Tri-power engine. Ram Air cars also had longer duration camshafts and heavy-duty valvesprings.

▲ This '66 Hardtop looks cool with the wire mesh grille and GTO badge.

1967 Chevrolet Corvette L-88

Of the many mean and nasty Corvettes unleashed during the half-century history of "America's Sportscar," among the meanest was the fabled L-88, built in limited numbers from 1967 to '69. Only 20 rolled out of Chevrolet's St. Louis assembly plant that first year, all clearly targeted for the track.

Anyone who tried to drive an L-88 on the street—and some fools did—were in for a rude awakening. For starters, there was no radio, heater, automatic choke, or fan shroud to aid underhood cooling. Also missing on the L-88, as was any semblance of emissions controls. A typical PCV valve wasn't even present; instead the 427 cubic-inch L-88 V-8 used an obsolete road-draft tube that vented crankcase vapors directly into the atmosphere. Anything that wasn't needed on a race track, anything that added unwanted extra pounds, wasn't included in the L-88 package, an off-road

Wheelbase:	98 inches
Weight:	3,200 pounds (approximate)
Original Price:	$5,675
Engine:	427 cubic-inch L-88 V-8 with aluminum cylinder heads
Compression:	12.5:1
Horsepower:	430 at 5,200 rpm
Induction:	single 850-cfm Holley four-barrel carburetor on aluminum open-plenum manifold
Transmission:	Muncie "Rock Crusher" (M-22) four-speed manual
Suspension:	independent A-arms w/coil springs in front; independent with driveshafts acting as upper links, lower lateral links, trailing arms and transverse leaf spring
Brakes:	power-assisted four-wheel discs
Production:	20 (coupes and convertibles)

option if there ever was one.

What was included was an impressive list of purposeful hardware, beginning with the L-88 427's weight-saving aluminum cylinder heads. Feeding things on top was a huge 850-cfm Holley four-barrel carb mounted on an open-plenum aluminum intake manifold that totally sacrificed low-speed cooperation for high-rpm flying. Atop all that was a unique air cleaner assembly that mated up with the Corvette's first functional ram-air hood. Ductwork bonded to the hood's underside directed air

flow from the high-pressure area normally created at the base of any car's windshield into the hungry Holley below.

Remaining standard L-88 features contributed further to the car's gnarly nature. All L-88 Corvettes built in 1967 were fitted with such mandatory options as the stiff F41 suspension, G81 Positraction differential, J56 power-assisted metallic brakes, and M22 "Rock Crusher" four-speed manual transmission.

The Goodwood Green coupe shown here is

one of the earliest L-88 Corvettes built, if not the earliest. Owned by noted collector Bill Tower, this curious machine exhibits more than one oddity that doesn't appear on other 1967 L-88s. Most noticeable are the "L/88" decals stuck on the hood and each valve cover. "An engineer at Chevrolet told me they were going to put these on the cars," recalls Tower, himself a former GM engineer. "They were going to use those decals, but they drew so much attention they decided against it.

◀ Corvette chief engineer Zora Arkus-Duntov (on left) grins as engineer Denny Davis dyno tests an L-88 prototype in May 1966.

▼ At Le Mans in June 1967 an L-88 topped 170 mph before a connecting rod disconnected.

They didn't want just anyone buying an L-88, they didn't want everyone knowing about it."

That same logic came into play when Chevrolet officials grossly underrated the L-88 427 at 430 horsepower. "They used that number so that guys wanting the fastest Corvette available in 1967 would notice the 435-horse [L-71] engine instead," said Tower. "Again, they just wanted to sell

▼ Prototype "L/88" identification was created then cancelled to downplay the car's race-ready nature.

MILESTONE FACTS

- L-88 Corvettes were built for three years. Production was 20 in 1967, 80 in 1968 and 116 in 1969.

- The L-88 was the first Corvette to use a functional hood scoop, this one pointed backward towards the cowl. Chevrolet engineers as far back as 1963 had discovered what tapping into the high-pressure area at the base of a car's windshield could do to free up a few more ponies on top end.

- Factory paperwork advised an L-88 buyer to steer clear of typical pump fuels: "This unit operates on Sunoco 260 or equivalent gas of very high octane. Under no circumstances should regular gasoline be used." Another label stuck inside the car repeated this warning. "Warning: vehicle must operate on a fuel having a minimum of 103 research octane and 95 motor octane or engine damage may result."

- Living with the optional J56 brakes in everyday operation was not easy. These fade-resistant clampers worked famously once warmed up. But when cold they were about as effective as Fred Flintstone's feet.

- Unlike the "stinger" hoods on typical big-block Corvettes in 1967, the L-88's lid was fully functional—it fed fresh air to the carb below.

- A transistorized ignition, RPO K66, was another mandatory L-88 option. The L-88 427 also used a mechanical-advance distributor.

- Special deep-groove pulleys were used on the L-88 427 to help prevent belts being thrown at high rpm.

the L-88 to real racers."

Eagle eyes might also notice the "wrong" Rally wheels with their deep-dish trim rings. Standard Sting Ray Rally rims in 1967 were 15x6 units with "skinny" trim rings. Like the decals on the hood, the wheels on Tower's L-

▲ Feeding the 430-horse L-88 427 was a huge 850-cfm four-barrel carb specially prepared by Holley for this application.

88 are experimental prototypes, and they're accordingly marked with "XP" identification. Measuring seven inches wide, they previewed the new rims introduced along with the restyled 1968 Corvette.

Anyone with eyes can see another "non-stock" feature: racing-style sidepipes. Originally manufactured by Stahl, these pipes and the full-race headers they're bolted to were also prototypes, in this case for the track-ready, wide-open exhausts that apparently were shipped in boxes to some L-88 Corvette buyers in 1967. Why all this special equipment?

Tower's car spent much of 1967 as a Proving Grounds testbed for the new L-88 package, during which time engineers thrashed everything from experimental high-speed Goodyear rubber to that functional fresh-air hood. Perhaps tested most thoroughly was the big Holley four-barrel, built specifically for the L-88 application. Holley engineer Marty Sullivan worked closely with GM people to iron out early bugs and maximize performance with both differing exhaust setups and that new fresh-air hood. "That was part of my job, too," recalled Sullivan. "I worked along with the Chevy engineers who developed that scoop." "That hood wasn't just thrown together," added Tower. "They did a lot of testing to identify the flow characteristics of the air coming off the windshield."

When testing was finally done, Tower's green L-88 went south to Jim Rathmann's dealership in Melbourne, Florida, home to the handling of the complimentary Corvettes delivered to NASA astronauts. Indeed, the L-88 arrived in Melbourne on a hauler loaded with Sting Rays earmarked for the space program. Rathmann then sold the unique coupe to an old racing buddy, who later resold it in 1976 to Tower.

◄ Chevrolet introduced the stunning Sting Ray coupe in 1963, and this body rolled on with minor updates up through 1967.

▲ These wheels are experimental prototypes measuring 15x7. Typical 1967 Corvette Rally wheels were 15x6 units.

Bill restored the rarity in 1995 after extensive research was performed to uncover its full background.

Is it the first L-88? He thinks so.

1967 Chevrolet Nova SS L79

The Nova had been dropped, briefly, in anticipation of the larger Chevelle SS, but public demand had resulted in a midyear return for the model, with two new engine options. These were the first V-8 for the Nova, and the 230 inline. The convertible and 3-seat station wagon were dropped, but the 2-seat wagon continued. The Chevy II 300 series trim was deleted. '65 had heralded minor trim changes, which were reinforced in '66. The installation of more serious engines to the car in the '64-'65 period began to establish a serious reputation for Nova SS as a muscle car.

Both the Chevelles and Chevy II Novas were completely restyled in 1966.

The hot ticket version of the car was the L79 version of the 327 V-8, which developed 350 horsepower. Officially, this engine option was dropped in 1967, to prevent sales being drawn away from the newly introduced Camaro range. But although the L79 option was officially deleted, production records show that six such cars were built in '67.

Only minor styling changes were introduced in 1967, to consolidate the car as one of the most clean-looking and collectible Chevys of all time. A new grille and side trim were the most visible changes to the car. Mechanically, the dual-pot barking system was fitted as standard, but disc brakes were available as an option. Revised for '67, the standard engine option for the Nova and Nova SS was a 187.6 six-cylinder inline. Optional engine variations were the RPO L22 250-cid 155 horsepower six-cylinder block, and the RPO L30 327-cid 275 horsepower V-8. The small, taut Nova Super Sport two-door hardtop coupe (series 117) continued to make an excellent high-performance car when equipped with these special options.

Engine: V-8 overhead valve, cast iron block,

Displacement: 326.7 cid

Horsepower: 275 at 4800 rpm

Compression Ratio: 10.0:1

Number Produced: 10,100

The exterior of the Nova SS was distinguished with a special blackaccented chrome grille, complete with SS insignia low on the driver's side.

Above a black painted sill area, there was an elegant chrome accent stripe, lower body moldings, and bright wheelhouse accents extending along the lower fender edges. The model had specific Super Sport full wheelcovers, fender scripts and full-width color accent deck lid trim panels. The car interiors were all vinyl, with front Strato bucket seats, optional Astro-bucket headrests, with bright seat end panels as standard. In cars where the transmission was upgraded to four-speed or automatic transmission, a floor shift trim plate was added. The cars also had a specific Nova Super Sport three-spoke steering wheel.

▲ One of only six '67 Nova Super Sports built with the L79 engine option, this red hardtop coupe is a rare car indeed.

151

1967 Chevrolet Z/28 Camaro

Introduced to the automotive press on November 26, 1966, at Riverside, California, Chevrolet's first Z/28 was nothing more than a street-going extension of Chevy's Sports Car Club of America racing effort. Initiated in 1966, the SCCA's Tran-Am sedan series had ended up being a one-horse show in its first year as Ford's Mustang took all the marbles running against a pack of Plymouth Barracudas and Dodge Darts.

And things almost ended right then and there—apparently race fans weren't too keen on watching Mustangs beat up on Barracuda and Darts all day long. Not until Chevrolet's Vince Piggins convinced SCCA officials that his company would honor Trans-Am competition with its presence did a 1967 race schedule become reality.

On August 17, 1966, Piggins, then an assistant staff engineer in charge of performance product promotion, issued a memo to upper brass outlining his plan to build an SCCA-legal factory racer based on Chevrolet's new ponycar, the Camaro. Once approved, Piggins' proposed package was given regular production order (RPO) number Z28, a label that stuck despite Vince's pleas for the name "Cheetah."

To meet SCCA homologation standards, the officially named

"Z/28" had to have a back seat (which made it a "sedan"), it had to have a wheelbase no longer than 116 inches, it had to have an engine no larger than 305 cubes, and it had to sold to the public no less than 1,000 times. The first two requirements were no problem, and the production quota scared no one at Chevrolet—"the sales department anticipates a volume of 10,000 such vehicles [for] 1967," wrote Piggins in his August 17 memo. It was the engine size limit that presented the real challenge.

A truly hot 302 cubic-inch small-block V-8 was created exclusively for the Z/28 Camaro

Wheelbase:	108 inches
Weight:	3,070 pounds
Base Price:	$3,380
Engine:	302 cubic-inch small-block V-8
Compression:	11:1
Induction:	single 800-cfm Holley four-barrel carburetor on aluminum high-rise intake
Horsepower:	290 at 5,800 rpm
Torque:	290 at 4,200 rpm
Transmission:	Muncie four-speed manual
Suspension:	independent A-arms w/coil springs in front; live axle with leaf springs and a radius rod in back, beefier springs and shocks at the corners
Brakes:	power front discs, rear drums
Performance:	14.9 seconds at 97 mph in the quarter-mile, according to Car and Driver
Production:	602

by stuffing a 283 crank into a 327 to stay within the 305-cid maximum. Though the cylinder block was a typical passenger-car unit with two-bolt main bearings (stronger four-bolt mains came along in 1969), the rugged crank was made of forged steel instead of nodular cast-iron. L79 big-port heads, 11:1 pistons, a radical solid-lifter cam, and an 800-cfm Holley four-barrel carb on an aluminum intake heated things up further. Advertised output was 290 horses. Seat-of-the-pants

▼ Chevrolet's Z/28 Camaro debuted somewhat quietly in 1967. "Z/28" fender badges didn't appear until 1968.

readings, however, went much higher, some as lofty as 400 horsepower.

Whatever the true number, the 302 impressed the press to no end. "The very-backdoor word is that [destroking the 327] has resulted in a happy and extremely potent screamer," wrote Sports Car Graphic's Jerry Titus, while Car and Driver simply labeled the 302 the "most responsive American V-8s we've ever tested." That was big talk for a small-block.

Deserving of similar raves was the 302's supporting cast. Per Piggins' original plan, Chevrolet's superb F41 sports suspension was

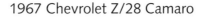

included as part of RPO Z28. So was a quick-ratio Saginaw manual steering box and 3.73:1 rear gears. A Muncie four-speed transmission with a 2.20:1 low was a mandatory option, as were RPO's J56 and J52—front disc brakes and power assist, respectively. Thrown in along with those discs were four smart-looking 15x6 Corvette Rally wheels. Other than these bright rims, the only other outward sign of a '67 Z/28's presence were twin racing stripes on the hood and rear deck. The legendary "Z/28" emblem didn't debut until midway through 1968.

In all, only 602 Z/28 Camaros were built in

▼ Twin racing stripes on the hood and rear decklid were included in the Z/28 deal in 1967.

MILESTONE FACTS

- Chevrolet's first Trans-Am ponycar carried no external identification. Those legendary "Z/28" badges didn't show up until 1968.

- Included as Z/28 standard equipment in 1967, the F41 suspension consisted of heavy-duty springs, stiff shocks, and a radius rod on the axle's right side to control wheel hop.

- An optional cowl-induction air-cleaner was shipped in the trunk of some '67 Z/28 Camaros. Headers too were offered, but few were sold.

- Z/28 production soared to 7,199 in 1968, then topped 19,000 the following year.

- Chevy's Z/28 legacy was briefly interrupted in 1975 and '76. Returning in 1977, the hot-to-trot Camaro remained popular into the new millennium.

- In 1970 the Z/28 received a stunning new body and a new engine based on the Corvette's LT-1 350 small-block.

◀ A huge 800-cfm Holley four-barrel fed the Z/28's 302 small-block.

1967. How then did Chevrolet take it racing on the Trans-Am circuit? Officials played a little numbers game by homologating the 350-cid Camaro—which darn near grew on trees compared to the Z/28—under Federation Internationale de l'Automobile (FIA, the world governing body over SCCA racing) Group I rules, then qualified that car equipped with RPO Z28 under Group II

◀ Chevrolet's Camaro joined Ford's ground-breaking Mustang in Detroit's ponycar corral in 1967.

specifications. Don't understand? Don't worry, neither did the competition back in 1967.

But they did pick up on the Z/28's nimble nature, which quickly proved itself more than worthy on SCCA tracks. Camaros dominated Trans-Am racing in 1968 and '69, action that thrust the Z/28 into the public limelight big-

time. In 1968, sales of this hot-handling ponycar increased nearly ten-fold to more than 7,000, and the legend continued rolling on from there.

Though briefly shelved for two years in the Seventies, the Z/28 Camaro continued running strong into the new millennium before GM recently cancelled its F-body platform. Apparently all good things must indeed come to an end.

◀ Rally wheels and front disc brakes were standard on Chevrolet's first Z/28.

▲ The interior and dash of the 1967 Z/28.

▼ The 1967 Camaro model line-up.

◀ The slightly-evolved Camaro Z/28 of 1969.

▲ This 1968 Camaro Z/28 looks like a full-up muscle car.

▶ A magnificent example of the 1967 Camaro.

◄   A fine Camaro from 1968.

▼   A pair of Camaros from 1967 and 1969.

◄   This 1969 Z28 Camaro RS is fitted with a DZ 302 engine and a Muncie four-speed transmission.

▲   This blue and white 1969 Z/28 Camaro Rally Sport is equipped with a 302 engine, and a four-speed manual gearbox. The interior is trimmed in black-and-white houndstooth cloth.

1967 Dodge Charger 426 Hemi

"Four-twenty-six Hemi." What made the this big, bad hunk of Mopar muscle so special? Just ask any SS Chevelle or Cobra Jet Ford owner who dared cross paths with one back in the Sixties. Chrysler officials weren't lying when they said it produced 425 horses. Well, actually they were. In truth, output was higher than that.

Brute force was its forte. On top of that, the thing just looked so mean and nasty. Save perhaps for Ford's Boss 429, no other American performance powerplant looked like the 426 Hemi. And very few ran like it.

Chrysler Corporation had introduced its milestone hemi-head V-8 in 1951, then dropped the design after 1958 in favor of lighter, equally powerful wedge-head V-8s that were easier and cheaper to build. The concept then reappeared six years later, though in vastly different form. Based on

Wheelbase:	117 inches
Weight:	4,160 pounds
Base Price:	$4,500
Engine:	426 cubic-inch Hemi V-8
Compression:	10.25:1
Horsepower:	425 at 5,000 rpm
Torque:	490 at 4,000 rpm
Induction:	two 650-cfm Carter four-barrel carburetors
Transmission:	four-speed manual with Hurst shifter
Suspension:	independent A-arms w/torsion bars in front; live axle with leaf springs in back
Brakes:	front discs, rear drums
Performance:	14.16 seconds at 96.15 mph in quarter-mile, according to Car Life magazine (test car equipped with Torqueflite automatic transmission)
Production:	59, with four-speed transmission—another 59 Hemi Chargers were built for 1967 with the Torqueflite automatic

1967 Dodge Charger 426 Hemi

▲ Adding the optional 426 Hemi V-8 to the Charger
body in 1966 and '67 helped put the fast in fastback.
Shown here is one of 118 Hemi Chargers built for 1967.

Chrysler's 426 cubic-inch wedge V-8, the '64 Hemi was an all-out competition engine never meant for the street.

The target was big Bill France's still-new superspeedway in Daytona Beach, Florida. In December 1962, engineer Tom Hoover had been asked to recreate the Hemi with the goal being to take it racing on the NASCAR circuit. Hoover's team then completed the job just in time to for the sixth running of the Daytona 500 in February 1964, a race it dominated with ease. And that domination continued throughout the NASCAR season.

Chrysler's advantage was so great, Bill France decided—in the best interest of parity—to ban the Hemi in 1965. It was not a regular-production engine and thus was not legal to compete on his "stock car" circuit.

Not ready to give up so easily, Chrysler officials then transformed the race Hemi into the street Hemi in 1966. By making the 426

MILESTONE FACTS

• Chrysler first reintroduced its hemi-head V-8 in race-only form in 1964. A second "race Hemi" appeared in 1965, then the "street Hemi" was introduced in 1966.

• Counting the truly rare race-ready versions of 1964 and '65, Dodge and Plymouth rolled out roughly 10,500 Hemi cars during that eight-year run.

• The 426 Hemi first appeared as a Dodge Charger option in February 1966.

• "If you missed the San Francisco earthquake, reserve your seat here for a repeat performance," began a Car and Driver review of the 1966 street Hemi. "This automobile is the most powerful sedan ever, bar none."

• A standard interior feature in 1966, the Charger's large center console became an option in 1967.

• Total Charger production in 1967 was 15,788, compared to 37,300 for 1966.

• Hemi Charger production in 1966 was 468; 250 four-speeds, 218 automatics.

Hemi a certified regular-production option, Chrysler then satisfied France's homologation requirements, and the Hemi was free to race again.

Taking the Hemi to the streets in 1966 required more than a little "detuning," beginning with a major compression cut. A less radical cam was stuffed in and the race Hemi's steel tube headers were replaced by cast-iron manifolds. On top, a heated aluminum intake mounting two Carter four-barrels superseded the exotic cross-ram manifold used previously.

The street Hemi was offered in a wide array

▶ Chrome-plated steel road wheels were optional for Dodge's 1967 Charger.

▲ The first-generation Charger's unique interior featured four bucket seats, with the rear pair folding down to increase usable storage space beneath that sloping rear window.

of Dodge and Plymouth models from 1966 to '71. But if there was any one car that first year that best matched the Hemi's hot performance with equally hot looks it was Dodge's sleek, new Charger, a veritable stunner that turned heads with ease.

Introduced in January 1966, the Charger was, in Dodge general manager Byron Nichols' words, "a fresh new concept in styling and engineering excellence from bumper to bumper." Innocent by-standers, however, couldn't help but notice that the '66 Charger was not much more than a typical Coronet sedan with a trendy fastback roof tacked on. The two did share the same unit-body platform, with its 117-inch wheelbase, so the resemblance was certainly there. But not so fast. Based on the Charger II dream machine—a sleek, sexy sensation that began touring the auto show circuit in late 1964—

▲ Beneath a 1967 Hemi's chrome air cleaner were two Carter four-barrel carburetors. Output was a conservatively rated 425 horsepower.

the regular-production Charger represented an exceptional job of face-lifting a rather mundane model into and exciting fun machine.

V-8 power was standard, beginning with a yeoman 318. At the top of the options list was 426 Hemi, which backed up all those fast looks with some serious performance. But all that muscle came at a price. The Hemi option alone ran in the $800 neighborhood. Throw in a long list of heavy-duty "mandatory options and the $3,100 base price began zooming

towards five grand in a hurry, explaining why only 468 Hemi Chargers were sold in 1966.

Even fewer hit the streets in 1967. Minor Charger updates included new fender-mounted turn signals and an additional performance option, the 375-horse 440 cubic-inch big-block. Buyers who didn't mind the Hemi's cranky disposition and higher insurance costs could still opt for the 425-horse big-block, but only a handful did. Hemi Charger production in 1967 fell to 118.

The Hemi Charger returned in 1968, this time with yet another sleek, new body. Dodge built its last 425-horse Charger in 1971, after which time the Hemi was retired for good.

◀ The sweeping rear view of the 1967 Dodge Charger.

▲ The final Hemi engine.

◣ This dark blue Dodge Charger from the previous model year (1966) is equipped with the 440ci engine and four-speed manual transmission. It has a black interior.

▼ This 1969 car is decked out as the General Lee Charger.

1969 Dodge Charger Daytona

◄ This USPS stamp celebrates the outrageously styled 1969 Dodge charger Daytona. Designed for the track, the car made its NASCAR debut in September, 1969 al Talladega, Alabama.

◣ The wide front view of the 1970 Dodge Charger.

▶ A 1967 Hemi, complete with factory-fitted carburetors.

▼ The complicated tail light assembly of the 1971 Dodge charger R/T.

◀ A 1971 Dodge Charger R/T.

▶ An original example of 1971's luxurious Charger R/T, complete with the black R/T decal.

▼ The Dodge Super Bee was a limited production muscle car, manufactured between 1968 and 1971.

◢ This Charger color was designated Lime Light Green in 1970, but had become Sassy Grass Green by 1971.

1967 Dodge Charger 426 Hemi

1967 Dodge Dart GTS (383 V-8)

Engines and cars got bigger in the mid-sixties, heavier and more complex.

Detroit had learnt the way to power through stock-car racing and gradually introduced what it had learnt to production models. The company's fortunes had also grown in these years, as it gradually climbed higher in the production league table. In 1967, they were at seventh place (on production of nearly half a million cars), but had made a brief stop at fifth in '66. R.B. Curry became the General Manager of Dodge in this year.

The Darts got a completely restyled unibody, 43 per cent of these were fitted with the V-8 engine option. The car was now America's largest compact and was styled with curved side glass and delta-shaped taillamps. Polara and Monaco were also extensively redesigned and built larger, riding a 122-inch wheelbase.

The restyle for the Dart was total, from the ground up. The cars retained the chassis of the previous year, but were restyled to look larger than the earlier model (although they were actually half an inch shorter). The full-width grille housed single headlights and featured a vertical bar arrangement with a largescale dividing bar in the center of the concave grille. The side profile was rather more rounded than in the previous incarnation of the car, but carried similar lines. At the back, the taillights were almost square and fitted into a flat section on the trunk lid. The cars were trimmed with chromed windshield and rear window moldings.

The Dart was the base model of the range, the Dart 270 was the intermediate trim level, and the Dart GT was the top-level model. The GT was fitted with all the options of the entry-level models, plus a padded instrument panel, special wheel covers and bucket seats. There were two GT models, a two-door hardtop coupe and two-door convertible. The cars were fitted with two basic engine options, the slant six-cylinder and the V-8 – available with various-sized engine blocks. The convenience options for GT models included an interior console, buffed paint, a tachometer and simulated 'mag' wheel covers.

Engine:	Overhead valve V-8, cast iron block
Displacement:	383 cid
Horsepower:	270 at 4400 rpm
Compression	Ratio: 9.2:1
Induction:	Carter two-barrel BDD-4125S
Weight:	3030 lbs
Wheelbase:	111 inches
Base Price:	$2860
Number Produced: (All Dart GTs)	38,200 (including 21,600 V-8s)

▲ This convertible Dart GTS proclaims its 383-cid V-8 status with pride.

1967 Mercury Cougar XR-7

Mercury entered the pony car race at full speed in 1967 with the introduction of the Cougar. The model was launched with some powerful performance packages.

The Cougar was one of the most handsome automobiles of 1967, and Cougar was a niche marketing success for Mercury in that it bridged the gap between the performance of the Ford Mustangs (and was slightly larger) and the luxury of the Thunderbird models. Overall, its probably leant more to comfort than performance. Its styling was more mature, featuring disappearing headlights, wraparound front and rear fenders and triple taillights (with sequential turn signals). The front and rear end styling were similar. Cougars came, equipped with all-vinyl bucket seats, three-spoke 'sport-style' steering wheel, deep-loop carpeting and deluxe seat belts. The standard transmission for the model was floor-mounted three-speed manual transmission.

There was a single base Cougar model, the two-door hardtop coupe. A Cougar XR-7 two-door hardtop coupe was introduced in the mid-model-year.

No convertible or fastback models were offered until 1969. Except for a medallion on the quarter panel of the roof, it looked just like the standard Cougar model. It was also embellished with a black-faced instruments set into a simulated walnut dashboard, and a more luxurious, simulated leather, interior.

Engine:	V-8, overhead valve, cast iron block
Displacement:	289 cid
Horsepower:	200 at 4400rpm
Compression Ratio:	9.3:1
Induction:	Autolite C7DF-9510-Z two-barrel
Body Style:	Two-door Hardtop Coupe
Number of Seats:	5
Weight:	3015 lbs
Wheelbase:	111 inches
Base Price:	$3081
Number Produced:	27,221

The Cougar was immediately successful, selling a total of 150,893 cars in its first model outing, accounting for nearly half of Mercury sales for the entire year. Only 7,412 of these were fitted with the optional front bench seat, and only 5.3% with the four-speed manual transmission. The most popular options were automatic transmission (96.2%), power steering (97%), tinted glass (69.7%) and power brakes (65.6%).

A GT performance package was also available for a further $323. This included a firmer suspension with bigger shocks, fatter anti-roll bars, power front disc brakes and a 390-cid V-8 (rated at 335 horsepower) that required premium fuel.

▲ The Cougar received *Motor Trend Magazine*'s 'Car of the Year' award for 1965.

1967 Mercury Cyclone 427

GTO clones were seemingly everywhere not long after Pontiac introduced the muscle car to the world in 1964. Oldsmobile's 4-4-2 appeared late that year, followed by Buick's Gran Sport and Chevrolet's SS 396 Chevelle in 1965. GM clearly had a great recipe cooking, but what about Chrysler and Ford?

While the two other Big Three players had the hot engines capable of running with the General's latest prime movers, the duo fell a bit short in the application department. Early on neither fielded a mid-sized muscle machine that matched up with the Goat or any of its corporate cousins.

At least Mercury tried. In January 1964, Ford's upscale corporate running mate introduced its Cyclone, a jazzed-up Comet wearing faux chrome-wheel wheelcovers, complete with chromed lug nuts. Bucket seats and console, a sporty three-spoke steering wheel, and a tach were included in the deal, which concentrated more on imagery than action. Standard power was the Super Cyclone 289 small-block, rated at 210 horsepower.

Mercury's Cyclone whipped its way back on the scene in 1965 with all the same standard goodies offered the year before, plus an exclusive grille treatment. The Super Cyclone 289 also returned, now rated at 225 horses. Those 15 extras ponies, however, by no means improved the Cyclone's position compared to GM's big-block intermediates. According to Motor Trend, the best this baby could do in the quarter-mile was 17.1 seconds at 82 mph. Maybe that new optional fiberglass hood with its two simulated scoops would've helped.... Not.

Okay, so maybe those early Comet-based Cyclones constituted more hot air than hot performance. But Mercury had to start somewhere, and storm clouds were building even as the '65 Cyclone was blowing smoke up the tailpipes of rival muscle cars. Although an optional 390-cube FE-series big-block appeared in 1966, it was still no match for the likes of Chevy's 396 and Pontiac's 400. Then came the answer to a fast-

Wheelbase:	116 inches
Weight:	3,600 pounds
Original Price:	$4,100
Engine:	427 cubic-inch FE-series V-8
Induction:	single Holley four-barrel carburetor
Compression:	11.1:1
Horsepower:	410 at 5,600 rpm
Torque:	476 at 3,400 rpm
Transmission:	four-speed "top-loader" manual
Suspension:	independent A-arms w/coil springs in front; live axle with leaf springs in back
Brakes:	power front discs, rear drums
Production : (with 410-hp 427 V-8)	8

▲ Save for easy-to-miss fender badges, no major external clues were present as to the 1967 427 Cyclone's true identity.

thinking Mercury man's prayers.

In 1966 Ford designers had started stuffing their biggest, baddest FE, the 427, into the Comet's mid-sized cousin, the Fairlane. From there the logic was almost impossible to miss. If the 427 fit into the Fairlane, it also could nestle between Cyclone flanks. Too bad it took a year for Mercury's movers and shakers to figure this one out.

For 1967, Comet customers were treated to two new big-block options, the 410-horsepower 427 with its single four-barrel carburetor and its 425-horse big brother, topped by two four-barrels. No production totals are available for the '67 427 Comet, but apparently at least eight 410-hp mid-sized Mercs were built that year, including the Jamaican Yellow Cyclone shown here. Like the 427 Fairlane, the 427 Mercury was created with drag racers in mind, leaving witnesses wondering why, in this case, a buyer would have opted for the top-shelf Cyclone coupe when he could have dropped the race-ready FE big-block into a cheaper, lighter, less frivolous base Comet sedan? Your guess is as good as ours—perhaps he wanted to be cooler than the competition at the strip.

Ordering the 427 option for the Cyclone in 1967 brought along a whole host of heavy-duty hardware, beginning with a knee-taxing 11.5-inch clutch. Behind that was a "top-loader" four-speed manual transmission that sent torque to a nodular 9-inch rearend filled with 31-spline axles and 3.89:1 non-locking gears. Additional additions included a heavy-duty battery, a 42-amp alternator, an extra-capacity radiator, and a clutch-fan.

FoMoCo's famous 427 need no introduction. But for those then living in caves, this beastly big-block was the same "side-oiler" engine that had taken no prisoners on NASCAR tracks in 1963 then followed that up with a milestone win at Le Mans three years later. Beneath a 427 Cyclone's hood in 1967 was

MILESTONE FACTS

- Mercury's mid-sized lineup for 1967 began with the bare-bones Comet 202, the progressed up the pricing ladder to the Capri, the Caliente, and the Cyclone, which among other things came standard with bucket seats.

- Ford's FE-series big-block family was born in 1958. In 1961, maximum FE displacement went from 352 cubic inches to 390, followed by 406 in '62, and 427 in '63.

- The 427 powered Ford's GT-40 racing machine to a 1-2-3 finish at Le Mans in 1966.

- Engine code for the single-carb 410-hp 427 was "R." It was "W" for the 425-hp dual-carb variety.

- The king of the FE-series big-blocks actually displaced more like 425 cubic inches, but engineers labeled it a "427," probably to make sure it could never be topped in size by a rival. In those days, 7 liters—or about 427 cubic inches—was the common maximum displacement in most racing classes, and the biggest FE was built for racing, period.

- Only one 427 V-8 option (fitted with a hydraulic-lifter cam and single-carb) was offered by Ford and Mercury in 1968 before being canceled midway through the model run. This 390-hp FE big-block was replaced by the 428 Cobra Jet V-8 in April that year.

the same cross-bolted block with its forged-steel crank, forged-steel Le Mans rods (with capscrews instead of bolts), and forged-aluminum pistons. Big valves, a bodacious solid-lifter cam and transistorized ignition were in there as well. A Holley four-barrel carb (with vacuum secondaries) fed things on top, and free-flowing cast-iron headers handled

◄ Ford Motor Company's famed 427 cubic-inch FE-series V-8 was born in 1963. It last appeared in 1968.

spent gases on the other end.

All told, the sum of these parts represented one of the meanest machines seen on the streets in 1967—a howling Cyclone if there ever was one.

◀ A single four-barrel carburetor fed the 410-horsepower 427 in 1967.

▶ Fitting a 1967 Merc with a 427 was done solely with competition in mind, and neither a radio or heater were needed at a dragstrip.

▼ Heavy-duty steel wheels adorned with no-nonsense "dog-dish" hubcaps were included when the 427 big-block was ordered for a 1967 mid-sized Mercury.

1967 Plymouth Barracuda Formula S 383-cid

The Barracuda had been launched by Plymouth in 1964, specifically designed to go head-to-head with Ford in the Mustang pony car race. It was a sporty new 'glassback' coupe with a large and distinctive wrap-over rear window treatment that gave the car a fastback shape. It also had a uniquely styled roof and deck, in which the deck lid bulged up to meet the glass. The car also boasted distinct trim features, that included a split, negative space grille with center insert and horizontal outer division bars, wide rocker sill panels and a chrome band across the base of the rear window.

A single two-door sports hardtop Barracuda model was offered in the model's first, second and third years. The news for '65 was the introduction of the Barracuda Formula S package. This included a Commando 273-cid V-8 engine, rally suspension, heavy-duty shocks, Goodyear Blue Streak tires, a tachometer and 'open wheel' covers.

For 1966, the Barracuda was offered as part of the Valiant series. The car was redesigned towards the font, but remained largely unchanged at the rear end and above the belt. It was now fitted with the split Valiant grille opening.

The 'S' option package continued to be offered, and the standard engines were either the 225-cid slant six, or 273-cid two-barrel V-8.

The Barracuda models shed their links with the Valiant family in '67, and three distinct body shapes were now on offer, a two-door notchback coupe, a two-door fastback coupe (the 'Sports Barracuda') and a two-door convertible.

The 'glassback' look was consigned to the past, and the cars were offered to the public with completely new styling. Barracudas now had curvy, flowing features with extremely restrained, modern trim. Contemporary motoring magazines compared the styling of the car to that of the Buick Riviera, but they were really worlds apart. The new Barracuda had single headlights, concave roof pillars (on the notchback coupe), curved side glass, a concave rear deck panel, wide wheel openings and a sleek fastback.

Standard equipment for the '67 Barracuda included three-speed transmission, and the 225-cid slant six or 273-cid V-8. The interiors were equipped with carpeting, front bucket seats (in the convertible), a fold-down rear seat (in the fastback), a padded dash and all standard safety equipment. The 'S' equipment package was still available in an up-rated form. Whatever the rationale, the '67 Barracuda doubled its sales from the previous model year.

Engine: Barracuda V-8

Displacement: 383-cid

Horsepower: 280

Transmission: three-speed manual

Number Produced: 28,196

▲ This Barracuda Formula S two-door notchback coupe was fitted with the up-rated 383-cid V-8.

1967 Plymouth Belvedere GTX

The year 1967 Plymouth production models were introduced to the market in September 1966. 638,075 cars were sold, putting Plymouth at number four in the league of production. Robert Anderson was the chief executive officer of the company in this year.

The 1967 Belvedere range grew to include another tier of performance, the GTX models. All '67 model year medium-sized Belvederes and the derivative models of the series were slightly face lifted. The horizontal grille blades were thinner and house side-by-side headlights with small grille extensions between them. The parking lamps were moved into the bumper, and the taillamps were redone. A new economy station wagon model was introduced to the range, simply known as the Belvedere.

Belvedere I models had a cigar lighter, padded dash, two-speed wipers with washers, back-up lights, front and rear armrests and rocker panel moldings.

The Belvedere II line had all of the above plus foam front seats, parking brake warning lamp, wraparound taillights, carpeting, wheel opening moldings and full-length side moldings. The Satellite models had additional extras including front bucket seats with console (or center armrest seat), deluxe wheel covers, glove-box light, fender-top turn signals, upper body accent stripe, courtesy lights and aluma-plate full-length lower body trim panels.

The high performance GTX had all this and more, including a 'Pit-Stop' gas cap, Red Streak tires, dual hood scoops, dual sports stripes, heavy-duty threespeed TorqueFlite transmission, brakes, suspension and battery. The standard engine for the GTX cars was the 440-cid four-barrel V-8 engine. They inherited the benefits of the racing heritage of the Mopar big-block engines, and were the muscle cars to beat on the streets.

Two GTX models were available, the two-door hardtop coupe and two-door convertible. 720 GTX cars were fitted with the Street Hemi option package in this year, 312 of which were fitted with four-speed transmission.

Engine:	GTX V-8, overhead valve
Displacement:	440-cid
Horsepower:	375 at 4600 rpm
Transmission:	TorqueFlite automatic
Compression Ratio:	10.1:1
Body Style:	Two-door Hardtop Coupe
Weight:	3615 lbs
Wheelbase:	116 inches
Base Price:	$3418
Number Produced:	30,328 (including Satellite Hardtops)

▲ The GTX hardtop coupe came complete with a muscle car heritage.

1968 Plymouth GTX

Plymouth remained at number four in the producers' league of 1968, on a production of 790,239, and had an 8.1 per cent market share. G.E. White was the chief executive officer of the company in this year. Retail sales for the Chrysler-Plymouth group hit an all-time high.

The GTX models were now part, and top of the Plymouth Intermediate model range, which also included the Belvedere, Satellite, Road Runner, Sport Satellite and Satellite Sport Wagon. Including the two GTXs (a two-door hardtop coupe and two-door convertible), the Intermediate line-up comprised sixteen different models that ranged from two-door convertibles to nine-seat station wagon options. The Road Runner was a newly introduced lightweight pillared coupe that was essentially a no-frills Belvedere equipped as a fullblown muscle car. A modified version of the car was driven to success by the Sox and Martin drag-racing team. The GTX models remained the powerful and expensive Intermediate cars, but considering their serious equipment, they were still quite reasonably priced. They were considered 'special' level cars.

All Intermediate cars were all given a sleek new body. The square look was gone, and the cars now had smooth-flowing 'coke bottle' lines that emphasised the low profile and width of the cars. The grille was different for each intermediate line. The taillamps were housed in sculptured fender extensions with a sideways 'U' shaped appearance. The rear deck lid was somewhat high and slightly 'veed'. GTX models were equipped like the Sport Satellites, and had the same grille style, but also had many standard extra.

They were fitted with 440-cid 'Super Commando' V-8 engines, heavy-duty brakes, suspension, battery and shocks, together with a fully-functioning dual scoop hood and GTX identification.

Despite their already sparkling performance, 446 Street Hemi packages were installed into Belvedere GTX hardtop and convertible models. 234 of these were also equipped with four-speed transmissions.

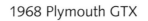

Engine:	GTX V-8, overhead valve
Displacement:	440-cid
Horsepower:	375 at 4600 rpm
Transmission:	TorqueFlite automatic
Compression Ratio:	10.1:1
Body Style:	Two-door Hardtop Coupe
Weight:	3520 lbs
Wheelbase:	116 inches
Base Price:	$3329
Number Produced:	17,914

▲   The 1968 GTX Hardtop Coupe sporting its racing lines.

1968 Plymouth Road Runner

Today the concept is known as the "biggest bang for the buck." This phrase, however, had yet to be coined in the fall of 1967 when Plymouth people woke up the masses with a muscle car that didn't require an arm and a leg to own.

By 1967 performance models were by no means collecting dust in showrooms, but more and more were becoming E-ticket rides. That year there were many factory hot rods priced above $3,300 that could reach 100 mph in the quarter-mile. Yet not one below that bottom line could score triple digits. Thus became Plymouth's "frugal" goal for 1968: "100 mph in the quarter for less than $3,000.

To meet this end Plymouth designers kept non-essentials to a minimum. A bare-bones Belvedere sedan, with swing-out rear windows instead of roll-up units, was initially chosen as the foundation for the project. That foundation was then typically beefed up with stiffened suspension components and F70 wide-tread rubber mounted on wide steel rims adorned only with low-buck "dog-dish" hubcaps. Inside, the basic interior was as spartan as a taxi-cab save for that tall, shiny floor shifter. As expected, a four-speed manual gearbox was standard—no wimpy column-shifted three-speed here. Image-conscious bucket seats were not offered, and frivolity was

Wheelbase:	116 inches
Weight:	3,880 pounds
Original price:	$4,400
Engine:	426 cubic-inch Hemi V-8
Compression:	10.25:1
Horsepower:	425 at 5,000 rpm
Torque:	490 at 4,000 rpm
Induction:	two Carter AFB four-barrel carburetors
Transmission:	three-speed Torqueflite automatic
Suspension:	independent A-arms w/torsion bars in front; live axle with leaf springs in back
Brakes:	front discs, rear drums
Production (coupe w/Hemi V-8):	
	840; 449 with four-speeds, 391 with automatics

limited to a blacked-out grille, a GTX hood, a couple of decals printed up with Warner Brothers' express permission, and that cute "beep-beep" horn. "Road Runner" was the name; speeding away from wily Goats was the game.

Customers of all ages loved every bit of it: the name, the horn and the nicely affordable muscle car behind it all. By paying attention were it mattered most, Plymouth designers were able to keep the Road Runner's base price at roughly $2,900—and without

skimping on the muscle. Beneath the hood was a clever combination of passenger-car power source and hot-ticket hardware. The Road Runner's standard 383 cubic-inch V-8 shared cylinder heads, crankcase windage tray, intake manifold and cam with the big-bully 375-horse 440. With next to no muss and very little fuss, Plymouth engineers had produced a relatively cheap performance V-8 able to make 335 horses on command, and that power fit the original plan nicely.

"Plymouth figures, and rightly so, that one

way to win you over this year is to give you lots of car for your money," raved a February 1968 Car Life review. "In the case of the Road Runner, Plymouth's idea is to give lots of performance for the money, and it does this partly by putting gobs of go-goodies into the car, partly by not charging tremendous amounts for it, and partly by keeping things simple."

Calling the new Road Runner "the world's fastest club coupe," the Car and Driver test crew pointed out that "this is the first car since the GTO to be aimed directly at American youth and it very probably is dead on target. But just wait till ol' Nader hears about it."

Fortunately American youth got wind of the Road Runner before Ralph (he wasn't that old then) and his consumer-conscious "Raiders" got a chance to spoil things. Demand for Plymouth's mainstream muscle car quickly skyrocketed with 1968 production reaching 44,599. Within a year the Road Runner was America's second best-selling muscle car behind (by only a few grand) the new leader, Chevy's SS 396 Chevelle. The former front-runner, Pontiac's GTO, ranked a distant third.

Clearly Plymouth had proven that less indeed could be more. Maybe so, but not all early Road Runners were low-buck bombs. Options were typically plentiful, and most prominent on the extra-cost shelf was the always-awesome 426 Hemi.

Talk about a budget-buster. The '68 Road

MILESTONE FACTS

- Plymouth introduced the Road Runner in 1968 and continued building it up through 1975.

- Total production in 1968 was 44,599—29,240 coupes and 15,359 hardtops.

- Adding to the Road Runner image was a horn that went "beep-beep" just like the cartoon character.

- Advertisements even referring to Plymouth's new muscle car species by its Latin name, "acceleratii rapidus maximus."

- Enough changes were made to the 426 Hemi in 1968 to earn the designation "Stage II." A slightly hotter cam and recalibrated carbs were the main revamps. Compression remained at 10.25:1 and output stayed at 425 horsepower.

- Domestic production of Hemi Road Runners in 1968 was 840 coupes and 169 hardtops. Of those coupes, 449 had four-speeds, 391 had automatics. The breakdown for the Hemi hardtops read 108 four-speeds, 61 automatics.

- An A833 four-speed manual transmission was standard for the '68 Road Runner. The Torqueflite automatic was optional.

- A Road Runner convertible was offered in 1969 for one year only.

- Motor Trend magazine named the 1969 Road Runner its "Car of the Year."

- Road Runner sales in 1969 soared to 84,420, second only by a couple grand to the muscle market leader, Chevy's '69 SS 396—and about 12,000 more than the former king, Pontiac's GTO.

◀ Plymouth did right by licensing the Road Runner cartoon image from Warner Brothers for its mass-market muscle car, one of the Sixties' best-remembered factory hot rods.

Runner's only optional power source, the Hemi wore a hefty price tag of $715, and the bottom-line beating didn't stop there. Adding those 425 horses into the mix also meant the mandatory installation (for four-speed cars; it was optional with the Torqueflite automatic) of the heavy-duty Dana 60 rearend with Sure-Grip differential and 3.54:1 gears, a package priced at $139. All Hemi Road Runners were also fitted with their own special K-member subframe and further-stiffened suspension, improved cooling, heavy-duty drum brakes, and big 15-inch wheels and tires.

Though it defeated the whole budget-minded purpose, mating high-rolling Hemi power with the plain-Jane Road Runner resulted in a predictably fast automobile. Low 13s were no problem, leading Motor Trend's resident muscle maven, Eric Dahlquist, to label the sum of the parts "probably the fastest production sedan made today."

On the flipside, the cost of all this earth-shaking speed was nearly $4,400, a figure well out of Average Joe's reach in 1968. But if you had the dough and the desire, could you name a better buy? Who cared about "biggest bang for the buck" when a Hemi offered the biggest bang, period?

▲ 1968 Road Runners were powered by either the standard 383 V-8 or the optional 426 Hemi.

◀ Though it defeated this budget-bomb's prime purpose, the Hemi fit nicely between Road Runner fenders, raising the bottom line by about a grand in the process.

▼ Plymouth's familiar Road Runner image ran from 1968 to 1974.

◀ Early Road Runners were initially offered only in bare-bones coupe form with flip-out rear quarter windows instead of roll-up units.

1968 Pontiac Firebird 400

Pontiac introduced the Firebird in 1967, as the Chevy Camaro-clone of the division. Both cars were designed to go head-to-head with Ford's Mustang.

The first car was made at Lordstown, Ohio in early January 1967, and was officially released in the February of that year. Two basic models were launched (the two-door hardtop coupe and two-door convertible), but the cars were marketed in five 'model-options' created by adding regular production options (RPOs) in specific combinations. All Tempest and GTO powertrains were available for the car, a total of four major engine types (two six-cylinders, and two V-8s). All others were described as optional equipment. Sales were excellent, with 82,560 model units being sold.

Styling for the second year Firebird models was almost identical to the original cars, and continued to be offered as two-door hardtop coupes and twodoor convertibles. Body styling was sculptural with twin grilles of a bumperintegral design, front vent windows, and three vertical air slots on the leading edge of rear body panels. Federal safety side-marker lights made use of the Pontiac logo. The only major change was that the vent windows were now replaced with one-piece side door glass. The cars were also fitted with outside mirrors, side marker lights, E70-14 black sidewall wide-oval tires with a Space Saver spare. Cordova vinyl tops were available, as were wire wheel covers.

Inside the car, apart from the standard GM safety features, front bucket seats continued to be fitted as standard, as was vinyl upholstery. The dash was simulated burl woodgrain. Astro-ventilation was now offered on the cars.

Engine:	Firebird 400 V-8
Displacement:	400 cid
Horsepower:	335 at 5000 rpm
Compression Ratio:	10.75:1
Base Price:	$3397
Number Produced:	90,152

▲   This Firebird 400 is identified as having the Ram Air
package by the twin hood scoops – functional of course.

The Firebirds were now offered with seven different engine options, ranging from a base 175 horsepower six-cylinder, to a fire-breathing Ram Air II 400-cid V-8, rated at 340 brake horse power. This top option (available for an extra $616) could blow even the Mustang GT off the strip, and was fitted with twin functional hood scoops and a de-

▲ This glamorous red Firebird 400 from 1968 is a convertible.

◣ A magnificent glowing red 1969 Firebird.

▶ The magnificent power plant of the 1968 Firebird

clutching fan. The V-8 options were revised to be more emissions-friendly. Technical changes

1968 Pontiac Firebird 400

to the '68 model included biasmounted rear shock absorbers and multi-leaf rear springs.

'68 Firebird sales were even better than in the launch year, with the model attracting a total of 107,112 buyers. This was despite the number of cars now competing for 'pony car' sales. Every major US car manufacturer was now in on this act. The Firebird sales were a significant contribution to Pontiac's total model year total of 910,977.

▲ A 1968 Firebird's magnificent 400 power plant.

◀ A side view of the 1968 Firebird complete with hood scoop and the iconic logo.

▲   A sleek black firebird from 1968, complete with the Ram air package.

▼   This 400cid turbo automatic Firebird from the 1969 model year is also equipped with wide track tires and an Edelbrock intake.

▶   The Ram Air hood from a 1969 Firebird convertible.

▶   The front light assembly of a convertible 1969 Firebird 400.

1968-½ Ford Mustang 428 Cobra Jet

Three years after Ford kicked off Detroit's ponycar race with a bang in April 1964, Dearborn officials found themselves choking on dust as rival copies of their wildly popular Mustang began galloping away with the burgeoning performance car market.

Introduced for 1967, GM's F-body Camaro and Firebird both offered loads of ponycar pizzazz, as well as optional big-block power. In response, Ford designers fattened the second-generation Mustang to make room for its own big-block, but the '67 GT with its 390-cube FE-series V-8 was no match for Chevy's SS 396 Camaro and Pontiac's Firebird 400.

Leave it to Robert F. Tasca. Credited with originating the phrase, "win on Sunday, sell on Monday," Tasca was no stranger to Ford performance, having promoted it openly from his East Providence, Rhode Island, dealership since 1961. First came sponsorship of a locally successful 1962

Wheelbase:	108 inches
Weight:	3,623 pounds
Original price:	$3,600, approximate
Engine:	428 cubic-inch Cobra Jet V-8
Compression:	10.6:1
Induction:	single 735-cfm Holley four-barrel carburetor
Horsepower:	335 at 5,600 rpm
Torque:	440 at 3,400 rpm
Transmission:	four-speed manual
Suspension:	independent A-arms w/coil springs in front; live axle with leaf springs and staggered shocks in back in back
Brakes:	power front discs, rear drums
Performance:	13.56 seconds in the quarter-mile, according to Hot Rod
Production:	2,827 (2,253 fastbacks, 564 hardtops, and 10 convertibles)

406 Galaxie, followed by a full-fledged drag race team that scored NHRA Winternationals championships in 1964 and '65. By then, Tasca Ford had established itself as the mecca in the East for Blue-Oval performance followers. If it was hot, it was on Tasca's lot at 777 Taunton Avenue.

Yet, despite great success as a speed merchant, not even Bob "The Bopper" Tasca could teach a new dog old tricks, a task put

before him as the supposedly strong '67 Mustang GTS began rolling onto his lot from Ford. As Tasca's performance manager, Dean Gregson, told Hot Rod's Eric Dahlquist, "we found the [390 Mustang] so non-competitive, we began to feel we were cheating the customer. We had to do something."

Actually the solution came about much by

luck after a Tasca employee trashed the 390 FE in a '67 GT coupe while street racing. In place of the grenaded 390 went a 428 Police Interceptor short-block wearing reworked heads and a 735-cfm Holley four-barrel, equipment that instantly transformed the car into a 13-second quarter-mile killer.

Called the "KR," for "King of the Road,"

Tasca's 428 Mustang inspired Hot Rod's Dahlquist to ask his readers if Ford should built a regular-production version. Once a few thousand positive responses began piling up on Henry Ford II's desk, Dearborn designers got the hint.

Following Tasca's lead, Ford engineers simply mixed and matched a collection of existing

MILESTONE FACTS

- Ford offered the 428 Cobra Jet as a mid-year "1968-1/2" option for Fairlanes, Torinos, Cougars and mid-sized Mercurys, but the CJ garnered the most attention as the brave new heart of a new, truly muscular Mustang.

- CJ Mustang production commenced at the Dearborn assembly plant on December 13, 1967. First came at least 50 specially prepared fastbacks: lightweight, strip-ready super-stock Mustangs with all sealers and sound deadeners deleted. These models, all painted Wimbledon White, were built for one job: to promote Ford's newest breed of ponycar performance at the drags.

- Regular production of street-going CJ Mustangs began after the run of super-stock drag cars was completed. Dealers received notice of the 428 Cobra Jet engine option on March 29, 1968. Its price was $420.

- The CJ Mustang Eric Dahlquist tested for Hot Rod was probably one of those first 50 super stock specials. Dahlquist does remember it lacking sealer and sound deadener.

- A team of white Cobra Jet Mustangs showed up in Pomona, California, for the NHRA Winternationals in 1968, and Al Joniec's CJ took top Super/Stock honors with a run of 12.12 seconds at 109.48 mph.

- A Car Craft track test of a super-stock Mustang CJ, driven by Dyno Don Nicholson and Hubert Platt, pushed the envelope even further to 11.62 seconds at 119.7 mph. To that Car Craft's John Raffa wrote that "Ford's new 428 Cobra Jet Mustang Super/Stocker can best be described as a car with hair!"

- The 335-horse 428 Cobra Jet remained a Mustang option up through 1970

- The 428 CJ became the Fairlane Cobra's standard powerplant in 1969.

◀ One of 50 specially prepared lightweight Cobra Jet Mustangs warms up at Pomona prior to the NHRA Winternationals in 1968.

FE-series big-block parts. Using a 428 passenger-car block as a base, they added 427 low-riser heads and a cast-iron version of Ford's aluminum Police Interceptor (PI) intake mounting Tascas's big 735 Holley. A 390 GT cam, PI rods, and 10.6:1 pistons went inside, while low-restriction dual exhausts completed the package, which debuted on April 1, 1968.

Passing on Tasca's suggested name, Ford's braintrust instead chose the "Cobra Jet" moniker for the hot new 335-horse 428, leaving Carroll Shelby to pick up on the KR

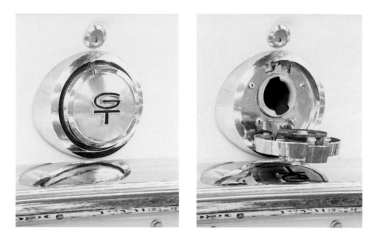

▲ Also among standard GT equipment was a competition-style flip-open gas cap.

▼ All Cobra Jets in 1968 were GT models, meaning they wore bright styled-steel wheels with trim rings and "GT" center caps.

▼ Ford's first Cobra Jet Mustang was offered with either a four-speed manual or Cruise-O-Matic automatic transmission.

label for his CJ-powered GT500 Mustang. Who was the mastermind behind the Cobra Jet label? It was more or less a team effort.

"We already had the snake idea in our heads," explained Ford engineer Bill Barr. "And we didn't do this like we normally did. We didn't just roll out the product with everyone standing around it scratching their asses trying to name it. The idea was already rolling by then. Some artist in Styling had already created a drawing of the Cobra emblem—the snake and the wheels and exhausts coming out of its tale. We had the

drawing, then the name came from there."

Offered in fastback, coupe and convertible forms, the CJ Mustang also featured a long list of standard performance pieces, including power front discs, braced shock towers, a beefy 9-inch rearend, staggered rear shocks (on four-speed models), and a black-striped ram-air hood. An 8000-rpm tach was standard with the four-speed, optional when a C6 automatic transmission was c hosen. Part of the deal, too, was the GT equipment group consisting of a heavy-duty suspension, F70 tires on styled-steel wheels, fog lamps, chromed quad exhaust tips, and "GT" identification.

Testing a specially prepared Cobra Jet prototype, Hot Rod reported a sensational 13.56-second quarter-mile time. Thoroughly impressed, Eric Dahlquist concluded that "the CJ will be the utter delight of every Ford lover and the bane of all the rest because, quite frankly, it is probably the fastest regular-production sedan ever built."

It was also the car responsible for saving Ford's bacon in the great American muscle car race.

◀ The striped hood scoop was fully functional. Ram-Air was standard.

1969 AMC Hurst SC/Rambler

Born in 1954 after the merger of veteran independents Nash and Hudson, American Motors Corporation seemingly always was off in its own world out there in Kenosha, Wisconsin. Affordable, economical, albeit bland transportation quickly became AMC's forte, and this main selling point proved to be just the ticket once money got tight around American households during the late Fifties.

Sales soared in 1959 and remained strong for a few more years. In 1963 Motor Trend magazine even named American Motors' compact Rambler its "Car of the Year." Then reality set in. AMC cars were dull and boring, while the Sixties scene was hip and happening. What was a Detroit outsider to do?

Why not jump up onto the muscle car

Wheelbase:	106 inches
Weight:	3,160 pounds
Base Price:	$2,998
Engine:	390 cubic-inch V-8
Compression:	10.2:1
Induction:	single Carter four-barrel carburetor with ram-air hood scoop
Horsepower:	315 at 4,600 rpm
Torque:	425 at 3,200 rpm
Transmission:	Hurst-shifted Borg-Warner t-10 four-speed manual
Suspension:	independent A-arms w/coil springs in front; live axle with leaf springs in back
Brakes:	power front discs, rear drums
Performance:	14.14 seconds at 100.9 mph in the quarter-mile, according to Road & Track
Production:	1,512

bandwagon? After some serious down times, AMC did just that, though a bit hesitantly at first. In 1967 the company became the last automaker to finally denounce the infamous AMA anti-racing edict of 1957, then followed that up with two all-new, all-exciting cars—the sporty Javelin and hot, little AMX two-seater—in 1968. But that was only the beginning. In 1969, with the help of the Hurst Performance people, the Kenosha company rolled out an outrageous super-stock Javelin

MILESTONE FACTS

• Hurst and AMC announced the SC/Rambler on February 13, 1969. The car then debuted at the Chicago Auto Show in March.

• "Well imagine the looks on the faces when you lay down an e.t. in the low 14s at say, 98 mph... right off the showroom floor!," read an AMC press release detailing the SC/Rambler. "And set it up for the strip with a little sharp tuning, who knows? You might be turning 12s."

• The 315-horse 390 V-8 breathed through a vacuum-activated ram-air hood scoop. On the other end was a unique dual exhaust system fitted with "Special-Tone" mufflers and chrome tips in back.

• The SC/Rambler's standard heavy-duty cooling package included a high-capacity radiator and a "Power-Flex" fan with shroud. Those flexible fan blades automatically decreased in pitch at higher speeds to save power and reduce noise.

• Tires were E70 Goodyear Polyglas Wide-Treads adorned with trendy red stripes.

equipped to go right to the dragstrip. Only about 50 of these red-white-and-blue factory race cars were built that year, with not one ever intended for daily driving chores.

More sociably acceptable was a second factory hot rod created in 1969 through cooperation between AMC and Hurst. Based on American Motors' diminutive Rogue coupe, the Hurst SC/Rambler was one of the flashiest fun machines ever let loose during the original muscle car era. In keeping with American Motors' established tradition, the car was done up in a patriotic finish that didn't have to beg anyone to take a look. On top of basic white paint went large red accent panels down each bodyside and a blue stripe up over the top. The wheel centers, too, were blue, as was the big "arrow" on the hood that directed air into a

◀ ▲ Two exteriors were offered for the SC/Rambler. Type A had red bodysides, while Type B had bare white panels.

somewhat odd, boxy scoop. For those who weren't sure what was going on, that scoop was appropriately labeled with red "AIR" lettering, and the arrow identified the engine that was sucking that atmosphere in: AMC's "390 cu. in." V-8.

The first 500 SC/Ramblers built for 1969 all

were done up in that same image. The next 500 off the line, however, were toned down by leaving off the red bodyside accents. The final 512 then appeared looking just like the first group. AMC enthusiasts today know those 1,012 cars with their red sides as "Type A" models. The other 500 without the red are, you guessed it, "Type B's."

Either way, A or B, the '69 Hurst SC/Rambler also represented one of the best buys from

213

prevent spring windup and wheel hop during hard acceleration.

Inside were bucket seats, a sport steering wheel, and a Sun tachometer strapped to the steering column. Along with all that pizzazz on the outside were dual racing mirrors, racing style hood tie-down pins and 14x6 five-spoke sport wheels.

The real star of the show, though, came beneath that functional boxy scoop. Fed by a Carter four-barrel carb, AMC's 390-cube V-8 produced 315 horses. Combine that power with roughly 3,100 pounds of lightweight Rogue and the results were predictable—the SC/Rambler could indeed run the quarter in roughly 14 seconds. A dip or two into AMC's

▲ A tachometer, strapped to the steering column in street-racer fashion, was including in the SC/Rambler deal.

▶ It was boxy and odd-looking, but this hood scoop did ram cooler, denser outside air into the carb below.

high-performance days gone by. Its base sticker was just short of $3,000, and that wasn't a stripped-down price for a stripped-down car. Standard equipment included a Borg-Warner T-10 close-ratio four-speed manual transmission with a Hurst shifter, a 10.5-inch clutch, power front disc brakes, a heavy-duty cooling package, a suitably beefed suspension, and a Twin Grip differential containing 3.54:1 gears. That stout suspension consisted of typically stiffened springs and shocks, a thickened front sway bar, and rear axle torque links to help

◀ Patriotic paint carried over to the SC/Rambler's wheels.

▲ The Hurst shifter people teamed up with various automakers, including AMC in 1969.

▼ The 1969 SC/Rambler's functional hood scoop.

hot parts bin could quicken that pace up in a heartbeat.

Yet as hot as the SC/Rambler was, it didn't quite attract the following AMC officials had hoped. Many critics loved its performance, but pooh-poohed all that "American-way" frivolity. Thus, the car ended up a one-hit wonder.

AMC designers, however, just couldn't leave well enough alone. They came back in 1970 with their Rebel Machine, another red-white-and-blue screamer wearing a boxy hood scoop—and yet another American Motors muscle car all but lost in the shadows of horsepower history.

1969 Chevelle SS396

In the beginning Chevrolet's legendary SS 396 Chevelle was a little-known, limited-edition teaser created to test the market waters that Pontiac had first splashed head-long into with its GTO in 1964. Only 201 "Z16" Malibu Super Sports were built in 1965, all fully loaded, and all wearing a price tag that would wilt the wallet of most muscle car fanatics.

With Chevrolet's new 396 cubic-inch Mk IV big-block leading the way atop a long list of standard performance and prestige features, the Z16 Malibu cost about $4,200, compared to $2,590 for a base small-block Chevelle. Most of those Z16s went to celebrities and prominent press people, all in the best interests of kicking off a high-powered bloodline with a high-profile bang.

When it returned in 1966, the SS 396 Chevelle was less potent in standard form, but was also less costly, all in the best interests of appealing to a mass audience. Although it was still based on the Malibu

Wheelbase:	112 inches
Weight:	3,900 pounds
Base Price:	RPO Z25, the SS 396 package, added $347.60 to the base sticker ($2,673)'69 Malibu sport coupe.
Engine:	396 cubic-inch L-78 V-8
Compression:	11.0:1
Horsepower:	375 at 5,600 rpm
Torque:	415 at 3,600 rpm
Induction:	single Holley four-barrel carburetor
Transmission:	Turbo Hydramatic automatic
Suspension:	independent A-arms w/coil springs in front; live axle with coil springs in back
Brakes:	front discs, rear drums
Production:	9,486 w/L78 396 (for both SS 396 and El Camino SS 396)

sport coupe (or convertible), it used a more civilized 325-horsepower 396 for standard power in place of the Z16's truly potent 375-horse Mk IV V-8. This power reduction, combined with the deletion of many of the Z16's standard feature, resulted in a more palatable base price of $2,776 for the '66 SS 396. This in turn resulted in sales of 72,000 Super Sport Chevelles that year. If a customer wanted Z16-type performance, all he had to do was ante up for various appropriate options, topped by RPO L78, the 375-horse 396.

By 1969, the popular SS 396 Chevelle had screamed past Pontiac's GTO to become Detroit's best-selling muscle car. Total production for all SS 396 varieties in 1969 hit 86,307, compared to 72,287 for Pontiac's "Goat."

In other news for 1969, Chevrolet changed the way it offered the SS 396 to power-hungry customers. In 1968, the SS 396 model lines included a Malibu sport coupe, convertible and El Camino. Beginning the following year, an SS 396 buyer had to check off RPO Z25, which was offered for those same three bodystyles, plus two new ones in the low-priced 300 series. Both the 300 Deluxe sport coupe and 300 Deluxe sedan could have been transformed into an SS 396

in 1969, the only year a Super Sport Chevelle could have been anything other than a top-of-the-line Malibu or Custom El Camino.

Priced at $347.60, RPO Z25 was basically the same SS 396 package offered from 1966 to '68, with a couple of nice additions thrown in for good measure. Standard power still came from the 325-hose 396 backed by a three-speed manual, and a beefed-up chassis remained as well. On top, the SS hood with its twin bulges carried over, as did the blackout

◄ Chevrolet's popular SS 396 Chevelle unseated Pontiac's GTO as America's best-selling muscle car in 1969.

MILESTONE FACTS

• Introduced in limited-fashion in 1965, the SS 396 Chevelle eventually rose up in 1969 to unseat Pontiac's GTO as this country's best-selling muscle car.

• Late in 1969 the 396 cubic-inch V-8 was bored out to 402 cubes. The name, however, remained "SS 396."

• For one year only, 1969, a Chevy customer could've ordered an SS 396 sedan. That year the Super Sport package became an option package, RPO Z25, available for Malibu sports coupes and convertible, Custom El Caminos, and 300 Deluxe coupes and sedans. All other SS 396s (save, of course, for the convertible and El Camino variety) built on other years were based on the Malibu sports coupe.

• The SS 396's base engine in 1969 was the 325-horse L35 396. Next on the options list was a 350-hp 396, RPO L34. At the top was the 375-horse L78.

• About 300 Chevelles were equipped with the Corvette's 425-horse L72 427 V-8 in 1969 by way of the clandestine COPO paperwork.

• Chevrolet introduced the L89 aluminum-head option for the Chevelle Super Sport's L78 396 only in 1969. These heads did not change the L78's 375-horse-rating; the idea was to shave off unwanted pounds from the potent big-block. L89/L78 production in 1969 was 400.

• Two radioactive Camaro paint choices were offered to SS 396 buyers in 1969: Hugger Orange and Daytona Yellow. Applying either shade added an extra $42.15 to the bottom line.

treatment for the grille and rear cove panel. "SS 396" badging once more graced both ends. Inside, the standard benchseat interior again featured "SS" identification on the steering wheel and "SS 396" tags on both the door panels and the dashboard's passenger side—actually, the dashboard emblem read "Super Sport" in 1966 and '67.

On the outside, the '69 Super Sport received new "SS 396" emblems on the fenders. And the deletion of all the excess lower body clutter used in 1968 (contrasting black paint, chrome trim delineation, various stripe treatments) helped clean things up

▶ Snazzy five-spoke sport wheels became standard SS 396 equipment in 1969. Typical steel rims with hubcaps had been standard from 1966 to 1968.

▲ A 325-horsepower 396 was standard for the 1969 SS396. Options included a 350-horse big-block and the top-shelf L78 V-8 (shown here), rated at 375 horses.

▼ Chevrolet kicked off its SS396 Chevelle legacy in 1965. This familiar badge last appeared in 1970.

considerably. A customer could add the contrasting lower-body paint at extra cost, but the standard scheme looked attractive enough without it. A more suitable choice was the D96 wide upper-body accent stripe.

The most prominent additions to the SS 396 standard equipment list in 1969 were power front disc brakes and a set of new five-spoke SS wheels. The former used 11-inch rotors and single-piston calipers. The latter featured small "SS" center caps and bright trim rings. Set off by chrome wheel opening moldings, these sporty 14x7 rims were the only wheels available for the '69 SS 396 and represented a marked departure from the "dog-dish" hubcaps that had been standard from 1966 to '68.

A nicely well-rounded package inside and out, the Chevrolet's SS 396 deserved its place as America's number-one muscle car in 1969. And the Super Sport Chevelle remained in the lead right up to the end in the Seventies. Did it get any better? Ask the man who owned one, like Fred Koss, of Pesotum, Illinois. He bought the red SS 396 shown here new in 1969—and still owns it today.

When you own the best, why give it up?

▼ An attractive sport steering wheel was one of many interior options for the 1969 SS396. Full instrumentation, buckets seats and a console were also offered.

▲ The M20 four-speed manual transmission.

1969 COPO/Yenko Camaro

When Chevrolet rolled out its big-block Super Sport Chevelle in 1965, GM edicts limited all its mid-sized A-body models to engines no larger than 400 cubic inches. The same lid applied to the new F-body Camaro when it was introduced in 1967.

Full-sized buyers could order the Corvette's 427 V-8 all they wanted for their Impalas and Bel Airs, but Chevelle and Camaro customers had to "make do" with the 396, at least officially.

More than one quick-thinking dealer picked up where the factory left off and began swapping Corvette engines into Camaros in 1967. Most notable were the 427-powered ponycars that rolled off the lot at Yenko Chevrolet in Canonsburg, Pennsylvania. An experienced Chevy racer, Don Yenko had first tried modifying Corvairs for his speed-sensitive customers in 1965. He then turned his attentions to the new Camaro two years later.

The process began with a typical small-block F-body. Once at Yenko's shop, the tame 350 was yanked out and an L-72 427 was dropped in, along with lots of additional heavy-duty hardware and a little touch of extra eye-catching imagery. Presto, instant "Camaro Super Car," a

Specs:	1969 Yenko Camaro
Wheelbase:	108 inches
Weight:	3,050 pounds
Engine:	427 cubic-inch L-72 Corvette V-8
Horsepower:	450 at 5,000 rpm (rated by Yenko Chevrolet)
Induction:	single 800-cfm Holley four-barrel carburetor
Transmission:	Muncie M21 close-ratio four-speed manual
Suspension:	independent A-arms w/coil springs in front; live axle with leaf springs in back
Brakes:	power front discs, rear drums
Production:	201 are known

1969 COPO/Yenko Camaro

▲ Pennsylvanian Don Yenko was one of various Chevrolet dealers to market hopped-up versions of the popular Camaro back in the Sixties.

MILESTONE FACTS

- Don Yenko won four SCCA national titles driving Corvettes before he started marketing his own personal breed of Bow-Tie performance in 1965. First came his red-hot Corvair "Stingers," race-ready compacts that proved unbeatable at any speed.

- One of the 200 '65 Stingers built by Yenko Sportscars—the performance division of Yenko Chevrolet—scored its own SCCA national crown in 1966 with Jerry Thompson driving.

- The Daytona Yellow paint on the Yenko Camaro shown here was a special-order item.

- Yenko Chevrolet also began offering 427-powered Chevelles and Novas in 1969. Novas fitted with the Corvette's 350-cube LT-1 small-block V-8 were introduced in 1970.

- Atlas aluminum wheels were Yenko Camaro options in 1969.

- Along with the L-72 427 V-8, the COPO 9561 package also included 4.10:1 Positraction gears, a Muncie close-ratio four-speed, F41 sport suspension, and power front disc brakes.

- Another COPO option, coded 9737, added a beefier one-inch front sway bar, a 140-mph speedometer, and 15-inch rubber on Chevrolet's popular 7-inch wide Rally wheels. COPO 9737 was known as the "Sports Car Conversion."

- Yenko Camaro production was 54 in 1967, 64 in 1968

- Yenko Chevrolet also marketed modified Vegas in 1971

Yenko's men made these time-consuming engine swaps for two years, using the SS 396 Camaro as a base the second time around in 1968. Then in 1969 they discovered Vince Piggins' central office production order (COPO) loophole, a somewhat clandestine paper trail normally used for special orders by fleet buyers, that is trucking firms, emergency groups, police departments, etc. COPOs didn't require upper office approval, so they represented an easy way to circumvent GM's

▼ A full complement of distinctive striping and badges played a prominent part in Yenko's Super Car conversion in 1969.

complete package sold directly to the public. Sold as well were various options, including such things as traction bars, headers, rear gears as low as 4.88:1, a Vette-style fiberglass hood, sidepipes, spoilers and aluminum mags. Ultra-exotic L-88 equipment was also advertised for Yenko's SC Camaro.

dreaded displacement limits.

As Chevrolet's performance products chief, Piggins cleverly used the COPO pipeline to create various 427-powered F- and A-bodies right on Chevrolet assembly lines in 1969. COPO code number 9561 delivered a '69 Camaro armed with the iron-block L-72 427. The same application in the Chevelle lineup was coded COPO 9562. A third code, COPO 9560, belonged to the outrageous ZL-1 Camaro with its all-aluminum 427. Reportedly, Don Yenko first met with Chevrolet officials in the summer of 1968 to discuss the use of COPOs to help simplify the

Yenko SC conversions. Although some believe that factory-built 427 Camaros might have been funneled from Chevrolet to Yenko in 1968, the accepted opinion holds that all 1967-68 Yenko Camaros were dealership swaps. All 1969 Yenko Camaros clearly were COPO cars.

A limited run of COPO 9561 Camaros were delivered to Canonsburg, where they were treated to a special dose of "Yenko/SC" (or "sYc" for short) imagery that made them all but impossible to miss on the street in 1969. "Yenko/SC" striping ran down the bodysides, and similar stripes (with "sYc" for short) went

▲ Chevrolet rated its L72 427 V-8 at 425 horsepower. Yenko upgraded it to 450 horses.

onto the hood. That same sYc nomenclature also was stenciled onto the bucket seat headrests inside. Back on the outside, "Yenko" badges appeared on the fenders and rear cove panel, and "427" emblems were slapped onto the hood and tail.

As to how many COPO Camaros made up that limited run, that is not clear. Before his death in March 1987, Yenko claimed he ordered 500 COPO 9561 Camaros in 1969. Apparently supporting his claim is a widely circulated photo showing a sign proudly announcing Yenko's "350th 1969 unit built." Yet only 201 '69 Yenko Camaros have been documented. Some say the "350th unit" photo may have referred to all Yenko products

(Camaros, Chevelles and Novas combined) for 1969.

All arguments aside, Yenko's Corvette-powered Camaro truly was a Super Car in 1969. Yenko rated the SC Camaro's 427 at 450 horsepower, more than enough muscle to make low 13s in the quarter-mile an easy reality.

Yenko continued toying with special performance conversions in 1970, in this case using only Novas. The Yenko Chevelle was a one-hit wonder for 1969, and the Yenko Camaro was dropped at year's end. As it was,

▲ The stencil on a Yenko Camaro's bucket seat head-rest was short for "Yenko Super Car."

▶ Five-spoke Atlas mags were optional for the '69 Yenko Camaro.

GM's displacement limit disappeared after 1969, making regular production of the awesome LS-6 SS 454 Chevelle possible. With Chevrolet offering so much performance right out of the catalog in 1970, how could hot-blooded dealers like Don Yenko compete?

Though the Yenko Camaro was only around for three years it left an impression that still has teeth to this day.

1969 Dodge Charger

The 1969 Charger continued to use the beautifully styled 'B' body introduced by Dodge in 1968. The styling of this classic hardtop shape is often compared to the coke bottle, being both slim and rounded. The main change in the second year was the new divided grille for this model year, and a new taillight treatment. Even though a mere 500 were built, the base engine for the model was the 225-cid Slant Six. The 318-cid V-8 was a much more popular base powerplant for these performance-orientated cars. The R/T was the sportiest of the lot; the most high-performance model in the range. This option featured all the standard Charger trim plus the Magnum 440 cid, 375 horsepower, four-barrel carburettor V-8. The car had dual exhausts with chrome tips, TorqueFlite automatic transmission and heavyduty brakes. Like our car, the model was fitted with F70-14 Red Line tires. The Charger SE was the sports/luxury model and was fitted with leather and vinyl front bucket seats, woodgrain steering wheel and instrument panel.

Coupled with the midyear-introduced R/T version of the Coronet Super Bee, the new models provided the Dodge division with a stable of fresh and exciting groundpounders. They were also members of the Scat Pack.

The Daytona Charger was an even scarier beast, a massive roof-high tail spoiler and projectile-shaped front end, gave the car shattering track performance. The latter was made from fibreglass and was fitted over the standard grille opening. Dodge was learning about aerodynamics on the job, anything to give them an advantage over the super-powerful Fords. The car could travel the super speedways at nearly 200 mph with their big 'Hemi' engines. The car was the direct ancestor of the 1970 Plymouth Superbird.

The Daytona Charger car won twenty-two out of fifty-four NASCAR races for 1969, and Bobby Isaac rode the car to victory in the Daytona 500.

Ironically, the most famous Dodge Charger manufactured in 1969, is the 'General Lee' driven by the Duke brothers in the Dukes of Hazard TV series.

Engine:	Overhead valve V-8, cast iron block
Displacement:	273 cid
Horsepower:	180 at 4200 rpm
Compression Ratio:	8.6:1
Base Price:	$3126
Number Produced: (All Chargers)	89,704

The car was orange-painted and decorated with the famous '01' decal. In fact, the producers wrecked over 1500 Chargers filming stunts for the series. But fifteen to twenty cars survived, and are now distributed around the country.

Dodge had had its fifth record sales year in 1968, but overall car sales were down in the US market for '69, and Charger numbers fell by over 6,000 units to 89,704. R.B. McCurry remained as General Manager at Dodge.

▲ This two-tone Charger was produced in the second best year in Dodge history so far.

1969 Dodge Coronet R/T

The Coronet R/T was one of Dodge's hot mid-size models. Powertrains were unchanged, but the new 'delta-theme' nose and tail treatments were interesting, and new grilles and taillights were included. The taillights were an unusual oval-shaped lenses. Essentially, however, the body was the same popular shape that had been introduced in '68, when the R/T version was introduced. Just 7,328 R/Ts were built, including the convertible version. As well as the base level Deluxe, there was also high-performance Super Bee model Coronet with 'Scat Pack' stripes highlighting the restyled rear. As the advertising slogan went, the Scat Pack models were 'Super Cars with the bumblebee stripes'. Both cars continued the honorable Mopar muscle tradition of offering the best in style and grunt for a modest price tag.

The big performance news for the '69 Cornets was the Magnum 440-cid 'six pack' V-8 engine. This engine was created by taking an existing 440 block, and replacing the single four-barrel carburetor with three two-barrel carburetors. The revised engine was also fitted with a fiberglass performance hood, and Ramcharger fresh-air induction was an option (this was standard on Hemi engines, that were available for a further $418).

The R/T continued as the highest-performance Coronet and the most expensive model in the range. It included all the features of the Coronet 500 but could also be fitted with a huge performance pack that included the Magnum 440-cid and TorqueFlite automatic transmission.

Coronets were also available with 426-cid Hemi V-8s, but these were more rare (around 166 two-door coupes and 92 door-door hardtops). This latter 'big block' engine option had been introduced by Chrysler in 1964 and proved that the company understood horsepower and all its implications as a production car seller. Outside, the cars were distinguished by bright sill moldings, R/T nomenclature (now in the rear black Bumblebee stripe rather than on the front fender, across the trunk lid and down the fendersides), twin simulated air scoops were also located on the rear fenders, just ahead of the rear wheelwell openings on each side of the car, and two intakes on the 'Power Bulge' hood.

The car's best dragstrip performance was 12.25 seconds for the quarter mile, at 112 mph. No wonder 'it looks guilty.'

1969 Dodge Coronet R/T

▼ 'Mother warned you there would be men like you driving cars like that', went the cheesy Mopar slogan.

Engine:	440 Magnum V-8
Displacement:	440 cid
Horsepower:	375 at 4400 rpm
Compression Ratio:	10.0:1
Wheelbase:	117 inches
Base Price:	$3442
Number Produced:	7328

1969 Dodge Dart Swinger

Dodge was at seventh in the auto producer's league for 1969, producing 611,645 cars. Despite a small fall in sales, the general upturn for the company was hailed as 'Dodge Fever'. Dart continued as the compact Dodge model, and the Swinger was the sports option for the base level Dart. The car was proudly introduced as the 'Newest Member of Dodge's Scat Pack'.

Taking a cue, no doubt from the infamous hipsters Martin, David, Sinatra, Lawford and Bishop – collectively known as the Rat Pack – Dodge planners decided that their stable of hot cars fit the good times, bad boy image of the original Packers quite well. With a reverent nod to the Vegas crew, Dodge fired up the coals and branded its performance screamers the Scat Pack. Like all good branding, the program needed a recognisable image to hold it all together. A rascally bumblebee replete with crash helmet, goggles and racing tires fit the bill nicely. The cars were also decaled with dual bumblebee stripes in black, defying the traditional industry trend to run racing stripes the length of the car body. The marketing initiative heralded the Dodge muscelcars, including the Swinger, as a specific group.

Effectively, the Swinger 340 was a modestly priced sports car, and proved to be a popular option for the economy-mind performance enthusiast. The car could be fitted with a whole gamut of Dodge powerplants, from the basic six-cylinder to the 383 Magnum V-8. The 340 was devoid of any creature comforts, like carpets, but was fitted with a performance option package that included the 340-cid 'high-winding, 4-barrel' V-8, Rallye Suspension, Firm Ride Shocks and a 'Power Bulge' hood with die-cast louvers. The car was also loaded with a manual four-speed gearbox with a Hurst shifter and bumblebee stripes. In fact, this all conspired to make the car a red-hot performance option, and one of the high points of the sixties Super Car Era. It could cover the quarter mile in fourteen seconds.

Despite the performance heritage that went into the car, the styling had let the model down until the de-chroming of the '67 model year, and seemed disparate with the youth movement the car was aimed at, but the whole package looked great in the '69 restyle. As the slogan went: 'If you can find a hotter car (for the money) buy it!'

Engine:	V-8
Displacement:	340-cid
Horsepower:	275 at 5000 rpm
Compression Ratio:	10.5:1
Body Style:	Two-door Coupe
Base Price:	$2879
Number Produced:	20,000

▲ Despite the underdog status of Dodge within the Chrysler Group, the spicy small-block V-8 of the Swinger lit up the small performance car market.

1969 Ford/Shelby Mustang GT 350

FoMoCo hitched up with ex-racer Carroll Shelby in late 1964 to build an allnew sports car, based on the Mustang fastback. The goal was to create a car with the grunt to compete directly with the Chevy Corvette. The first Shelby GT350 was launched on January 27 1965. At first glance, the car looked just like an ordinary fastback Mustang, but that was the only similarity.

The car's drive train and technical equipment was all seriously beefed-up, and the engine power raised considerably. Effectively, the GT350 was a full-bred race car that could be purchased direct from a Ford dealer. The car underwent some minor changes in '66, which Ford directed in an attempt the make line financially viable. This meant making the specifications of the car closer to those of the production Mustangs. Hertz ordered 1,000 GT350s in '66, which were known as Hertz Shelby GT350s, and had gold-stripe decals.

In 1967, the Shelby body styling was quite a radical departure from that of '66, with the extensive use of fiberglass to modify its appearance. The car was given a big rear spoiler and dual hood-mounted air scoops. The driving lights were moved to the outside of the grille. '67 also saw the introduction of the Shelby GT500s, equipped with a big-block 427-

cid Medium Riser engine.

The range was virtually unchanged for '68 but the cars were now known as the Shelby Cobra GT350 and GT500. A production convertible was now added to the model range, and the Cobra Jet 428-cid engine was introduced.

1969 saw the introduction of the final Shelby Mustangs (though some of the cars were held over until 1970). But, effectively, this was the last year of this fine heritage line-up. This was due to a change of thinking at Ford, who now believed that sales were less relative to high-performance marketing.

Engine availability was changed from '68. The 302-cid V-8 was still fitted as standard, but the GT350s were also offered with a 351-cid four valve Ram Air cooled engine. The

GT500s were offered with a single engine option, the Ram Air cooled 428. This was also the year of 'scoops' – the NASA styled hood was equipped with five, there was one on both front fenders, and one on both rear quarter panels. The Lucas driving lights were now mounted below the front bumper and the dual exhausts now exited through a massive aluminum outlet mounted in the center of the rear valance panel. The cars were fitted with five-spoke Shelby mag wheels. Technically, the car was equipped with power disc brakes and steering. Safety was accommodated with an integral rollbar and shoulder harness seat belts.

Engine:	V-8
Displacement:	351 cid
Horsepower:	290 at 4800rpm
Compression Ratio:	10.7:1
Wheelbase:	108 inches

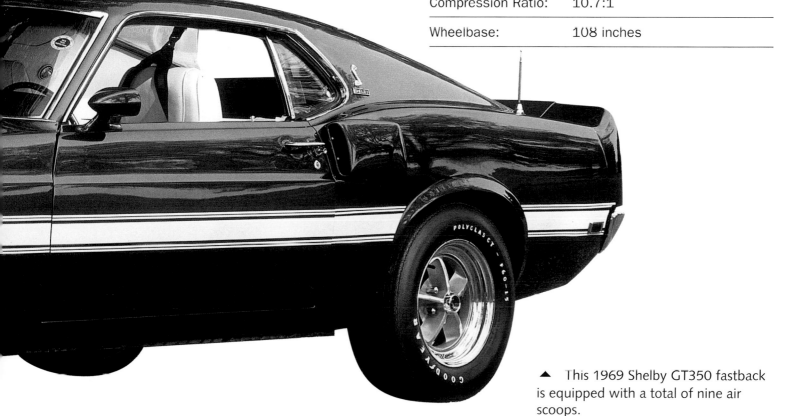

▲ This 1969 Shelby GT350 fastback is equipped with a total of nine air scoops.

1969 Ford Torino Talladega

The 1968-69 Fairlanes were a new body style altogether. Depending on the model, the new cars were designated as either Torinos or Fairlanes… or Fairlane Torinos. Torinos were at the higher end of the range, and the performance options. Torino Talladegas were made by Ford for the 1969 model year to compete in NASCAR racing. Like Chrysler with its winged cars, Ford had turned it attention to the potential of aerodynamics. The car was based on the Torino SportsRoof model, but the Talladegas had fared-in headlights and a more aerodynamic grille design.

So that the car could qualify for the NASCAR series, FoMoCo was obliged to build at least five hundred examples of the car and to put them on general sale to the public. Around 754 cars of this type were actually built, making the Talladega one of the most rare and exotic performance cars ever made.

The Mercury division of FoMoCo built a similar model that was based on the Mercury Montego model and called the Cyclone Spoiler II.

The original racing version of the cars was fitted with the 427-cid racing engine at the start of the NASCAR season, but this was later switched to the semi-hemi 429-cid racing engine. The racing version of the car, known as the Talladga was designed to raise the profile of the SportsRoof (Fastback Coupe) Torino model and boost their sales. More than this, the Talladega was to become a racing legend.

NASCAR race-inspired models put on sale to the public had the 335 brake horsepower Cobra Jet 428 engine, this production model was sold as the Torino Cobra. These cars were fitted with some of the most fierce 'showroom stock' performance engines ever built, together with four-speed manual transmission as standard equipment, 735- cfm carburetion, dual exhaust, beefed up suspension and F70-14 wide oval tires. These cars were part of the Fairlane Torino GT series, which was the sporty version of the Fairlane 500 series and included all of the features of the less expensive cars plus larger engine options, factory bucket seats and console. They were available as two-door hardtop or car with fastback roofline. A ram-air functional air hood scoop was available, as was a 'Traction-Lok' differential.

From the beginning, the car was recognised as a 'screamer', and is a rare collector's car to the present day.

1969 Ford Torino Talladega

▼ Ford's stock cars for 1969 were streamlined Torino Talladega Specials. They won the NASCAR championship with 26 Grand National victories.

Engine:	Cobra Jet V-8, overhead valve
Displacement:	428-cid
Horsepower:	335 at 5200 rpm
Transmission:	Four-speed manual
Compression Ratio:	10.6:1
Base Price:	$3680
Number Produced:	574

1969 Mercury Comet Cyclone Spoiler II

The Comet had been restyled for 1968. It is described as looking like a fullsize Mercury that had gone on a diet. The new car had a horizontal grille, rocker panel moldings, side market lights and chrome-encase vertical taillights.

Among the standard safety features for the car were an energy absorbing steering wheel and column, padded dashboard and sun visors, plus front and rear seat belts. Two speed windshield wipers and washers were also fitted. '68 Cyclones had a mid-tire level body tape stripe. Those with the GT option had an upper body racing stripe, bucket seats, wide tread whitewalls, special wheel covers, all-vinyl interior and a special handling package.

The '69 Comet Cyclone was lightly face-lifted, and only the Fastback body style returned for this model year. The GT option was reduced to just an appearance group option. The hot new Cyclone was the CJ. The Cyclone had a special blacked-out grille, Cyclone emblem, wheelwell opening moldings and a dual exhaust. The car came with the 428 Cobra Jet rated engine, which eveloped 335 horsepower. It was also fitted with the Competition Handling Package, and a plain bench seat interior.

Engine:	Windsor V-8
Displacement:	351-cid
Horsepower:	290 at 5200 rpm
Transmission:	FMX Cruise-O-Matic
Induction:	Autolite four-barrel
Body Style:	Two-door Hardtop
Number of Seats:	6
Weight:	3273 lbs
Wheelbase:	116 inches
Number Produced:	519

But the hottest of the hot was the Cyclone Spoiler II, which was modified to improve its aerodynamics for NASCAR drag racing. A total of 519 Spoiler IIs were built.

Spoilers came in two trim versions, both named after Mercury NASCAR drivers. The Dan Gurney Spoiler had a dark blue roof and striping, with a signature decal on the white lower portion of the car. The Cale Yarborough edition featured red trim and a signature decal. These Spoiler signature editions had

Windsor 351-cid engines, rated with 290 horsepower, and FMX Cruise-O-Matic.

The Cyclone was based on the Mercury Montego for 1970, and thus became bigger and heavier. It is said that this changed the car from a true contender to a full size pretender… The model was discontinued in 1971.

▲ The Cale Yarborough Cyclone Spoiler II models enjoyed special striping, badging, and a rear spoiler.

1969 Oldsmobile Hurst

By the end of the sixties, Oldsmobile's market share was wavering slightly, they were now at sixth position in the auto manufacturers' league, and would begin the seventies at seventh position.

Continuing their muscle-car collaboration, Hurst/Oldsmobile again offered a Cutlass-based hardtop coupe. The car was a fine example of a pure-bred muscle car. Hurst was (and still is today) one of the premier U.S. gearbox manufacturers. When they teamed their expertise with that of Oldsmobile, a truly memorable product was born. The car was based on the Cutlass 4-4-2 two-door 'Holiday' hardtop, and was equipped with a massive 455-cid V-8 engine, and had a special Firefrost Gold and White paint scheme. The engine power output was a tasty 380 horsepower. Nine hundred and six cars were produced for this model year.

The Cutlass models were offered in three ranges for '69, the base Cutlass, the Cutlass Supreme and the 4-4-2s. The Cutlass was the next step up the Oldsmobile ladder from the base level F-85 models. The two-door Cutlass SS had a shorter wheelbase than the four-door models. A potent W-31 performance package was available for both the Cutlass and Cutlass Supreme models, as performance became important throughout the range. It was based on a 'Force-Air' inducted 350-cid V-8 with special equipment included hood louvers, an insulated fibreglass hood blanket, nylon blend

Engine:	V-8 overhead valve, cast iron block
Displacement:	455 cid
Horsepower:	380 at 4800 rpm
Transmission:	Hurst Dual-Gate Shifter
Induction:	Rochester 4GC four-barrel
Weight:	3900 lbs
Wheelbase:	112 inches
Base Price:	$4500 - $4900
Number Produced:	906

▲ This 4-4-2 based Hurst/Oldsmobile two-door hardtop
sports its special White and Firefrost Gold paintjob.

carpeting, special molding package and Deluxe steering wheel. Upholstery was vinyl or cloth.

Cutlass Supremes were the ultimate luxury in the range. This three-model series was one of Oldsmobile's best sellers and was equipped with standard supreme equipment plus a few luxury extras.

The 4-4-2 series was now in its second year. Not only could the buyer for this series order the classic 4-4-2 option, but they could also order the superstock drag racing package, the W-30. Properly tuned, these cars were among the fastest show room stock cars available on the domestic market. The Hurst/Oldsmobile two-door hardtop was included in this four-model range, and was the most expensive option by far.

▲ The 1969 Hurst was equipped with a 455 cubic-inch Rocket V-89 produced 380 horsepower and 500 pounds of torque.

▶ This car is an Oldsmobile Cutlass.

▲ The 1969 car received a functional mailbox fiberglass hood scoop.

▼ The 1969 Oldsmobile Hurst had a new paint scheme of Firefrost gold and white.

▲ The 1969 Oldsmobile Hurst interior included painted gold stripes on the headrests and an Oldsmobile Hurst emblem on the glove box door.

▲ The 1969 Cutlass was updated with a split grille with vertical bars and vertical tailgates.

▼ The Cutlass was a huge success for Oldsmobile. This 1972 model was available with several distinct trim levels and a multitude of different options. It was equipped with a 7.5 liter V-8.

▲ The 1969 Oldsmobile Hurst 442 Edition.

▼ The convertible version of the Oldsmobile Hurst 442. Only 4,295 convertibles were built.

▶ An immaculate convertible 442. In 1968, the 442 became a model in its own right.

▶ A detail of the convertible. The car had a 112-inch wheelbase.

1969 Plymouth 'Cuda 440-cid

By the late 1960s, the Plymouth Barracuda was a quintessential muscle car, and the bigger engined versions were difficult in insure. But the original car was quite a different, milder creature all together. The model was launched in '64 as a fastback version of the Valiant Sedan, and aimed at young, sporty American drivers, who wanted some fun transport. These sound just like Mustang drivers… Handily, the car was fitted with a fold-down rear seat that offered 7 feet of fully carpeted 'anything' space.

The original model was by no means hot, available with a single 273-cid V-8, developing a modest 180 horsepower. Eve so, a four-speed manual gearbox with a Hurst shifter was available. Handicapped by this low performance rating, the car got off to a rather slow start, selling only 23,000 in their first eight months of production.

Luckily, Plymouth soon realised where they were going wrong, and revamped the model considerably. The V-8 remained at 273cid, but with a four-barrel carburetor and higher compression ratio, the car could now push out 235 horsepower, and was tested at 0-60mph in 8.2 seconds. The car was also offered with a Formula S performance package, with stiffer suspension, wide wheels/tires and rally stripes. The car now appealed to the market far more, and sold 64,000 in this incarnation.

For '67, the Barracuda became a line in its own right, and had a bigger and hotter engine – the 383-cid, 280 horsepower engine, coupled with a Carter four-barrel carburetor and front disc brakes.

By '69, the 'Cuda was available in three models (two-door hardtop, two-door fastback and two-door convertible). The cars were hardly changed from the '68s, except for slightly face-lifted hoods and grilles. The cars also had new side marker lamps that were rectangular. The standard engine V-8 engine option was the 318-cid, but the tried-and-tested 225-cid Slant Six was also on offer. However, higher performance options were also available, including the 440-cid Hemi V-8. The cars were fitted with standard government-required safety equipment (deep dish steering wheels and padding), all-vinyl interiors, bucket seats, Pit-stop gas cap, rally lights and red or white stripe tires.

Engine:	GTX V-8
Displacement:	440-cid
Horsepower:	375 at 4600rpm
Compression Ratio:	10.1:1
Weight:	2987lbs
Wheelbase:	108 inches
Base Price:	$2813
Number Produced:	17,788

▲ This '69 'Cuda 440 is the fastback, complete with red stripe tires. Cars fitted with this powerful engine had a reputation for poor handling and braking.

1969 Pontiac GTO Judge

Pontiac's still at number three, and 'Here come da Judge' – a new $332 option package for Pontiac's '69 GTO, complete with 366 horsepower, Ram Air III induction, 400-cid V-8. For $390, the buyer could step up to 370 horsepower with Am Air IV. With this option, the car could go from 0-60 mph at 6.2 seconds, and cover the quarter mile in 14.5. The car was decorated with loud 'The Judge' decals, and was a 'hairy' looking car indeed. The first 2,000 Judges were finished in a true pop-art color, Carousel Red, and came complete with extrovert spoiler, and stripes. This in-your-face decorative style was becoming a muscle car tradition, and buyers were almost as interested in the 'look' as they were in the power under the hood.

The Judge model was introduced to try and halt the decline in GTO sales. The LeMans-based car was falling between two stools – it wasn't a budget muscle car, but neither was it a premium model. Other Pontiac models, such as the HOpowered Tempest developed almost as much power, and were cheaper to insure.

An important consideration for the young drivers these cars were aimed at. The Judge was designed to be a top-of-the-range GTO, to mop up customers who were looking for something with more style and power than the regular models.

For an extra $332 over the price of a standard GTO, the car came fully loaded with Ram Air III induction (later upgraded to Ram Air IV for $558), the '68 400-cid HO power unit, three-speed gearbox with floor shifter, (automatic was optional), Rally II wheels, heavy duty suspension and 14-inch tires. The cars were offered in hardtop and convertible forms, but the convertible sold only a meagre 108 units, whereas the hardtop scored nearly 7000 sales. Considering that the convertibles were over a thousand dollars more, this isn't too surprising. As well as the standard equipment, Pontiac also offered the cars with an enormous range of options, ranging from the handy to the downright bizarre (including a litter basket in several color choices, and a reading lamp). Inside the car, carpeting was fitted as standard, and there was a choice of bucket or notchback seats.

'Here come da Judge'

Although the Judge was now the best-equipped muscle car available for the money, it was only temporarily successful in halting the slide in GTO sales. The car was reasonably successful in it's own right, but its image did not seem to reflect on the rest of the range, and GTO sales slid by nearly 20 per cent to just over 72,000 for the '69 model year. Worse was to come. Sales really slumped as the '70s arrived, falling to fewer than 40,000 in 1970, and to just over 10,000 in '71. This was largely due to the spiralling insurance costs generated by the car's own scary performance image.

Engine:	Ram Air V-8
Displacement:	400-cid
Horsepower:	370
Number Produced:	6725

1969 Pontiac Trans Am

General Motors recent cancellation of its fabled F-body platform, found beneath Chevrolet's Camaro and Pontiac's Firebird, also ended one of Detroit's lengthiest high-performance legacies.

Discounting Chevy's Corvette, which stands on its own as "America's sports car," Pontiac's Trans Am Firebird was the only muscle car to run uninterrupted from horsepower's heydays in the Sixties up into our new millennium. No, the Trans Am's cousin, Chevy's Z/28 Camaro, couldn't claim a similar streak: it was temporarily cancelled after 1974 then returned as a midyear model in 1977.

The Z/28 did come first, however, debuting in 1967. Pontiac's original Trans Am then followed two years later. Both cars were low-production, special-edition vehicles created with stock-class racing in mind—specifically the Sports Car Club of America's Trans American Sedan Championship series, originated in March 1966. In order to legally compete a certain model on the SCCA circuit, a manufacturer had to sell a minimum number to the public. Additional SCCA specifications included a maximum displacement limit: 5 liters, or about 305 cubic inches.

SWheelbase:	108.1 inches
Weight:	3,654 pounds
Base Price:	$3,887
Engine:	400 cubic-inch Ram Air III V-8
Horsepower:	335 at 5,000 rpm
Induction:	single four-barrel carburetor
Transmission:	four-speed manual
Suspension:	independent A-arms w/coil springs in front; live axle with leaf springs in back
Brakes:	power front discs, rear drums
Performance:	14.1 second at 100.78 mph in the quarter-mile (for Ram Air IV version)
Production:	689 coupes, eight convertibles

Ford's Mustang, with its 289 cubic-inch small-block, fit comfortably into that category and dominated Trans-Am racing during its first two years. Chevrolet's Z/28 then sped past the Mustang to become the new SCCA champ in 1968 and 1969, and the "Trans-Am ponycar" race was on. By 1970 Dodge, Plymouth and even American Motors were selling hyped-up "homologation" hot rods intended to allow the parent company entry into the SCCA field.

Let's not forget Pontiac Motor Division, the firm that introduced the muscle car to America. In December 1968 the PMD boys introduced their Trans Am Firebird to the automotive press at Riverside International Raceway in California, then followed that up with a public unveiling at the Chicago Auto Show in March 1969. Initially Pontiac's plan was to build enough T/A Firebirds to make them legal for SCCA competition, however long that roller coaster ride ran. Little did company officials at the time know that they were creating a long-running legend.

Curiously the car's Trans-Am racing career didn't take off as planned as a suitable SCCA-legal small-block V-8 never reached regular production. The only engine offered for the 1969 Trans Am Firebird was a big-block V-8 that displaced 400 cubic inches, 95 more than SCCA rules allowed. But, while the 400-powered Trans Am didn't qualify for the competition series it was named after it did delight the street-racing crowd and continued doing so better than the rest throughout the

performance-starved Seventies and Eighties.

Listed under option code WS4 in 1969, the original "Trans Am Performance and Appearance" package was priced at about $1100 depending on transmission choice and bodystyle (coupe or convertible). Imagery was plentiful, what with that blue-accented Cameo White paint, fender-mounted air extractors, twin-scooped hood and rear spoiler.

Beauty beneath the '69 Trans Am's skin included a beefed up chassis consisting of a

▼   Like so many American performance cars, Pontiac's original Trans Am experienced severe frontal lift at high speeds.

MILESTONE FACTS

- According to Pontiac engineer Herb Adams, the Trans Am's 60-inch-wide rear wing created 100 pounds of downward force at 100 mph.

- Pontiac's Trans Am was the only muscle car to run consecutively from the sizzling Sixties into the new millenium.

- With a big-block V-8 beneath its hood, the nose-heavy 1969 Trans Am's weight bias was 58 percent up front, 42 percent in back.

- F70 fiberglass-belted rubber on 14x7 steel rims were standard for the 1969 Trans Am.

- Pontiac engineers originally planned to produce the Trans Am with a 303 cubic-inch small-block V-8 to make it legal for SCCA racing. This engine did not make into production, leaving officials no choice but to install the 400-cube big-block, an optional Firebird power source since the 1967.

- Though engineers claimed the 1969 Trans Am's rear wing worked well creating downforce at speed, the car's nose did the opposite—unwanted front end lift was a real problem.

- Of the 697 Trans Am Firebirds built for 1969, eight were highly prized convertibles.

- Of the 634 L74-equipped Trans Am coupes built for 1969, 520 had four-speeds, 114 automatics. The model shown here features a four-speed

heavy-duty three-speed manual transmission was standard. Optional trans choices included wide- and close-ration Muncie four-speed manuals and GM's ever-present Turbo-Hydramatic auto-box. Only 55 of the 689 Trans Am coupes built for 1969 featured the hot L67. All eight '69 Trans Am convertibles were L74-equipped; four with automatic transmissions, four with manuals.

As a straight-line performer, the nose-heavy

▼ Production of L74/four-speed Trans Am coupes (shown here) in 1969 was 520.

thickened one-inch front sway bar, heavier front coils and rear leaf springs, stiffer shocks, and a limited-slip Safe-T-Track differential. Brakes were power front discs, and quick, variable-ratio power steering was standard, too.

The base 400-cube engine was Pontiac's 335-horsepower "Ram Air III" rendition, coded L74. Another big-block, the 345-horse L67 Ram Air IV, was available at extra cost. A

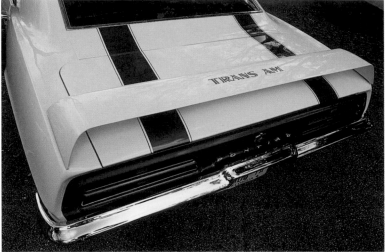

◀ Trans Am buyers in 1969 could chose between four-speed manual and automatic trans-mission options.

▲ Pontiac engineers bragged about the downforce created by the Trans Am's rear wing.

▼ Sport wheels were standard.

1969 Trans Am was a real screamer, running in the low 14-second bracket for the quarter-mile. And itt also did amazingly well in the twisties. Calling the new Trans Am "an animal; a souped-up, sharp-horned, hairy mountain goat, Sports Car Graphic magazine's road testers couldn't say enough about what was going on underneath. "We can't imagine

▲ The engine block of the 1969 Trans Am convertible.

where Pontiac learned how to set up a suspension, but this one is a good illustration that a nose-heavy car doesn't have to be a tragic understeerer." Added Hot Rod's Bob Swaim, " we feel safe in saying that, not counting Corvettes, the Trans Am is possibly the best handling production car made in this country."

True or not, this claim garnered little support on Mainstreet U.S.A. because so few first-edition Trans Ams were built in 1969. Production delays then almost left an even better T/A to a similar fate in 1970. But popularity soared from there, and Pontiac was selling more than 100,000 Trans Am Firebirds by 1979. In 1999, GM celebrated the Trans Am's 30th birthday with a special blue-accented white anniversary model.

A few years later the long, legendary tale came to a close.

◄ An advertising post for the smaller-engined 1969 Trans Am.

▼ A 1970 Trans Am dash. This car is fitted with air conditioning at an added cost of $376. The pushbutton AM radio cost $61.

1969-70 Ford Boss 302 Mustang

In February 1968 Henry Ford II hired former General Motors executive Semon "Bunkie" Knudsen to run the show in Dearborn. Knudsen, the son of William Knudsen, the man who had left Ford for General Motors back in 1921, had become GM's youngest general when he'd started out at Pontiac in 1956.

Almost overnight, he then transformed your grandpa's car company into a builder of true excitement. "You can sell a young man's car to an old man," went his prime motto, "but you'll never sell an old man's car to a young man." In Bunkie's mind, young men liked hot cars, and the hotter the better.

"When Mr. Knudsen came from GM, he brought along a strong belief in the power of performance," explained Motor Trend's Eric Dahlquist.

Wheelbase:	108 inches
Weight:	3,260 pounds
Base Price:	$3,500
Engine:	302-cid Boss V-8 with canted-valve "Cleveland" heads
Compression:	10.5:1
Induction:	single 780cfm Holley four-barrel on an aluminum high-rise intake with optional "Shaker" hood scoop
Horsepower:	290 at 5,800 rpm
Torque:	290 at 4,300 rpm
Transmission:	four-speed manual only
Suspension:	independent A-arms w/coil springs in front; live axle with leaf springs and staggered shocks in back, thick sway bars at both ends.
Brakes:	power front discs, rear drums
Performance:	14.62 seconds at 97.5 mph in the quarter-mile
Production:	7,013

Knudsen also brought along a strong belief or two concerning the Mustang. In his words, the popular ponycar was "a good-looking automobile, but there are a tremendous number of people out there who want good-looking automobiles with performance. If a car looks like it's going fast and doesn't go fast, people get turned off."

Knudsen took one look at Ford's ponycar and decided it was time for a change. The Mustang had just been redesigned for 1967 with an eye towards making more room up front for more engine, but initial results were disappointing. Though the Cobra Jet Mustang did debut in

April 1968, Bunkie wanted more, he wanted a hot machine that was as fast in the curves as it was in a straight line. That summer he demanded that his engineers produce "absolutely the best-handling street car available on the American market."

Something like Chevrolet's Z/28 Camaro perhaps?

Knudsen wasn't above stealing things—concepts or people—from his former employer. More than one GM genius also jumped over to Ford at Bunkie's invitation, and they brought more than one GM idea along with them. One of the more notable defectors was designer Larry Shinoda, the man who had created the Z/28's sporty image in 1967. When Knudsen hired Shinoda in May 1968, his first assignment was to best that hot, little Camaro.

Shinoda's contributions included the new Mustang's stripes, spoilers and window slats, as well as its name. "I suggested they call it 'Boss,'" a groovy label his superiors initially had a tough time relating to. But once they were tuned in as to how hip it was to be "boss," they began diggin' it, man.

Ford contracted Kar Kraft Engineering, in Brighton, Michigan, to develop the Boss Mustang, and the first prototypes were completed by August 1968. Ford Engineering

▶ Ford's Boss 302 Mustang was the Trans-Am racing champ in 1970, with Parnelli Jones' number 15 car taking top individual honors. Teammate George Follmer drove Boss number 16 during pre-season testing.

MILESTONE FACTS

• Along with the Boss 302's high-profile image, designer Larry Shinoda was also known for his work on Chevrolet's stunning Corvette Sting Ray, introduced in 1963.

• Shinoda also named the car, but not without an argument. "They were going to call it 'SR-2,' which stood for 'Sports Racing" or 'Sports Racing—Group II,' which I thought was a dumb name," he recalled in 1981. "I suggested they call it 'Boss.'" His idea won out.

• Both the Boss 302 and Boss 429 Mustangs were developed by Ford contractor Kar Kraft Engineering in Brighton, Michigan.

• According to Ford engineer Bill Barr, the Boss 302 dyno tested at 314 horsepower with all equipment in place and working. In bare-bones form with no air cleaner and headers in place of the stock exhausts, the Boss 302 produced more than 390 horsepower.

• Boss 302 production in 1969 was 1,628.

• Race-car quick 16:1 manual steering was standard, as were big 11.3-inch front disc brakes. Ten-inch drums handled braking chores in back. Power assist for both brakes and steering was optional.

• Boss 302 updates for 1970 included expanded color choices; from the four offered in 1969—Bright Yellow, Acapulco Blue, Calypso Coral, Wimbledon White—to 13, including the truly radioactive trio of "Grabber" colors: Grabber Blue, Grabber Green and Grabber Orange.

• Appropriate "Boss 302" decals apparently were in the works for a third rendition in 1971 before the the Boss 302 V-8 was dropped.

that took over production work from there. Engineer Matt Donner was the man responsible for the excellent Boss 302 chassis, which quickly impressed critics with the way it hugged the road. "Without a doubt the Boss 302 is the best-handling Ford ever to come out of Dearborn and may just be the new

1969-70 Ford Boss 302 Mustang

standard by which everything from Detroit must be judged," claimed a Car and Driver report.

How did the Boss 302 stack up to Chevy's hot-handling Z/28? "In showroom trim, car for car, the Mustang was close, but I can't really say [it] was superior," said Shinoda. On the track, the battle between the two arch-rivals was a toss-up. Chevrolet's Trans-Am Camaro took home SCCA racing laurels in 1969, while Ford's Boss 302 put the Mustang back on top in 1970.

As for street performance, both rivals relied on special 290-horsepower 302 cubic-inch small-block V-8s. Base for Ford's Boss 302 was a modified Windsor block featuring four-bolt main bearings. On top of that went new cylinder heads then being readied for the upcming 351 Cleveland V-8. With their big ports and large, canted-angle valves, these heads were excellent breathers.

The Boss 302 suspension package developed by Donner involved, in his words, "mostly adjustments." Star of the show were super fat F60 Wide-Oval tires on wide 15x7 Magnum 500 wheels. To make room for all that extra tread, the Boss 302's front wheel arches were re-rolled to increase clearance. Remaining tweaks included typically stiffened springs and

◀ The Boss 302 V-8 (left) was rated at 290 horsepower.

▼ Designer Larry Shinoda added the blacked-out panel surround the Boss 302's gas cap

shocks, the latter coming from Gabriel.

In 1970, the second-edition Boss 302 Mustang received a sway bar at the rear end, and that was about it as far as mechanical advancements underneath were concerned. On top came a slightly revised image and more color choices. Easily the hottest new image item was Ford's optional Shaker hood scoop, which as functional at it was "boss-looking," it rammed cooler outside air into the carburetor whenever pedal met metal.

And that happened a lot in a Boss 302 Mustang, one of Detroit's best all-around performers of the original muscle car era.

◀ The super-cool "shaker" hood scoop (below) was optional.

▼ the rear spoiler and back window slats

1969-70 Boss 429 Mustang

When Ford married its big, bad Boss 429 V-8 to the Mustang in 1969, it did so to legalize the so-called "Shotgun" motor for NASCAR racing. According to NASCAR rules, any model or engine could compete as long as at least 500 regular-production examples were made available for public sale.

Those rules didn't specify that the two be built together, leaving Ford a loophole to roll right through. As long as the Blue-Oval boys brought 500 or more Boss 429 V-8s to the dance, it didn't matter how they were dressed. On the street, the big Boss satisfied homologation standards beneath ponycar hoods. On NASCAR tracks, it then threw its weight around behind the extended snout of Ford's odd-looking Talladega, which, by the way, came standard in regular-production trim with a 428 Cobra Jet V-8. Confused? You should be. Some things never change; NASCAR rules moguls still have heads spinning to this day.

Like the Boss 302, the Boss 429 Mustang was originally developed by Ford's performance contractor, Kar Kraft Engineering, in Brighton, Michigan. Kar

Wheelbase:	108 inches
Weight:	3,870 pounds
Base Price:	$4,868
Engine:	429 cubic-inch V-8 with aluminum cylinder heads
Compression:	10.5:1
Induction:	single 735-cfm Holley four-barrel carburetor on a dual-plane aluminum intake
Horsepower:	375 at 5,200 rpm
Torque:	450 at 3,400 rpm
Transmission:	four-speed manual only
Suspension:	independent A-arms (suspension geometry modified to make room for big Boss 429 V-8) w/coil springs in front; live axle with leaf springs and staggered shock absorbers in back
Brakes:	power front discs, rear drums
Performance:	14.09 seconds at 102.85 mph for the quarter-mile, according to Car Life test
Production:	857

Kraft then handled final production duties, rolling out its first Boss 429 in January 1969, nearly three months ahead of Ford's first Boss 302.

Development of the Boss 429 V-8 dated back to 1968 after Ford had introduced its 385-series big-block family for its luxury lines. To take this mill racing, engineers recast a special reinforced cylinder block, then topped it off cast-iron heads featuring hemispherical combustion chambers. In production, those iron heads were traded for weight-saving aluminum units with revised combustion chambers that weren't quite hemispherical. Thus another nickname: "Semi-Hemi."

▲ Complementing the Boss 302 Mustang was its big, bad brother, the Boss 429.

Whatever the name, the big Boss 429 did not drop easily into the ponycar platform, thus the reasoning behind Kar Kraft's involvement. Various labor-intensive modifications were required, including widening the engine compartment by two inches, and these changes were best made on a small, specialized assembly line.

Ford started delivering '69 Mach 1s to the Kar Kraft works in December 1968. There the cars were stripped of their engines, and specially reinforced shock towers were engineered to supply the extra underhood room needed to allow the Boss 429 V-8's entry. Upper A-arm location points in turn were moved outward an inch and lowered another inch. Beefier spindles were also installed, as was a modified export brace on top to firmly tie the restructured shock towers to the cowl.

On the outside went "flared" front fenders, needed to supply extra clearance for the standard F60 Wide-Oval rubber mounted on 15x7 Magnum 500 wheels. Other exterior mods were minor in comparison. The most prominent add-on was a huge functional

MILESTONE FACTS

- According to Car Life magazine's critics, the Boss 429 Mustang was "the best enthusiast car Ford has ever produced."

- Unlike the Boss 302's super-clean shell, the Boss 429 body retained the 1969 SportsRoof Mustang's rear roof pillar medallions and fake rear quarter scoops.

- No striping or black-out treatment was added to the Boss 429, just simple, straightforward "Boss 429" decals for the front fenders.

- Standard Boss 429 equipment included power front disc brakes, power steering, staggered Gabriel shocks in back, and thick sway bars at both ends.

- Included with the Boss 429 V-8 was a Drag Pack-style oil cooler to help keep lubricants within their effective temperature range.

- Also standard was a close-ratio four-speed that delivered torque to a Traction-Lok differential with 3.91:1 gears out back.

- Clearance was tight beneath a Boss 429 Mustang's hood. A thinned-down power brake booster was used to avoid a conflict on the driver's side with the Shotgun motor's huge valve cover. And the battery was relocated to the trunk, where it also conveniently transferred weight from the front wheels to the rears.

- Production of 1970 Boss 429 Mustangs was 499.

- Changes to the 1970 Boss 429 Mustang were few. Most noticeable was low-gloss black finish for that huge hood scoop. Mechanical upgrades included the addition of a standard Hurst shifter and the relocation of the rear sway bar from below the axle to above.

These NASCAR-style Boss big-blocks featured beefy connecting rods with large 1/2-inch bolts. The remaining Boss 429s for 1969 and most for 1970 got the "T-code" engine, which traded those heavy, rev-limiting rods for lighter pieces with 3/8-inch bolts. The first T engines featured the same hydraulic cam and magnesium valve covers found inside and on top of the S rendition. But early in the T run, the magnesium covers were replaced with aluminum units and a slightly more aggressive solid-lifter cam superseded the hydraulic stick. The third Boss 429 rendition, found in very few 1970 models, was the "A-code" engine, which was basically a T motor with revised smog controls. All three versions were conservatively rated at 375 horsepower.

▼ There was no mistaking the Boss 429 V-8 with its "semi-hemi" heads.

hood scoop.

Beneath that scoop went three different variations of the Shotgun motor. The first 279 cars built were fitted with "S-code" engines.

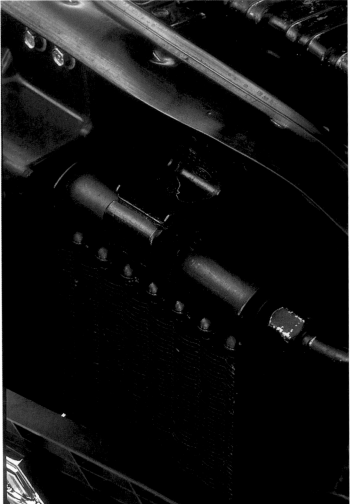

◀ Big, sticky F60 Goodyear tires on 15-inch Magnum 500 five-spoke rims were standard for the Boss 429 in 1969 (shown here) and 1970.

▲ A competition-conscious oil cooler, mounted just ahead of the radiator core support on the driver's side, was also standard.

As mean as the Boss 429 looked on paper, real-world results didn't quite measure up, at least in some opinions. More than one magazine road tester called the NASCAR-engined ponycar "a stone." In designer Larry Shinoda's words, the Semi-Hemi "was kind of a slug in the Mustang." On the other hand,

Car Life's critics claimed that the big-block Boss "ranks as one of the more impressive performance cars we've tested."

Why the difference of opinions? Most in the know knew that the Boss 429 Mustang should have been running well into the 13s. Hell, Ford's Semi-Hemi was a full-fledged race engine unleashed on the street. But therein lay the problem. Engineers were forced to defeat their own purposes to make this monster streetable. The Boss 429's big valves and ports were designed to make lots of power at high rpm. Yet the cam, although aggressive by most perspectives, was not up to the task of fully filling those ports with fuel/air. On top of all that, the factory-installed rev-limiter turned off the juice just when the big Boss was just starting to show off its true potential.

As was the case with the Boss 302, the Boss 429 was built for two years only. Kar Kraft

shipped off its final Shotgun-motored Mustang on January 6, 1970. Later that year Ford pulled the plug on its racing activities, and that was that. Such was life in the fast lane.

◀ Ford people laughingly rated the Boss 429 big-block V-8 at 375 horsepower.

▲ The Boss 429 V-8 was basically a race engine let loose on the street.

▼ This functional hood scoop was painted to match the Boss 429's body in 1969. It became black in 1970.

1969-70 Mercury Cougar Eliminator

Mercury division always has offered quite a bit more prestige than its corporate cousin Ford. Yet it still has continually encountered difficulties earning its due regardless of how much quality awaited its customers. Then again, isn't that the fate of most middle children? Lower-priced Fords always sell like hotcakes, and the top-dog Lincolns will forever garner all the attention from top-shelf shoppers.

Whether or not Mercury will finally find its fair share of the limelight soon remains to be seen. As intriguing as Mercury's new performance sedan, the Marauder, was in 2003, it still rolled right into the shadows, much like so many other muscular Mercury models before it.

Take for example the Cougar Eliminator of 1969-70. As cool as they came during the days of Purple Haze and groovy go-go boots, Mercury's hottest-ever ponycar offered it

Wheelbase: 111 inches

Weight: 3,610 pounds

Base Price: $3,200

Engine: 302-cid Boss V-8 with canted-valve "Cleveland" heads

Compression: 10.5:1

Induction: single 780cfm Holley four-barrel on an aluminum high-rise intake

Horsepower: 290 at 5,800 rpm

Torque: 290 at 4,300 rpm

Transmission: four-speed manual

Suspension: independent A-arms w/coil springs in front; live axle with leaf springs in back, sway bars front and rear

Brakes: front discs, rear drums

Performance: 14.4 seconds at 98 mph in the quarter-mile, according to Cars magazine

Production (with Boss 302 V-8): 450

all: pizzazz, performance and prestige. Being a Cougar, the Eliminator was inherently more roomy and luxurious than its Mustang running mate, and even more class and convenience was available by way of a long, long options list.

Like the Boss 302 Mustang, the Cougar Eliminator was the work of the late Larry Shinoda, the design genius who had previously penned the '63 Sting Ray for Bill Mitchell at Chevrolet. When Bunkie Knudsen fled GM's executive offices for Ford's in 1968, he enticed Shinoda to make a similar

defection, with the goal being to one-up Chevy's Z/28 Camaro with the Boss 302. Shinoda's bitchin' Boss image went over so well, Lincoln-Mercury officials then decided they should try the same tack.

Taking its name from the dragstrip, a prototype Cougar "Eliminator" was prepared for an October 1968 debut at the Los Angeles Auto Show. Spoilers front and rear fit the beautiful Cougar body like a glove and reportedly worked. Also part of the package was an aggressive hood scoop, bodyside striping, a blacked-out grille and wide Goodyear rubber on American Racing mags. Positive public response convinced L-M execs to rush this Boss Mustang knock-off to market as a mid-year 1969 model. Regular-

production examples were introduced in March that year.

Save for the mags, the first Eliminator was essentially a carbon copy of the prototype. As much as Shinoda campaigned for a suitably sporty set of standard wheels for the '69 Eliminator, cost-conscious execs wouldn't budge; conventional 14x6 stamped-steel rims with mundane dog-dish hubcaps were included as part of the base package. At least attractive styled-steel wheels were offered at extra cost.

Standard equipment did include F70-14 Goodyear Polyglas tires and the Competition

▲ A prototype Eliminator debuted at the Los Angeles auto show.

Handling Suspension group, which included heavy-duty front and rear springs and shocks and a large front anti-sway bar. A rear sway bar was optional. And like the flaming orange prototype, all regular-production Eliminators turned heads with ease thanks to six available eye-popping "Competition" paint choices.

Unlike its Mustang counterpart, which relied solely on the Boss 302 small-block, the '69 Cougar Eliminator was offered with various power sources. Base was the 351 four-barrel V-8, the latest concoction of Ford's Windsor small-block family. A 320-horse 390 cubic-inch big-block was next up the ladder, with the 335-horsepower 428 Cobra Jet big-block topping things off. Ordering the Cobra Jet added an even stronger suspension with higher rate springs, a thicker front anti-sway bar and staggered rear shocks. The Eliminator's big hood scoop could've also been made functional atop a Ram-Air 428 CJ.

The bone-jarring Cobra Jet suspension was also included in a fourth Eliminator package, this one using the high-winding Boss 302 small-block with its superior canted-valve heads. Like its Boss Mustang brethren, the

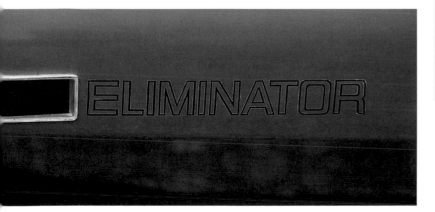

MILESTONE FACTS

- In 1970, Ford Motor Company's hot, new 351 Cleveland V-8 became the Eliminator's standard powerplant.

- As in 1969, the 428 Cobra Jet big-block V-8 was an Eliminator option in 1970.

- Total Cougar Eliminator production (all engines) in 1970 was 2,200. Eliminator production in 1969 (again with all engines) was 2,411.

- Mercury's Competition Handling Package was standard beneath a 1970 Eliminator. Included was a thicker 15/16-inch front sway bar and a half-inch rear bar.

- Boss 302 Eliminators were sold only with four-speed manual transmission in 1970.

Boss 302 Eliminator represented a wonderful combination of straight-line strength and hot handling that made it one of the muscle car era's best all-around performers. While Cobra

▲ Shinoda's favored rear-deck spoiler was a popular option for 1969 and 1970.

◀ The Eliminator name also appeared in those years only.

Jet Cougars were among Detroit's fastest machines of the day—forays into the 13-second bracket for the quarter-mile were no problem—they were no match for their small-block cousins on the long and winding road. The nose-heavy big-block Eliminator handled nowhere near as nicely as the better-balanced Boss 302 variety.

Yet as attractive as the Boss 302 Eliminator was in both 1969 and '70, it still fell well short of its Mustang cohort as far as popularity was concerned. The 1970 Boss Cougar shown here is one of only 450 built that year.

Clearly both the Eliminator and its Mustang counterpart had a lot to offer in 1970: great looks, lots of muscle and ample road-worthiness. But apparently there was only room in Ford Motor Company's ponycar corral for one Boss. And it was again left to a Mercury muscle car to lose its way in the shadows.

▲ Distinctive sport wheels with trim rings were Eliminator options in 1970.

▼ Noted designer Larry Shinoda supplied the image for both Ford's Boss 302 Mustang and its Cougar Eliminator cousin. Distinctive striping and a blacked-out grille were part of the Eliminator package in 1969 and 1970, as was a chin spoiler.

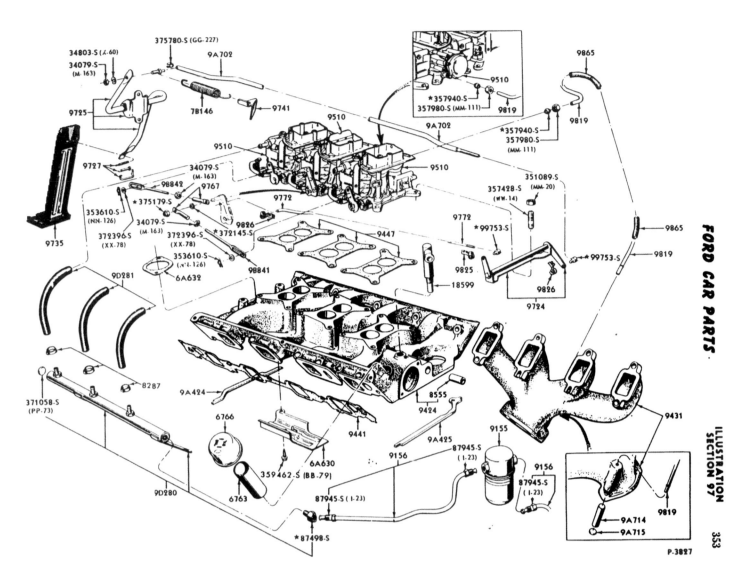

▲   Ford's engine diagram for the 1969 Cougar Eliminator.

▼   A four-speed stick was included behind the optional Boss 302 V-8 (◀).

1970 AMC Rebel Machine

AMC were at tenth position in the auto producers' league in 1970, on an output of 242,664 cars. The company was determined to continue its muscle car legacy, and launched a new, gaudy muscle car, the 'Rebel Machine' out of nowhere. Their first muscle car offering was the 1966 Rambler Rogue, fitted with the Typhoon V-8. This engine was fitted in the Marlin the following year, but it wasn't really until the AMX was launched in '68 that AMC joined the exclusive muscle car club.

Through the development of these models, AMC had acquired a reputation for the ability to create eye-catching, high-performance machines at bargain prices. The Rebel Machine was a classic example of this combination. The car was developed with the input of the Hurst Products Company, and was based on the relatively ordinary Rebel model. But at least 1,000 Machines boasted a flamboyant red, white and blue paint scheme, and a massive shoebox-like hood. Later editions of the model were finished in a choice of solid colors and featured a blackout hood treatment with silver pin striping, plus optional red, white and blue graphics that could be added on to the grille and body.

AMC launched the car at the National Hot Rod Association's World Championship Drag Race in Dallas, Texas, during October 1969.

What AMC had saved in trim and appearance goodies for the Rebel Machine (though they were fitted with cool wheels) were spent to good effect on performance extras. Customers got a Ram Air induction set-up, heavy-duty shocks, and springs, front and sway rear sway bars, four-speed close ratio manual transmission complete with four-speed Hurst shifter and power front disc brakes. Power was supplied by AMC biggest ever publicly offered power plant, the 390-cid V-8, rated at 340 horsepower and capable of a quarter mile time of 14.4 seconds at 98 mph. Rather bizarrely, the car was also equipped with a hood-mounted tachometer. The interior was fitted with high-back bucket seats.

However, Rebel Machine sales proved disappointing, so this proved to the one and only year that the car was offered as part of the AMC line-up.

Engine:	V-8
Displacement:	390-cid
Horsepower:	340 at 3600 rpm
Compression Ratio:	10.0:1
Body Style:	Two-door Hardtop Coupe
Weight:	3650 lbs
Wheelbase:	114 inches
Base Price:	$3475
Number Produced:	1936

▲ The Rebel Machine was a gaudy muscle car from an unexpected source.

1970 American Motors AMX

During the Sixties you could count the number of American-built two-seaters using only a couple digits, one finger for Chevrolet's Corvette, the other for American Motors Corporation's almost forgotten AMX. While the Corvette just celebrated 50 years on the road in 2003, the hot, little AMX lasted a mere three years, 1968 to '70, although AMC's diminutive machine probably deserved a much more noteworthy fate.

What was an AMX? Wags still commonly refer to it as little more than a cut-down Javelin, itself a sporty new AMC offering for 1968. At 97 inches, its truncated wheelbase was one click shorter than the Corvette's, and designers had achieved this short stance by simply wacking out 12 inches (in the area in front of the rear wheels) from the same unit-body platform found beneath the Javelin. With no room left for a backseat, the AMX simply featured a carpeted storage area in the shortened rear compartment. From there the two siblings from Kenosha, Wisconsin, shared fenders, doors, bumpers, rear deck lid, windshield and rear glass.

Wheelbase:	97 inches
Weight:	3,495 pounds
Base Price:	$3,560
Engine:	390 cubic-inch V-8
Induction:	single Carter four-barrel carburetor
Compression:	10:1
Horsepower:	325 at 5,000 rpm
Torque:	420 at 3,200 rpm
Transmission:	four-speed manual
Suspension:	independent A-arms w/coil springs in front; live axle with leaf springs in back
Brakes:	power front discs, rear drums
Performance:	14.68 seconds at 92 mph in the quarter-mile, according to Motor Trend
Production:	4,116

Though optional V-8 power was available for the Javelin (a six-cylinder was standard), the AMX came with nothing else.

Argument also still persist to this day as to which actually came first, although it must be said that the Javelin was introduced in the fall of 1967, with the AMX debut following nearly six months later. But the AMX was conceived first, its roots running back to January 1966 when the original AMX (for American Motors Experimental) concept-car appeared at the Society of Automotive Engineers annual gathering. This fiberglass-bodied flight of fancy featured seating for two and a short 98-inch wheelbase, and it also inspired the evolution of a steel-bodied, regular-production spin-off. A few evolutions later, the real-world AMX was unveiled to rave reviews on February 15, 1968, during Daytona Beach's famed Speed Weeks

◀ AMC's 325-horse-power 360 cubic-inch V-8 became the AMX's standard engine in 1970.

Styling wizard Richard Teague, who was responsible for the AMX's exceptional good looks, called American Motors' two-seater, "a hairy little brother to the Javelin." Group vice-president Vic Raviolo, himself directly responsible for once-staid AMC's startling walk on the wild side, referred to it as "a Walter Mitty Ferrari." And although the AMX—like the Camaro, Cougar and Firebird—essentially followed in the Mustang's hoofprints, its truly distinctive long-hood/really-short-deck profile nearly redefined the ponycar image. Toss in a decent dose of standard performance and the AMX almost qualified as a breed apart.

spectacular. Along the way designers also morphed the new platform into the longer, roomier Javelin. In truth, referring to the Javelin as a stretched AMX is probably the correct thing to do.

AMC officals foresaw great things ahead for their sawed-off runt, projecting sales of 10,000 for he abbreviated 1968 model year, and 20,000 for each year thereafter. Despite some positive early press, despite semi-

▼ Craig Breedlove established 106 speed and endurance records at a Texas test track with two 1968 AMX coupes.

stunning looks, despite impressive American-style performance, the AMX never took off as expected. A minor revamp for 1970 couldn't stave off fate, and sagging sales convinced the guys in Kenosha to make a short story even shorter. But blaming the quick disappearing act on the car itself isn't at all fair, especially when you consider the improvements made for 1970 to an already nice package.

Paying due homage to Teague's somewhat timeless sheetmetal lines, not a crease was touched or a bauble added to clutter things up, with the possible exception of 1970's new

MILESTONE FACTS

- Total two-seal AMX production for 1968 to '70 was 19,134: 6,725 in 1968, 8,293 in 1969 and 4,116 in 1970.

- According to Mechanix Illustrated's Tom McCahill, American Motors' two-seat AMX was "the hottest thing to ever come out of Wisconsin."

- Mechanically speaking, the '70 AMX was updated with a switch from AMC's old trunnion setup to ball-joints in the front suspension.

- After the two-seat AMX was retired after 1970, American Motors continued using the name for its top-shelf Javelin model—which did have a backseat.

- A Hurst shifter was standard equipment for four-speed AMX's in 1970.

- AMC also offered its coveted "Go Pac" options group for the '70 AMX. Included were power front disc brakes, a special handling package, a 3.54:1 Twin-Grip differential, E70 Goodyear red-line tires, and exterior "C-stripes."

◀ Functional ram-air equipment was included as part of AMC's "Go Package" options group.

▲ A "rim-blo" steering wheel and simulated wood-grain appointments were new for the 1970 AMX.

▲ This AMX is finished in Golden Lime Metallic. It is equipped with the 390 Go-Package and Machine wheels. Surprisingly, the AMX was seen as a competitor to the Corvette.

hood, which was lengthened two inches and crowned with an aggressive "power bulge." Unlike the 1968-69 hood, which was fully non-functional, the '70 AMX bonnet could be put to work once the optional ram-air equipment was in place.

Beneath that new hood was new standard power as the previously installed 225-horse 290-cid "Typhoon" V-8 was replaced by a 360 V-8 rated at 290 horsepower. The top

option continued to be AMC's big 390, but it was now rated at 325 horses, 10 more than in 1968 and '69.

Elsewhere, simulated "sidepipe" rocker trim was added and the parking lights were moved from the bumper to the grille, supposedly leaving the bumper openings to supply

▶ AMC's two-seat AMX was built for 1968-70 only.

▲ This 1968 model is one of the early AMXs.

▼ The 1970 AMX was the only American-built steel-bodies two-seater of its time. Its short wheelbase made it even more unique.

cooling air to the brakes. Anyone with eyes, however, could see the ducts installed for that purpose didn't extend close enough to the brakes to make any real difference.

But most who looked at the '70 AMX liked what they saw. And in 1985, the Milestone

Car Society recognized American Motors' intriguing two-seater as an American milestone, citing its styling, engineering, performance and innovation. If only it had

▼ A fine example of an AMX from 1970.

been born in Detroit instead of Kenosha—we might still be talking about the AMX today.

▼ The 1970 AMX was produced in a fantastic array of flamboyant paintjobs.

1970 Buick GSX Stage 1

General Motors dominated the early supercar race with Pontiac's GTO and Oldsmobile's 4-4-2 kicking things off in 1964. In 1965 Buick followed that lead with the first of its long-running Gran Sports, a classy machine based on the division's mid-sized Skylark model.

Born in Flint, Michigan, where "better cars" were built, Buick's gentlemanly GS, in the opinion of Car Life magazine's editors, came "off stronger, more distinctive [than its GM cousins] and with something its owners can appreciate"—that being a humble asking price. Priced at a tidy $200, the GS option added a 325-horse 401-cube V-8, a beefier convertible frame, and those ever-present heavy-duty chassis upgrades.

But don't kid yourself. Just because it was a Buick didn't mean a Gran Sport's appeal was totally intended for gentlemen. Performance escalations in Flint during the Sixties included the 1969 introduction of the division's revered "Stage 1" engine package, offered that first year for the firm's 400 cubic-inch

1970 Buick GSX Stage 1

Wheelbase:	112 inches		Torque:	510 at 2,800 rpm
Weight:	3,920 pounds		Transmission:	Turbo Hydramatic automatic
Base Price:	$3,700		Suspension:	independent A-arms w/coil springs in front; four-link live axle with coil springs in back
Engine:	455 cubic-inch Stage 1 V-8			
Induction:	single Rochester Quadrajet four-barrel carburetor		Brakes:	power front discs, rear drums
Compression:	10.5:1		Performance:	13.95 seconds at 100.50 mph for the quarter-mile
Horsepower:	360 at 4,600 rpm		Production	(w/Stage 1 455 V-8): 400

big-block V-8. Among other things, Stage 1 parts included a hotter cam and a modified Rochester Quadra-Jet four-barrel carburetor topped with a ram-air hood. Output for the Stage 1 400 was a laughable 350 horses, though few got the joke. Not many muscleheads took Buick performance seriously, so even the super-strong Stage 1 was commonly overlooked—
that is, until it left an unsuspecting victim eating dust at a traffic light. "If the [Stage 1 Buick] had a GTO sheetmetal wrapper on it," wrote Hot Rod's Steve Kelley, "you couldn't build enough of 'em."

▼ Either gleaming Apollo White or snazzy Saturn Yellow paint adorned the GSX in 1970. No exterior engine identification was included.

Token Stage 1 output went up 10 horses in 1970 as cubic inches for Buick's biggest big-block zoomed to 455. After watching a 455 Stage 1 Gran Sport scorch the quarter-mile in a scant 13.38 seconds, Motor Trend's Bill Sanders called this ground-shaking Buick an "old man's car inbred with a going street bomb." Continued Sanders, "It may be some vague sort of incest, but the results are pretty exciting. Performance verges on a precipitous mechanical hysteria. The first time you put your foot to the boards a premonition of impending whiplash emanates from the base of the Achilles tendon."

Exciting words indeed. And this was before Buick designers started dressing up their Stage 1 455 in a shocking sheetmetal wrapper the

MILESTONE FACTS

- Total Buick Gran Sport production in 1970 was 20,096. Of these, 9,948 were powered by 350-cid small-block V-8s. Buick also built 1,416 GS convertibles that year, all with 455-cid big-blocks.

- All GSX Buicks were hardtops. Total GSX production for 1970 was 678, followed by 124 in 1971.

- Buick's Stage 1 455 Gran Sport was one of the last Seventies muscle cars standing around Detroit. It was still in the scene in 1974.

- Like Oldmobile's 4-4-2, Buick's Gran Sport was treated to a 455 cubic-inch big-block V-8 in 1970 after General Motors dropped its 400-cid limit for its mid-sized model lines.

- Buick parts books also listed even more outrageous "Stage 2" components for its big-block V-8s. Yet as potent as these parts were, they garnered little attention 30-odd years back. Even fewer horsepower hounds recall them today.

▶ Buick's Gran Sport first appeared in 1965 as a "gentleman's hot rod" of sorts. There was nothing gentle about the new GSX in 1970.

likes of which performance buyers had never seen before. On February 9, 1970, Buick introduced its gonzo-looking GSX at the Chicago Auto Show. Along with a hot suspension, 15x7 sport wheels shod in fat G60 Goodyear Polyglas GT rubber, and power front disc brakes, the GSX featured what may well rank as the muscle car era's highest profile image treatment.

Included were front and rear spoilers, color-coordinated headlight bezels (standard GS units were chromed), black bodyside accent stripes and twin black hood stripes (all trimmed in red pinstriping), a hood-mounted tachometer, dual racing mirrors and "GSX" identification. Accompanying all this was either Apollo White or Saturn Yellow paint. Inside, black was the only available shade. Bucket seats, a consolette, a Rallye steering wheel, gauges and a Rallye clock were also present and accounted for.

Beneath that bodacious skin was Buick's Rally Ride Control Package, consisting of heavy-duty front (1-inch) and rear (0.875-inch) sway bars, boxed lower control arms and performance-tuned springs and shocks.

Standard power came from a 350-horsepower 455 big-block backed by a four-speed and a limited-slip differential carrying 3.42:1 gears in back. The sum of these parts, identified by Buick options code "A9," added roughly $1,100 to a Gran Sport's bottom line in 1970.

For those with a little pocket change left over there were some interesting options, the foremost being the fabled Stage 1 V-8. Beneath a yellow or white GSX hood, the Stage 1 option was priced at $113 in 1970. It cost $199 when ordered for a "typical" GS. But unlike the GS Stage 1, the GSX version carried no exterior identification, meaning most challengers on the street never even knew what hit them.

▲ "GSX" identification appeared in the grille, on the rear quarters...

▼ ...and on the rear spoiler's trailing edge.

▲ Buick's Stage 1 455 V-8 was optional for the GSX.

◀ Fat Goodyear rubber on 15x7 sport wheels was standard for the GSX.

▼ The hood-mounted tach was standard.

▼ The Stage 1 interior, complete with rally clock.

1970 Chevrolet Chevelle LS-6 SS 454

Determining which car ruled during the muscle car era of the Sixties and Seventies is not an easy task—so many hot cars, so much hot-to-trot horsepower. Yet as tough as this task appears, it simply begs to be done. After all, competition was the muscle car's main claim to fame. The race had to have a winner, right?

Being the quickest from point A to B alone, however, did not a champion make. Granted, raw speed and power were top priorities. But not all performance-minded car buyers 30-something years back wanted to go racing. Most simply wanted to play the Walter Mitty part while driving to work, cruising the town, or picking up the younguns from John F. Kennedy Elementary.

If elapsed times are used as the only measuring sticks, Detroit's factory super-stocks of the early Sixties come out on top hands down. But these wild beasts were never meant for the street. In the civilized world they were nothing more than warranty work waiting to happen. Then again, so too were many of the mass-marketed muscle cars to follow. Living with a fully pumped-up performance car in the

Sixties was never easy, especially so when the package included solid lifters, lumpy cams, metallic brake linings, knee-bending clutches, and locking differentials. More muscle almost always meant more headaches. No pain, no gain, right?

So where does this leave us as far as crowning our king?

Many believe that honor belongs to the Chevy clan. From a popularity perspective, Chevrolet's Super Sport Chevelle ranked as the muscle car era's front-runner. After finally

Wheelbase:	112 inches
Weight:	3,885 pounds
Original Price:	$4,475
Engine:	454 cubic-inch LS-6 V-8
Induction:	single four-barrel carburetor
Compression:	11.25:1
Horsepower:	450 at 5,200 rpm
Torque:	500 ft-lbs at 3600 rpm
Induction:	single 780-cfm Holley four-barrel carburetor
Transmission:	Muncie "Rock Crusher" (M-22) four-speed manual
Suspension:	independent A-arms w/coil springs in front; live axle with coil springs in back
Brakes:	power front discs, rear drums
Performance:	13.12 seconds at 107 mph for the quarter-mile, according to Car Craft magazine
Production:	4,475 (coupes and a few convertibles)

▲ Free-breathing closed-chamber heads with big valves (2.19-inch intakes, 1.88 exhausts) and huge ports were key to the 450-horsepower LS6 454 V-8's success.

succeeding the GTO as America's best-selling muscle car in 1969, the SS Chevelle outsold its rival from Pontiac by 37 percent before the axe came down on high-performance in 1972.

Chevrolet's SS 396 Chevelle rose to the top because it offered decent performance at a decent price in base form. "Although [the SS 396] is not the fastest machine right off the showroom floor, it does possess much more potential than any other car in its field," concluded Popular Hot Rodding's Lee Kelley in 1968. "The best-selling Supercar isn't the quickest," added a 1970 Car Life review. "But

it looks tough. And it's kind to women and children. With the handling package, brakes, etc., the SS 396 makes a fine family car." By 1970 the SS 396 legacy had grown so respected, Chevrolet's hype-masters didn't dare toy with it after the Turbo-Jet big-block had been bored out to 402 cubic inches late in 1969. "Ess-Ess-four-oh-two?" Nah. It was "Ess-Ess-three-ninety-six" or nothing at all— unless, of course, "it" was the new SS 454, the supreme evolvement of the breed.

The SS 454 Chevelle came into being after GM finally dropped its 400-cube maximum displacement limit for its intermediate models after 1969. Two widely different SS 454s were offered for 1970, beginning with the relatively tame LS5, rated at 360 horsepower. The other

▲ Called "Cowl Induction," Chevy's ram-air system was optional on both the SS 396 and SS 454.

MILESTONE FACTS

- The LS6's 450-horsepower factory rating was the highest ever assigned during the muscle car era of the Sixties and Seventies. Estimates put actual output as high as 500 horses.

- LS6 454 V-8s were equipped with three different types of air cleaners in 1970: a conventional dual-snorkel unit, a jazzy chrome-topped open-element type, and the Cowl Induction design that sealed to the hood's underside to direct cooler outside air into the carburetor.

- Estimates put LS-6 convertible production for 1970 at between 20 and 70.

- Although magazines road-tested a 1971 LS-6 Chevelle, it never reached production. Instead, Chevrolet transferred the LS-6 option over to the Corvette lineup, where it too was offered for one year only.

- Chevrolet produced the SS 454 Chevelle from 1970 to 1972.

- Chevrolet later revived the LS-6 engine identification when it introduced the Z06 Corvette in 2001.

was the legendary LS6, a burly big-block that Car Life called "the best supercar engine ever released by General Motors." Many other critics considered the LS6 to be the best supercar engine, period.

Put together with care at Chevrolet's big-block V-8 production plant in Tonawanda, New York, the LS6 was specially built from oil pan to air cleaner with super performance in mind. Unlike the LS5, which was based on a two-bolt main bearing block, the LS6's bottom end was held together with four-bolt main bearing caps. The LS6 crank was a tough

▲ A standard speedometer could barely hold the LS6, which was equipped with either a four-speed or automatic transmission.

forged steel piece cross-drilled to insure ample oil supply to the connecting rod bearings. Rods too were forged steel, and they were magnafluxed for rigidity.

The real attraction of the LS6 show was a pair of closed-chamber cylinder heads that could breathe with the best of them thanks to large rectangular ports and big valves. A huge 780-cfm Holley four-barrel fed this beast, which was conservatively rated at 450 horsepower. Some claim actual output was more than 500 horses. Whatever the number, the results on the street were outrageous.

"Driving a 450-horsepowe Chevelle is like being the guy who's in charge of triggering atom bomb tests," claimed a Super Stock

▲ Hood pins with tie-down cables were standard for the Super Sport Chevelle in 1970.

report. "You have the power, you know you have the power, and you know if you use the power, bad things may happen. Things like arrest, prosecution, loss of license, broken pieces, shredded tires, etc."

Even so, your mama probably could've driven this car down the quarter-mile in a click more than 13 seconds. Dipping into the 12s was only a matter of letting mom slap on a pair of slicks and bolt on a set of headers while her cookies cooled on the ledge. Either way, the LS6 Chevelle was all but unbeatable on the street. "That's LS as in Land Speed Record," concluded Motor Trend's A. B. Shuman.

But the LS6 SS 454 was not only a mean machine, it could also get along relatively well with everyday use. Evidence of just how well this wild animal could survive in domestication appeared in production figures. Even though the 450-horse 454 alone cost $1,000 extra, the slightly cranky LS Chevelle actually outsold its more affordable, less disagreeable

▲ The 454 large block engine developed 450 horsepower.

▼ This car is a 1970 Chevy Chevelle SS LS-6 454.

LS5 brother, 4,475 to 4,298. Relatively speaking, Detroit's most powerful musclcar was also its greatest sales success.

▲ A convertible version of the Chevrolet Chevelle SS 454 LS-6.

▼ An all-original Chevelle interior.

◀ Equipped with Chevrolet's big block V-8, the 1970 Chevelle SS developed 450 horsepower.

◣ This hardtop white Chevelle SS 454 drag car achieved a quarter mile time of 11.20 seconds.

▲ A superb convertible 1970 Chevelle SS 454 LS-6.

▼ A concourse standard Chevelle from 1970.

1970 Chevrolet Corvette LT-1

Corvette production dropped by half in 1970, due to a prolonged workforce dispute at the St. Louis factory. This had had the knock-on effect of extending dealer delivery times to over two months, which reduced orders to only 17,316 cars. This was the lowest Corvette production volume for over a decade, and means that cars from this 'limited-production' model year are now both rare and sought after. Other market factors were also mitigating against the success of high-performance cars at this time. High gas and insurance prices, together with a general feeling of economic uncertainty made selling this kind of luxury/power auto package tricky. In real terms, the cars were becoming bsolete. But despite their problems, Corvette continued to subtly revise the car to keep it in the forefront of design and performance.

Corvette's big block V-8 engine grew even bigger in this year – to a high point of 454-cid (producing 465 horsepower). This LS-7 option was designed for competition, and could cover the quarter mile in around 13 seconds at 110 mph.

The LS-7 package wasn't fitted to regular road cars. The LT-1 engine option was also introduced to the range in '70. This was a solid-lifter 370 horsepower version of the small block engine. The LT-1 package included sharper valve timing, a bigger bore exhaust, and the same carburetion as the big-block with cold air induction. The LT-1 was actually advertised as a 350-cid set-up to accommodate Federal emissions regulations. These anti-performance government restrictions were to negatively affect all the pony car runners in the 1970s, obliging them to put an increased emphasis on comfort and luxury features to sell the cars.

The basic aerodynamic styling introduced to the Corvette in 1968 effectively persisted until 1983, but it was refined and revised for 1970. Corvettes were available as sport coupes and convertibles in this model year. The car's four fender gills were replaced by an ice cube tray grille, which was echoed in the (nonfunctional) radiator intakes at the front of the car. Corvette designers were aware that the lower portion of the car was susceptible to stone-chip damage from material flicked up by the

wheels, so they flared the wheel arches to offset this problem.

The twin tail-pipes were squared-ff to become rectangular rather than round. Inside the car, the seats were improved, in an attempt to give better support and more headroom, and improved access to the luggage area. This was crucial, as the cars still weren't fitted with trunk lids. Inertia-reel seatbelts were now fitted as standard.

Engine:	LT-1 V-8
Displacement:	350-cid
Horsepower:	370
Weight:	3153lbs
Wheelbase:	98 inches
Base Price:	$5469
Number Produced:	10,668

▲ This 1970 Corvette inadvertently became a limited-production model, and is now extremely desirable.

1970 Chevrolet El Camino SS 454

Chevrolet didn't limit their muscle car talents to passenger cars, they even worked their magic on their pick-ups. The El Camino was a Chevelle/Malibuderived truck, introduced to the market in 1958, in the wake of the '57 Ranchero.

The truck shared most of the major mechanicals of the car, including the underpinnings and trim. By 1966 almost all the muscle car options offered on the Chevelle SS models were also offered on the El Camino including the hairy 366-cid Mk IV big-block V-8, complete with 375 horsepower. Interior appointments were also sports-orientated with bucket seats, a console and mag-style wheel covers. But the SS imagery was not awarded to the El Camino at this point.

This all changed in 1968 when Chevrolet finally began to offer an SS 396 El Camino complete with the revered 'SS 396' badging, blacked-out grille and bulging power hood. Production for this first Super Sport El Camino was 5,190, helping total El Camino sales shoot up by at least twenty per cent to a new high of 41,791. A similar jump in sales was achieved in '69 when the final tally soared to 48,385.

Maximum performance also leapt in 1970, as the SS 454 option debuted for both the Chevelle and El Camino. As well as sharing many of the same goodies, including a power-bulge hood and four-speed manual transmission, El Caminos also shared the SS power plants. Most SS 454 option El Caminos for '70 were equipped with the 360 horsepower LS-5 454 big-block V-8, but a few customers ordered the higher-powered 450 horsepower LS-6 454. This latter option is considered by some pundits to be the most intimidating engine ever to be produced in the entire muscle car era. By this time, work had definitely given way to play in the car-truck field, and people were buying both the El Camino and Ford Ranchero models for enjoyable driving, rather than hauling. 'People all over the country are getting on the band-wagon' wrote Lee Kelley in the December '67 issue of Motorcade magazine. El Caminos were even seen at the drag strip, and could cover the quarter mile in under 15 seconds at around 98 mph.

With or without the high performance option, the El Camino continued to be a hot seller throughout the seventies, and was a common sight both on and off the road. The SS 454 made the El Camino the ultimate muscle truck, and the ever-present SS models reflected glory on the entire range. Even so, trucks kitted out in this way made up only a small percentage of El Camino sales.

▼ Leading the hard lives they do, trucks don't survive in great numbers, so the SS 454s are ultra-rare.

Engine:	Turbo-Jet V-8
Displacement:	454-cid
Horsepower:	360 at 5400 rpm
Induction:	Single Four-barrel carburetor
Body Style:	Car-truck
Wheelbase:	116 inches
Number Produced:	47,707

1970 Dodge Challenger R/T

Short for "Road and Track," "R/T" was to Dodge what "SS" was to Chevrolet, though in comparatively smaller doses. Dodge built nowhere near as many R/T models as Chevrolet shelled out Super Sports during the Sixties and Seventies, nor did the former cars pack as much of a high-profile whallop as the latter.

Those "R/T" badges were cool, and they did signify the presence of a special machine. But they never attained the status of, say, "SS 396" or "SS 454."

From its humble beginnings in 1967, the R/T package included, first and foremost, a high-powered big-block Magnum V-8. Chassis beefs were thrown as part of the deal, too, to better handle the R/T's extra muscle. First came the Coronet R/T that year, followed by a Charger R/T in 1968, both of which were fitted with either the "standard" 375-horse 440 cubic-inch V-8 or the optional 426 Hemi. A third R/T, this one based on Dodge's all-new ponycar platform, debuted for 1970.

1970 Dodge Challenger R/T

Wheelbase:	110 inches		Transmission:	four-speed manual
Weight:	3,820 pounds		Suspension:	independent A-arms w/torsion bars in front; live axle with leaf springs in back
Base Price:	$3,266 (with "standard" 383 V-8)			
Engine:	440 cubic-inch Magnum V-8		Brakes:	four-wheel drums, standard; power front discs, optional
Induction:	single Carter four-barrel carburetor			
Compression:	9.7:1		Performance:	14.8 seconds at 95 mph in the quarter-mile, according to Sports Car Graphic
Horsepower:	375 at 4,600 rpm			
Torque:	480 at 3,200 rpm		Production (w/440 V-8 and four-speed):	916

MILESTONE FACTS

- Dodge built 76,935 Challengers in various forms (coupes and convertibles, six-cylinder and V-8 power, etc.) in 1970.

- Total Challenger R/T hardtop production (import and domestic) in 1970 was 14,889. Of that figure 2,802 were fitted with the 440 V-8—1,886 with automatic transmission, 916 with four-speeds.

- Another 3,979 R/T hardtops with the upscale Special Edition package were also built for 1970, as were 963 R/T convertibles.

- The Special Edition package included a vinyl-covered roof with a small rear window, though the vinyl top (with normal-sized glass) could be ordered individually for the basic Challenger R/T hardtop.

- Standard on a 1970 Challenger R/T was the Rally instrument cluster, which included a simulated woodgrain panel, a 150-mph speedometer, a tachometer, a trip odometer, clock, and gauges for fuel, oil and temperature. An ammeter and three-speed variable wipers were also part of the package.

- Dodge unveiled an interesting new pallet of exterior shades for the 1970 Challenger, including such eye-catching colors as "Plum Crazy" (shown here), "Sublime," and "Go-Mango."

▲ Striping was standard for the Challenger R/T in 1970. The vinyl roof and rear spoiler were options.

Plymouth's ponycar, the Barracuda, had been around since 1964, and in 1967 it had graduated up into Chrysler's A-body ranks, home to Dodge's Dart. Along with this slight upsizing came the opportunity to stuff big-block V-8s beneath the Barracuda's long hood, although that optional addition left little room for anything else under there. Say, like a compressor for optional air conditioning.

Merry Mopar men then set out to rebuild their ponycar platform with an eye towards creating more space up front for both more engine and more equipment. Though overall size remained compact as ever, the all-new E-body foundation they came up with relied on a cowl structure borrowed from Chrysler's mid-sized B-body line (Coronet, Road Runner, etc.), which meant for a wider, roomier engine bay compared to the A-body Barracuda's. From there followed a truly spunky little car conveying a rakish image accentuated by its abbreviated tail perched high above the road out back.

Dodge designers, led by Bill Brownlie, managed to create a slightly different slant on the same long-hood/short-deck theme by using slightly more wheelbase, 110 inches compared to 108 for Plymouth's remade 1970 Barracuda. They then named their E-body "Challenger," and they offered it in three forms: the basic six-cylinder model, the more sporty V-8, and the aforementioned R/T. All three model lines in turn featured three different bodystyles: a hardtop, a convertible, and a "sports hardtop" featuring Dodge's

Special Edition package, which among other things included a vinyl-covered roof with a downsized rear window.

Contrary to its midsized predecessors, the Challenger R/T was powered in base form by Dodge's 383 cubic-inch Magnum four-barrel V-8, rated at 335 horsepower. Next up the extra-cost pecking order was the 375-horse 440, followed by the 390-hp triple-carb 440 and the ever-present Hemi. Both of the 440 big-blocks and the 425-horse 426 were offered as options for the R/T only.

A three-speed manual was the standard

▼ Dodge's 375-horsepower 440 Magnum V-8 (above) was one of three engines offered for the Challenger R/T.

gearbox behind the 383 Magnum, but Chrysler's always-tough three-speed Torqueflite automatic was optional, as was a preferred four-speed. Buyers opting for the Hemi or one of the 440s got a choice between the four-speed or the Torqueflite.

Additional standard Challenger R/T features in 1970 included Dodge's Rallye suspension, heavy-duty drum brakes, and Wide-Tread F70x14 tires (Hemi models rolled on larger 15-inch wheels and tires). The Rallye instrument cluster was part of the deal inside, and the

▲ Dodge first offered its "R/T" performance package in 1967.

◀ The popular Rallye wheels were optional.

R/T's outside could be dressed up with either a longitudinal stripe or Dodge's popular "bumble-bee" stripe around the tail.

Among popular options were Dodge's familiar Rallye road wheels and the too-cool "Shaker" hood scoop, added midway through the 1970 model run. The Shaker was both functional and fun; when it was doing its dance you knew that things below were really cookin', and all that heat was helped along by the cooler, denser ambient atmosphere sucked in through that vibrating scoop. The Challenger R/T's basic twin-scooped hood looked downright dull in comparison.

Dodge picked out a handful of professional race drivers to promote its 1970 model line,

▲ A sporty interior was standard fare on all 1970 Challengers.

▼ As was the competition-style fuel filler.

and drag racing's "Big Daddy" Don Garlits was assigned the Challenger R/T. As Garlits was quoted in company ads, "Now Dodge has gone and done the real thing. They watched the whole ponycar thing develop, then built their own super-tough version. Compact like a Dart. Wide like a Charger. Just the right size for anyone who likes his own personalized backyard bomb. Dodge should sell a million of 'em."

While production fell a bit short of that prediction, the Challenger R/T nonetheless didn't disappoint—whether you were a Dodge dealer or a customer in search of the hottest thing out there wearing a Pentastar in 1970.

1970 Dodge Coronet Super Bee

The Dodge Coronet Super Bee was a member of Dodge's 'Scat Pack' a collection of fun cars offering high performance. The Scat Pack was marketed to the American youth car market, and the cars were a great success. They were available in a selection of eye-scorching psychedelic-inspired colors, including Hemi-Orange, Go-Mango, Plum-Crazy and Sublime.

Introduced as a Coronet option in 1968, The Super Bee launched a flurry of advertising copy, 'Scat Pack performance at a new low price. Beware of the hotcammed, four-barrelled 383 mill in the light coupe body. Beware the muscled hood, the snick of the close-coupled four-speed… Beware the Super Bee. Proof that you can't tell a runner by the size of his bankroll'. It was as though Dodge was worried that the dowdy exteriors of the regular production cars would lull buyers of the Super Bees into a false sense of security. The Coronet Super Bee continued as the high-performance intermediate-sized counterpart to the Dart Swinger 340s for 1970. Super Bees included as the Coronet Deluxe features plus a special 383-cid Magnum V-8 engine; three-speed manual transmission with floor-mounted shifter; heavy-duty, automatic adjusting drum brakes; dual horns; heavy-duty front shock absorbers; Rallye Suspension with sway bar (or extra-heavy front duty suspension); three-speed windshield wipers; carpeting; F70-14 fiberglass belted white sidewall or black sidewall tires with raised white letters; and a three-spoke steering wheel with partial horn ring.

The 1970 Super Bee was fitted with a 383-cid Magnum V-8, complete with three-speed manual transmission. A Hurst gear shifter was optional. Priced at $3074, the car was actually cheaper than the previous year's model, and was equipped with more standard features. The Hemi engine was also offered for an additional $712, and 166 Super Bee buyers chose to order cars fitted with this option. In fact, the acceleration for the Hemi was very similar, taking just 0.2 of a second off the Magnum's 0-60 mph of 6.8 seconds. But Hemi-equipped cars could cover the quarter mile in just 14 seconds – a full second faster than the Magnum. But sales for the

Super Bee slumped to 15,506 in 1970, and the Coronet models were cancelled. The value-for-money Super Bee option was available only for the Dodge Charger in '71.

▲ This was the final year for the Coronet, and the Coronet Super Bee.

Engine:	Magnum V-8
Displacement:	383-cid
Horsepower:	350
Body Style: T	wo-door Super Bee Coupe
Weight:	3425 lbs
Wheelbase:	117 inches
Base Price:	$3012
Number Produced:	3,966

1970 Mercury Cyclone Spoiler

As Ford's luxury line, you might think that Mercury would have little interest in performance, racing and muscle. But you would be wrong – for the sixties and seventies at least.

Mercury morphed their Comet into a full-blown Cyclone through various stages, starting with the Comet Cyclone hybrid in 1965. The car was by no means in the Hemi road-racing class, being more of an 'econo-racer' hot sedan. Although Mercury developed a strong interest in developing a line of strip racers in the sixties, they never got into the flashy presentation common at the time – stripes, wings and spoilers just weren't their thing.

In '68 the car was restyled as the Cyclone Spoiler II, as a true fastback, or 'Sportsroof' as Ford called it. This was one smooth curving line from the top of the windshield backwards. It looked good, and cut the air like a knife. The car strongly resembled a Ford Torino Talladega, but had more luxury trim. It was built with the NASCAR racing series in mind. A special edition of the '69 model was also built, the Cyclone Cale Yarborough, complete with special striping, badging and a rear spoiler. Signature cars were great marketing tools in the sixties, and Cale Yarborough was one of the most famous drivers of the time, driving for Lincoln-Mercury in the SCCA Trans-Am series. Dan Gurney was also honoured with an eponymous vehicle. Power for the Cyclone II came from a 290 horsepower four-barrel Windsor 351. Buyers also got FMX Cruise-O-Matic transmission and 3.25:1 Traction-Lok gears.

The 1970 Cyclone Spoiler continued the quest for aerodynamic lines, and the car grew by seven inches. It also had a strange protruding centre section of the grille, front and rear spoilers, exposed headlights, mid-bodyside stripes, traction belted tires, a scooped hood and dual racing mirrors. In NASCAR, the Dodge Daytona and Plymouth Superbird were the main competition, so engine power was beefed up for this Cyclone, and the cars were fitted with a competition handling package. The race-ready power plant was the 370 horsepower Ram Air 429-cid V-8. Regular Cyclones came with a choice of the 370 horsepower Cobra Jet or the 375 Super Cobra Jet. The model lasted just two years, being discontinued in 1971.

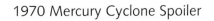

Engine:	Ram Air V-8
Displacement:	419-cid
Horsepower:	370 at 5400 rpm
Compression Ratio:	11.3:1
Weight:	3464 lbs
Wheelbase:	117 inches
Base Price:	$3530
Number Produced:	1631

▲ The Spoilers were aptly named with front and rear
spoilers fitted as standard.

1970 Oldsmobile 4-4-2 W-30

'Dr Oldsmobile' has the longest historical record of any US Car manufacturer.

The division had moved back into the performance field with the iconic 4-4-2 option package, first fitted to the F-85/Cutlass models, appearing later as a fully-fledged series. Originally, the numbers stood for four barrel, four-speed, twin exhaust. 4-4-2 was marketed as a separate series in 1968, and continued as such until 1971. The car was a serious hit with high-performance lovers, and its popularity continued to grow as long as it was offered to the buyers. Later in the sixties, the seriously powerful W-cars came on stream. Oldsmobile continued to develop the 4-4-2 series so that by the beginning of the seventies, the engine was used to power the whole Oldsmobile hi-po crew.

The 1970 4-4-2 is the car that epitomises all that is good about Oldsmobile in that year. The division had now been able to overcome the GM ban on engine blocks larger than 400 cid for intermediate-sized models, and the car was equipped with a 455. The 'W-30' package offered on these 455-cid 4-4-2s was an extra performance package of go-goodies including power front disc brakes, twin-scoop fibreglass hood and a variety of transmission options. This all added up to a powerful car that also handled really well. A W-31 package was offered on the Cutlass S.

The 455 cid block had been officially off limits until this model year, and had only been available as a Hurst-fitted limited production model. Cars now equipped with the W30 option of the 455 big-block could cover the quarter mile in 14 seconds, hitting 100 mph. Top speed for the car was defined as 115 mph.

4-4-2 continued for its third year as a separate Olds series for 1970, and was the performance leader for the division. A 4-4-2 equipped convertible was the pace car for the 1970 Indy 500. High performance cars continued to sell well for the company. Three models were now offered in the series, the two-door Holiday hardtop, the two-door sports coupe and two-door convertible. There had been a fourth member, the two-door Hurst/Olds in 1969. This had been the limited production 455-cid engine model, but was

Engine:	V-8 overhead valve, cast iron block
Displacement:	455-cid
Horsepower:	370 at 5400 rpm
Compression Ratio:	10.50:1
Wheelbase:	112 inches
Base Price:	$3376
Number Produced:	19330

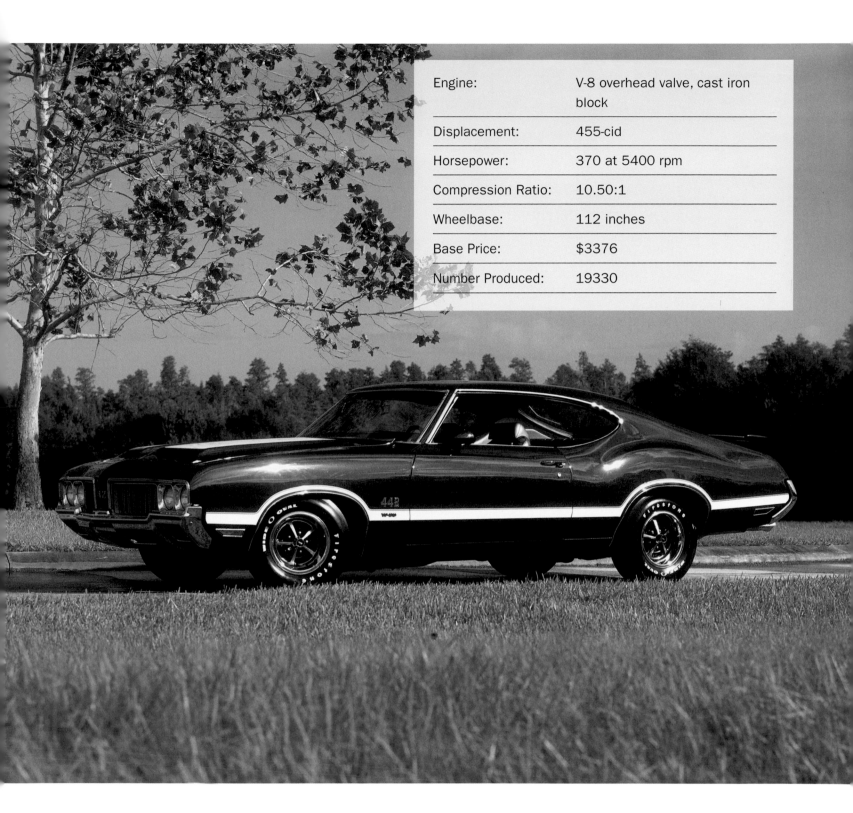

now superfluous. Standard equipment included everything fitted to the Cutlasses, plus foam padded seats, a special handling package, external and internal emblems, deluxe steering wheel, low-restriction exhaust system, and paint stripes. The standard tires were G70-14 with raised white letters. Interior upholstery was in vinyl or cloth.

▲ This W-30 4-4-2 was the top of the tree for Oldsmobile power and performance for 1970.

1970 Oldsmobile Cutlass SX

Olds first introduced the Cutlass in 1964 as part of the F-85 series. In 1965 it was the three-model top-of-the line F-85 option, and remained so for 1966 with four models. The car was restyled for 1966. In 1967, the Cutlass achieved series status of its own with six-cylinder and V-8 engine options spreads over ten different models. These ranged from a two-door convertible to a four-door station wagon. The Cutlass would now begin the climb that would eventually make it the most popular name-plate on a US car. Upholstery was in cloth or vinyl. Standard equipment included carpeting, courtesy lamps, a chrome molding package, foam seat cushions and a deluxe steering wheel. Their standard tire size was 7.75 x 15 inches. Cutlasses were assembled in the same factories as the F-85s.

The Cutlass Supreme had been originally introduced as a one-model series in 1967, and was the only Cutlass offered with the high-performance 4-4-2, before this option also became a series in its own right (with or without Ram Air induction), and the high-mileage Turnpike Cruising package). 24,829 4-4-2 Cutlass Supremes were sold in this year.

For 1970, Oldsmobile introduced three models in the Cutlass Supreme series, including a convertible model. The opulent SX was available as the top

Engine:	V-8 Rocket
Displacement:	455-cid
Horsepower:	365
Transmission:	three-speed manual floor shift standard
Induction:	Two-barrel carburetor
Body Style:	Two-door Convertible
Number of Seats:	5
Weight:	3614 lbs
Wheelbase:	116 inches
Base Price:	$3335
Number Produced:	4867

of the line two-door model for the Supreme series. The car was equipped with highway cruising in mind. Oldsmobile gave the car the full luxury treatment, while ensuring that it also offered excellent fuel economy and comfortable cruising. This was achieved by a specific combination of a two-barrel carburettor on the 'Rocket' 445-cid V-8 and a 2.56:1 rear axle set up. This gave the car excellent turnpike manners and relatively low fuel consumption. Pick-up wasn't great, but the car could cover the quarter mile in a respectable 15 seconds or so. Top speed for the car was estimated at 117 mph. The tires for the cars were the G70-14 Firestones, made from polyester and fiberglass, and designed to offer less rolling resistance that, in turn, improved the gas mileage of the car.

The interior was fully fitted for luxury with a simulated walnut dash, and cloth or vinyl upholstery. The car also had Flo-Thru ventilation, adeluxe steering wheel and Custom Sport seats.

▲ This SX equipped Cutlass Supreme convertible is identified by special badges.

1970 Oldsmobile F-85 Rallye 350

Olds had launched the F-85 in 1961, as an entry-level car to it's range. This was the first time that the company had broken with its three series format. Smaller than any other post-war Oldsmobile, the first F-85 models were powered by a unique aluminum 215-cid V-8. It was launched to compete with the small car offerings of Buick and Pontiac. The Cutlasses were launched as part of the F-85 series in 1962. The cars were restyled and re-sized over the years, and went from compact to midsize in 1964. The cars gained a handsome new 'A' body platform, which was shared with the Buick Special and Skylark, the Pontiac Tempest and Le Mans and Chevy's new Chevelle. F-85s were also used as the platform for several of Oldsmobile's high-performance options, including being the first body for the 4-4-2 in 1965. This was the Oldsmobile answer to the Pontiac GTO option. The full name for the option was 'Option B- 09 Police Apprehender Pursuit'. 25,003 4-4-2s were ordered in that year.

By 1970 the F-85 line was reduced to a single model sports coupe, and Cutlass was by now the next level Oldsmobile intermediate series. The F-85 was available with both a six-cylinder and V-8 engine option. At the performance end of the scale, the W-45, Rallye 350 package was installed on 3,547 Cutlass 'S'/F-85 coupes. This enabled Olds to offer a range of what might be called 'junior muscle cars'. Although cars like this were sometimes eclipsed by the 'big-block' tire burners, the Rallye 350 was actually 'big-block quick'.

Oldsmobile launched the Rallye 350 in 1970, as a kind of bargain bruiser muscle car in the tradition of Pontiac's GTO Judge. Like 'da Judge', the car also had eye-catching livery, including an eye-scorching Sebring Yellow paint job with black and orange stripes and cool black decals. You also got hood louvers and a spruced-up interior trim. Power for the car was a 310 horsepower 350-cid V-8.

This engine could also be up-graded with the scary W-31 forced induction system that boosted the horsepower rating by 15 – up to 325. A typical 310 Rallye with a three-speed manual shifter could cover the quarter mile in around 15.5 seconds at speeds of just below 90 mph. It could get from

1970 Oldsmobile F-85 Rallye 350

0-60 mph in just under eight seconds.

The low sales of the F-85 Rallye 350, a mere 1020, meant that the model did not return in 1971. The hallucinogenic graphic treatment had scared off too many buyers.

▲ These wildlooking muscle cars draw a premium from collectors today.

Engine:	V-8
Displacement:	350-cid
Horsepower:	310 at 4600 rpm
Compression Ratio:	10.25:1
Wheelbase:	112 inches
Base Price:	$2676
Number Produced:	1020

1970 Plymouth Road Runner 426 Hemi

Plymouth had gone to Hollywood in 1969, adopting the popular Warner Brothers Road Runner cartoon character as both the name and symbol for a new range of low-priced, medium-sized, high-performance muscle cars. The Road Runners were instantly popular. The base price for a GTX was below $3000 and this was for a car that featured a 383-cid, 335 horsepower V-8 Hemi.

Performance was shattering and the cars had loads of personality, complete with their jolly 'Beep! Beep!' horn.

The Road Runner, and 'Superbird' models were developed in a wind tunnel to develop a body that would cut through the air, straight to NASCAR stock car race victory. Qualifying speeds of over 190 mph were recorded at the super speedways like Daytona and Talladega, and highly tuned cars were capable of around 200 mph. The model dominated the 1970 NASCAR season. Pete Hamilton won the 1970 Daytona 500 in a Superbird at an average speed of 150 mph, and Superbirds rode to victory in 21 Grand National races. Plymouth was obliged to manufacture in excess of 1500 cars to homologate the model for the NASCAR series. They actually produced around 1,935 of these 426-cid Hemi V-8 fitted race-going cars, but they was obliged to discount the price of the model to stimulate demand.

The cars were replete with Plymouth heavy-duty 'fuselage' styling, which included loads of vents and scoops, both dummy and functional. The car was derived from the 1969 Dodge Charger Daytona, and employed an identical, massive aerodynamic, front-end extension that covered the headlights, and a towering rear spoiler mounted on struts above the trunk.

Production models of the car were equipped with the 383-cid V-8 that developed 335 horsepower. They also had a four-barrel carburetor and TorqueFlite automatic transmission. Options included a four-speed manual transmission and a 390 horsepower, 440-cid Street Hemi with the 440 'Six pack'.

Engine:	Superbird V-8
Displacement:	440-cid
Horsepower:	375 at 4400 rpm
Compression Ratio:	9.7:1
Wheelbase:	116 inches
Base Price:	$2896
Number Produced:	15,716

A Super Trak Package designed with racers in mind was also available, this constituted of a heavy-duty manual four-speed transmission (instead of the standard three-speed) and a 9¾-inch Dana Sure Grip rear axle.

But sadly, 1970 was the third and final year for the Road Runner body style.

NASCAR changed their rules to bring the Superbird's brief reign to an abrupt end. But the iconic status of the car was assured.

▲ Only 74 Road Runner Coupes were fitted with the Hemi engine option in 1970. Forty-four of these had the fourspeed manual transmission upgrade.

1970 Plymouth Superbird

When a factory wants to go racing it must meet certain "homologation" standards. Various sanctioning bodies have had different standards over the years, but most have involved a minimum production requirement. In NASCAR's case back in the late-Sixties, the sanctioning body belonged to big Bill France.

And his homologation rule was simple: build 500 regular-production examples of any given engine or body style and you could race them all day long on his tracks.

That requirement, instituted in 1967, inspired Detroit to create some of the wildest street machines ever seen. Easily the wildest were Dodge's Charger Daytona and Plymouth's Superbird, built in 1969 and '70, respectively.

Both looked like they were travelling 200 mph even while standing still. But unlike so many other fast-looking cars that were only imposters, these two high-flying machines did actually run that fast, in racing trim that is. Those bodies were fully function from an aerodynamic perspective, this because Detroit designers had finally discovered that brute force wasn't the only key to speed. Five-hundred or more horses could only do so much with a stock body, and apparently 175 mph was the limit. Breaking through that buyer required something more—something like a wind-cheating body.

Ford Motor Company racers breached that wall first when

Wheelbase:	116 inches
Weight:	3,840 pounds
Base Price:	$4,298
Engine:	426 cubic-inch Hemi V-8
Compression:	10.25:1
Horsepower:	425 at 5,000 rpm
Torque:	490 at 4,000 rpm
Induction:	two Carter four-barrel carburetors
Transmission:	three-speed Torqueflite automatic
Suspension:	independent A-arms w/torsion bars in front; live axle with leaf springs in back
Brakes:	front discs, rear drums
Performance:	14.26 seconds at 103.7 mph for the quarter-mile, according to Road & Track (440 cubic-inch V-8 model tested)
Production :	135; 77 with automatic transmission, 58 with four-speed manual

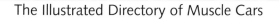

▲　Aerodynamic improvements made at both ends of Plymouth's 1970 Superbird translated into 200-mph speeds on NASCAR superspeedways.

the sleek Fairlane and Cyclone fastbacks appeared in 1968. The Dodge boys then responded that fall with their slicked-up Charger 500. Taking its name from Bill France's production requirement, the aerodynamically refined '69 Charger 500 was put together at Creative Industries in Detroit. Using the grille from a '68 Coronet, the Creative fellows transformed the Charger's recessed frontal cavity into a flush nose, complete with fixed headlights. In back, they

fabricated a steel plug to fill in the rear window tunnel. Presto! An additional 5 mph on top end.

While it initially looked promising from NASCAR perspectives, the Charger 500's early announcement, made before the 1968 season, only helped inspire quick retaliation from the competition. As Dodge was showing off its new aero-racer in Charlotte, Ford was busy building a similar machine, the Fairlane-based Talladega, which featured a downward sloping nose that reduced frontal area and induced the air flow up over, not under. This helped the Talladega stay exceptionally stable

MILESTONE FACTS

- Differences between the Charger Daytona and Plymouth Superbird were many, but perhaps most noticeable was the Superbird's vinyl roof—added to hide the hand-leaded seams around the flush rear window's mounting plug.

- The metal noses on the Daytona and Superbird differed in various ways. The Superbird's nose cap sweeps upward slightly; the Daytona's snout doesn't. Air inlets were also located differently. The chin spoilers, however, were identical.

- Compared to the Daytona's spoiler, the Superbird's wing was taller and swept backward at a sharper angle. Its pedestal bases were also wider. Daytona wings used three-piece tape stripes done in three contrasting colors; red, white or black. Superbird wings were always body-colored.

- Though they're commonly referred to as "air extractors," the scoops on a Superbird's fenders were actually used in NASCAR configuration to allow extra clearance for the huge tires used in stock car racing. On the street, these rounded scoops were for looks only. The "flat-topped" scoops on the Daytona actually covered a meshed opening that allowed trapped air to exit from the front wheel wells.

- Three different engines were offered for the 1970 Superbird: the 375-hp 440 with single four-barrel, the 390-hp 440 Six Barrel, and 425-hp 426 Hemi.

- Total Superbird production in 1970 was 1,935: 1,084 with the 440 four-barrel, an additional 716 with the 440 Six Barrel V-8, and 135 with the vaunted 426 Hemi.

while busting the 190-mph barrier on NASCAR superspeedways. Mercury also manufactured a kissin'-cousin to the Talladega in 1969, the Cyclone Spoiler Sports Special, or Cyclone Spoiler II.

Debuting in February 1969, the Talladega

overwhelmed its counterparts from Dodge as LeeRoy Yarbrough's long-nose Fairlane won the Daytona 500. Talladega drivers claimed 26 races in 1969, Charger 500s 18, and Spoiler IIs four.

Then Dodge regrouped, returning in April 1969 with an even more aggressive aero-racer, the Charger Daytona, the product of some serious wind-tunnel testing. To better beat the breeze, Creative Industries added a pointed steel beak with a chin spoiler, a fully functional modification that stretched the car by about a foot and a half. In back went a cast-aluminum "towel rack" wing towering

▼ The unmistakable Road Runner graphics.

over the rear deck. And like the Charger 500, the Daytona was also fitted with a leaded-in steel plug to allow the installation of a flush rear window. Reportedly the new nose could produce nearly 200 pounds of downforce; that huge rear wing, 650 pounds. In full-race form, the Daytona was the first NASCAR competitor to surpass the 200-mph barrier.

Not long afterward, Plymouth designers kicked off their own aero-car project. Born in June 1969, then temporarily canceled in August, the Superbird was rapidly readied for the 1970 NASCAR season. As in the case of the Talladega-Spoiler II relationship, Plymouth's winged street racer looked similar to its Daytona forerunner from Dodge, but was very much of a different feather. For starters, the Road Runner front clip wouldn't

▲ The 425-horsepower 426 Hemi was optional for the 1970 Superbird. Plymouth's 440 was standard.

accept that nose graft as easily as the Charger's did. Thus, a hood and front fenders were copped from the Coronet line for this application. Various measurements also differed at the nose and tail.

Production figures too differed greatly as NASCAR homo-logation standards changed for the 1970 season. The minimum production requirement was now either 1,000 or a number equal to half of that company's dealers, whichever was higher. Plymouth officials were then faced with the task of creating nearly four times as many Superbirds as Dodge did Daytonas.

Once on the track, the two winged Mopars

▲ Air extractor scoops on Superbird fenders were non-functional.

▼ A "towel-rack" rear spoiler adorned with Road Runner graphics was an unmistakable standard feature on the 1970 Superbird.

took command in 1970. Superbirds won eight races, Daytonas four. Another victory was scored by a Charger 500. The tally at Ford was four wins each for the Talladega and Cyclone Spoiler II, these recorded before Henry Ford II finally decided to cancel his corporation's competition programs late that year.

Bill France did the rest, instituting a carburetor restrictor plate rule for the high-flying Hemi-powered Mopars to help keep speeds (and the cars themselves) down to earth. This restriction then helped convince Chrysler officials to give up on the Superbird. Like the Daytona, it was a one-hit wonder.

▲ Plymouth's popular Rally wheels only complemented the high-flying image further.

1970-71 Ford Torino Cobra

After paying dearly for the rights to Carroll Shelby's "Cobra" image, Ford officials wasted little time sticking Shelby's revered snake label on almost everything that moved. Make that everything that really moved.

First came the famed 428 Cobra Jet V-8 in 1968. That was then followed in 1969 by a CJ-powered mid-sized muscle machine intended to follow in the Plymouth Road Runner's tracks. This new beast's name? What else?

With low-buck investment being the goal, the '69 Cobra was based on the yeoman Fairlane (in both formal-roof and fastback forms), not the top-dog Torino as is often commonly mistaken. Forget what you saw on NASCAR tracks; David Pearson's 1969 Grand National champion Talladega may have screamed "Torino" in on its quarter-panels, but there was nothing Torino about its street-going, long-nose counterparts. And the same was true for the non-aerodynamic Fairlane Cobra.

This confusion, however, was cleared up in 1970 when Ford's Better Idea guys did what they probably should have done in the first place, that is elevate the Cobra into the upscale Torino ranks. But this time only one bodystyle was offered, the newly restyled and renamed "SportsRoof," a sleek, sloping shape that had simply been called a fastback in previous years. As for the name game, the second-edition Cobra was unmistakably a Torino, it said so right there on the hood.

Beneath that hood, perhaps as a trade-off for the Cobra's newfound top-shelf surroundings, was a little less standard venom. In place of the formidable 428 Cobra Jet was the 360-horse 429 Thunder Jet, a torquey 385-series big-block best suited for turning pulleys on air conditioning compressors and power steering pumps for the LTD/Thunderbird crowd. Called "Ford's new clean machine" by Motor Trend, the 385 big-block family was a product of Washington's increasingly more demanding mandates to reduce

Wheelbase:	117 inches
Weight:	4,185 pounds
Base Price:	$3,249 (429 Cobra Jet option added $229 to this amount)
Engine:	429 cubic-inch Cobra Jet V-8
Horsepower:	370 at 5,400 rpm
Induction:	single 715-cfm Rochester Quadra-Jet four-barrel with "Shaker" hood scoop
Transmission:	four-speed manual with Hurst shifter
Suspension:	independent A-arms w/coil springs in front; live axle with leaf springs in back
Brakes:	front discs, rear drums
Performance:	0-60 mph in 5.8 seconds, 13.99 seconds at 101 mph for the quarter-mile.
Production:	7,675

MILESTONE FACTS

- Ford's 385-series big-block engine family was first offered in 1968 in both 429- and 460-cube forms.

- Motor Trend named the new Torino SportsRoof model its "Car of the Year" for 1970.

- The 429 Super Cobra Jet Torino Cobra ranked right up with the strongest muscle cars ever built during the Sixties and early-Seventies.

- The SportsRoof body was 1.2 inches lower and 5.1 inches longer than the mid-sized fastback shell seen in 1969.

- Both the Magnum 500 wheels and "Shaker" hood scoop appearing on this '70 Torino Cobra were options.

- Ford introduced its Cobra as a Fairlane model in 1969. In 1970, it was elevated to topline Torino status and the optional 429 Cobra Jet replaced the standard 428 CJ used the previous year.

- A Hurst-shifted four-speed manual transmission was standard for the Torino Cobra in 1970. High-back bucket seats and a center console were optional.

- Torino Cobra production was 7,675 in 1970, 3,054 in 1971.

- Engine breakdown for 1970 Torino Cobra productionw as 3,213 base 429 Thunder Jet V-8s, 974 429 Cobra Jets without optional Ram-Air equipment, and 3,488 429 CJ big-blocks with Ram-Air.

emissions. "Racing and research not only improve the breed," wrote MT's Dennis Shattuck, "they also clear the air."

While the typical 429 was kind to the environment, it did have an alter-ego, a dark side that better suited the jet set. To keep up with a box-stock '69 Fairlane Cobra, a '70 Torino Cobra customer had to shell out an extra $164 for the 429 Cobra Jet, a 370-horse

variation on the 385-series big-block theme. Dearborn engineers took the relatively tame 429 Thunder Jet and added a 715-cfm Rochester Quadra-Jet four-barrel on a cast-iron, dual-plane intake. They also bolted on a pair of Cobra Jet cylinder heads, they with their large rounded intake ports and big valves—2.242-inch intakes, 1.722-inch exhausts. Compression was upped to a whopping 11.3:1, and a long-duration cam was stuffed inside.

The 429 Cobra Jet also could've been ordered with or without ram-air equipment. Even though that distinctive "Shaker" hood scoop surely helped whip up a few more ponies on the top end, engineers chose not to adjust the ram-air 429 CJ's advertised output, which mattered very little anyway considering that 370 horsepower was undoubtedly an understatement to begin with.

Equally understated was the output figure assigned to the 429 Super Cobra Jet, a truly beefy big-block that came along as part of the Drag Pack group. The Drag Pack option transformed a 429 CJ into an SCJ by adding a big 780-cfm Holley four-barrel and a long-duration, solid-lifter cam. Additional heavy-duty hardware included forged pistons, four-bolt mains and an external oil cooler. Completing the Drag Pack cast was either a 3.91:1 Traction-Lok or 4.30:1 Detroit Locker rearend. Like the "basic" CJ, the underrated 375-horsepower Super Cobra Jet could've been crowned with the Shaker scoop, which again failed to change the advertised output

▲ Introduced as a Fairlane model in 1969, Ford's mid-sized Cobra became a top-shelf Torino offering the following year. A blacked-out hood with tie-down pins was standard.

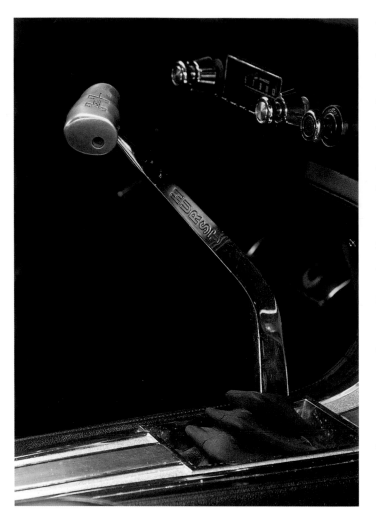

figure. After Super Stock's hot-foots managed a sensational 13.63-second quarter-mile blast in a '70 SCJ Cobra, it became more than clear that quite a few more horses were hiding in there somewhere.

All CJ Cobras in 1970, Super or otherwise, were fitted with the Competition Suspension package, which typically added higher rate springs. Included as well was a stiff 0.95-inch front stabilizer bar and heavy-duty Gabriel shocks. On four-speed cars, the Gabriels in back were staggered, with one mounted in front of the axle, the other behind. This was a

▼ The Cobra's optional tachometer may have been a failure (it was tiny and poorly located).

◀ But there was no knocking the standard Hurst shifter.

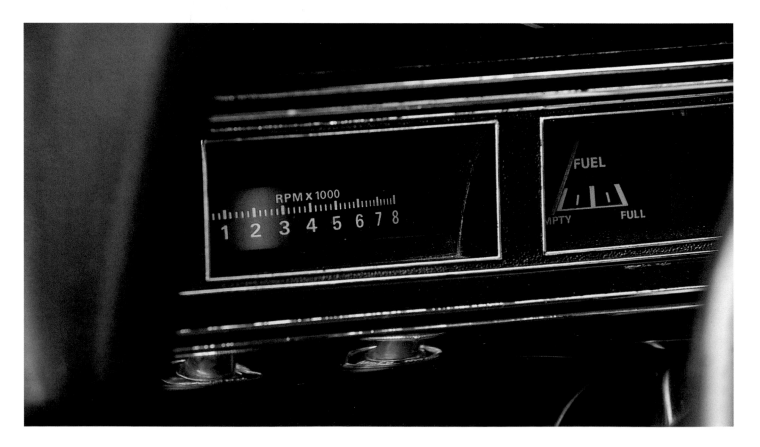

▲ Bright Magnum 500 wheels were optional for the 1970 Torino Cobra.

▶ Though not as dramatic as Chrysler Corporation's "Shaker," Ford's similarly designed optional ram-air hood scoop nonetheless fit the Cobra image to a "T."

▼ Ford paid Carroll Shelby for the rights to his "Cobra" image.

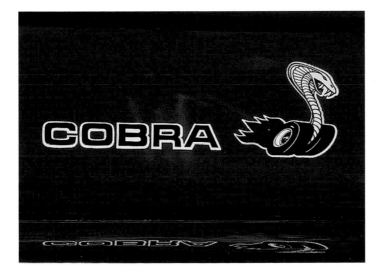

popular Ford trick used to hopefully control rear wheel hop created by axle wind-up during hard acceleration.

Like its Super Cobra Jet big brother, the CJ Cobra was no slouch when it came to putting those staggered rear shocks to the test in 1970. A February 1970 Motor Trend road test produced equally sensational performance figures for the 370-horse/four-speed Cobra.

1971 Dodge Charger R/T Hemi

By 1971 the muscle car era was drawing to a close, but Dodge decided to integrate both Super Bee and R/T muscle cars into their newly restyled Charger series. The changes to the Charger series were largely instigated to further segregate the models from the lower-level Coronets. The cars now rode on a new 115-inch chassis, and the model range was expanded to six coupes and hardtops in three series, the Chargers, Charger 500 series and Charger R/T (one car) series. All Chargers were now semi-fastback coupes featuring rear quarter window styling that swept up from the fender to meet the sloping upper window frame. The full-width bumper-grille shell was split by a large vertical divider on all Chargers and the rear end of the car featured a small trunk lid spoiler. Six square taillights were located in the oval rear bumper.

The top-of-the-range R/T model was the most luxurious and high-performance Charger model. It included all the standard equipment fitted to the 500s, together with a 70 amp/hour battery, heavy-duty brakes and shock absorbers; pedal dress-up kit; extra heavy duty Rallye suspension; Torqueflite automatic or four-speed manual transmission. Interiors were kitted out in keeping with the contemporary trend, and were awash with white-pleated vinyl and plastic wood.

The exterior of the car was dressed with a black R/T decal.

Engine options were the 440 Magnum (fitted as standard) and the Hemi was available as a $707 option. Some cars (178) were also equipped with the 440- cid 'Six Pak' V-8. The Hemi Chargers were equipped with twin Carter four-barrel carburetors and had a compression ratio of 10.25:1 producing 425 horsepower.

According to Mopar authority Galen V. Govier, 63 R/Ts were fitted with the Hemi engine option (30 four-speed manuals, and 33 TorqueFlite automatics). These cars were feared at dragstrips up and down the country.

NASCAR performance limitations severely reduced Dodge's interest in this race series, and they cut back heavily on their factory backing of stock car racing. Following 22 Grand National wins in 1969, and 17 in 1970, there were only eight Dodge victories in 1971. 1971 also marked the final year when the Hemi engine was offered for sale to the public, in either the street or racing form. Insurance premiums were astronomical on these high-performance cars and beginning in 1972, all cars had to be run on regular gas. Dodge decided to retire the Hemi while it was still in front. It returned in 1992, for sale to racers and restorers via the Chrysler Performance high-performance parts division.

▼ The R/T was one of the last cars equipped with a Hemi for over twenty years.

Engine:	Street Hemi V-8, overhead valve with hemispherical combustion chambers
Displacement:	428-cid
Horsepower:	425 at 5600 rpm
Compression Ratio:	10.25:1
Number Produced:	3,118

1971 Ford Mustang Boss 351

Fans of Ford ponycar performance were hit hard when both the small-block (302) and big-block (429) Boss Mustangs were unceremoniously cancelled in 1970. But not all was lost. In November that year, Dearborn officials rolled out their new Boss 351, a truly hot 1971 Mustang based on the totally restyled SportsRoof body, as fast a fastback as yet come down the pike.

The heart of the '71 Boss 351 was the 351 High Output (HO) Cleveland V-8, an able small-block that could throw its weight around like most big-blocks. Rated at 330 horsepower, the HO featured superb free-flowing heads, which were nearly identical to those used by the Boss 302 save for revised cooling passages. Those excellent canted valves carried over from Boss 302 to HO right down to their diameter, as did much of the valvetrain. Both engines also shared screw-in rocker studs, hardened pushrods, and guide plates. The Boss 351's solid-lifter cam, however, was more aggressive than the Boss 302's.

The 351 HO's lower end was also more stout. As was the case inside the Boss 302's modified Windsor block, the HO's crank was held in place by four-bolt mains, but the latter had four-bolt caps at all five main bearings, not just three. The HO crank was cast (of high nodular iron) instead of forged, and it was specially tested for hardness. Forged connecting rods were shot peened and magnafluxed and were clamped to the crank by super-strong 3/8-inch bolts. Pistons were

Wheelbase:	109 inches
Weight:	3,625 pounds
Original Price:	$3,746.90
Engine:	351 cubic-inch "Boss 351" V-8
Compression:	11:1
Horsepower:	330 at 5,400 rpm
Induction:	single 750-cfm Autolite four-barrel carburetor
Transmission:	Hurst-shifted four-speed manual
Suspension:	independent A-arms w/coil springs in front; live axle with leaf springs in back
Brakes:	power front discs, rear drums
Performance:	13.8 seconds at 104 mph in the quarter-mile, according to Motor Trend
Production:	1,806

▲ ▼ Able to smoke through the quarter-mile in the 13-second range, the Boss 351 Mustang ranked among Ford's hottest all-time muscle cars.

cooling package with a flex fan, and a Hurst-shifted wide-ratio four-speed. In back was a Traction-Lok 9-inch rearend with 31-spline axles and 3.91:1 gears. Underneath was the Competition Suspension package, which featured heavier springs, staggered rear shocks, and sway bars front and rear. Power front disc brakes were standard, too, as were F60 raised-white-letter rubber tires on 15x7 steel wheels adorned with the flat hubcaps and trim rings. Ford's flashy Magnum 500 five-spoke wheels were optional.

forged-aluminum pop-up pieces. On top was a 750-cfm Autolite four-barrel on an aluminum dual-plane manifold.

The Boss 351's standard supporting cast included a ram-induction hood, a special

The Boss 351's standard appearance features were all but identical to those found on the 1971 Mach 1. Included up front was Ford's functional "NASA hood, a chin spoiler and a honeycomb grille with color-keyed surround. That ram-air hood incorporated twist locks and was done in either an argent or blacked-out finish, depending on the body paint choice. Like the hood, Boss 351's standard

MILESTONE FACTS

- Ford's 351 Cleveland small-block V-8 would carry on as the company's top performance powerplant after the 429 Cobra Jet big-block was cancelled in 1971.

- According to Lee Iacocca, Ford's Mustang had grown into "a fat pig" by 1971. But apparently bigger was better in the mind of Ford chief Semon "Bunkie" Knudsen, who had given the go-ahead for the "SportsRoof" restyle before he had been fired in 1969.

- Nearly everything about the 1971 SportsRoof was bigger compared to the 1970 fastback Mustang. It was three inches wider, two inches longer and 400 pounds heavier. Wheelbase was stretched an inch and both front and rear tracks increased two inches.

- Lee Iacocca took over for Knudsen atop Ford in 1970, and four years later he rode herd over a new breed of ponycar, the compact Mustang II, a car that he felt ran closer to its roots.

- The Boss 351 and Mach 1 Mustangs shared numerous appearance features, but the 351 HO small-block was exclusive to the Boss in 1971.

- Ford's use of the term "NASA hood" was actually a misnomer. The scoops on those hoods were actually known as "NACA" ducts around aviation circles. NACA, the National Advisory Committee for Aeronautics, was superseded by NASA, the National Aeronautics and Space Administration, in the late Fifties. Apparently Ford officials felt the American public in 1971 would recognize NASA, but not NACA.

▲ The 330-horse 351 V-8 was standard

lower-body paint accents and accent tape stripes were either black or argent, again depending on the chosen exterior finish. Black or argent treatment once more showed up at the rear. And among remaining features were dual racing mirrors and "Boss 351 Mustang" decals on the fenders and tail. A rear deck spoiler was optional. The coveted Mach 1 sports interior was optional inside, while full

instrumentation was standard.

Inside or out, from nose to tail, the Boss 351 Mustang was a big winner in most critics' minds. Sure, some reviewers complained about visibility problems inherent to the 1971 SportsRoof restyle. But they couldn't deny the Boss 351's aggressive appearance and high-spirited nature. Few rivals could keep pace. As Car and Driver reported, the Boss 351 "offers dragstrip performance [14.1 seconds at 100.6 mph] that most cars with 100 cubic inches more displacement will envy." Enthusiastic

▲ 15-inch Magnum 500 wheels were optional.

▶ A Hurst-shifted four-speed was standard

Motor Trend testers pushed the envelope even further, producing a 13.8-second run, a figure that put the Boss 351 right up there with the hottest Fords ever built.

Many witnesses at the time recognized too that the Boss 351 probably represented the end of the road for Ford's brand of muscle. "This is probably the last chance you'll have to buy a machine of this kind," began Sports Car Graphic's March 1971 Boss 351 road test. "Ford is now diverting all its racing talent and dollars into solving safety and pollution problems and trying to satisfy government mandates. We have heard from reliable sources that for the '72 new model release, all Ford products will be detuned to run on regular fuel. That means lower compression. The current exhaust-popping 11:1 [ratios] will probably be lowered 15 to 20 percent, and

▼ Like its Boss 302 forerunner, the Cleveland-head Boss 351 V-8 also featured a rev-limiter to help keep a lid on things.

the only way to regain the lost power is through expensive modifications—which will probably become illegal. Perhaps we'll just learn to live with the situation, like war and taxes, which we accept as facts of life. But we have few years left. We might as well take what we can get and live it up while we can."

A few years? Who was kidding whom? Although the 351 HO did survive for one more year—albeit in detuned form—the Boss 351 Mustang came and went as quickly as it ran from stoplight to stoplight. One year here then gone.

At least the Boss Mustang legacy went out with a bang.

▲ Full instrumentation was standard on the 1971 Boss 351, while the upscale Mach 1 sports interior (with its high-back bucket seats) was an option.

▼ Boss 351 engine hoses.

1971 Ford Mustang Mach 1

Ford had broken the mold to offer the first Mustang to the American public in April 1964. The car was a completely unique fusion of Detroit's power and comfort, with the styling of the classic European sportscars. The Mustang was an immediate run-away success, and for the moment, the first of the ponycars was ahead in a one horse race.

One of the main reasons for the success of the Mustang range was always the breadth of its appeal. Ford was careful to offer a selection of cars to appeal to different kinds of buyers, from the boy-racer to the more sedate middle-aged customer interested more in image than performance. The first Mach 1 was introduced in 1969 as a middle-of-the-road Mustang, with muscle car heritage in a relatively civilised road-going package. The car was styled with the new Ford Sportsroof (the latest version of the fastback). Mach 1s were immediately successful, and sold 70,00 units in their introductory year.

By 1971, Mustang production peaked at 149,678 unis, and the division was known as the Ford Marketing Corporation. The Boss Mustang 351 was now the most serious package on offer. But for buyers who wanted something slightly less hairy, but still with a sporty flavor, the Mustang Mach 1 remained the streetfriendly alternative for this model year. The car came complete with a full sports appearance package and was available with a range of power plant options. These varied from the relatively mild 210 horsepower 302-cid V-8 all the way through to the Cobra Jet 429, or even the completely wild 370 horsepower 429-cid Super Cobra Jet fitted with Ram Air induction. In fact, only five othese cars were reputedly built, and 1971 was the final year that this big-block 429 engine was on offer. The 351-cid Cleveland four-barrel V-8 was another engine on offer with the Mach 1, and developed an impressive 285 horsepower. Other sports

Engine:	Cleveland V-8
Displacement:	351-cid
Horsepower:	285 at 5400 rpm
Number Produced:	36,499

goodies could also be included in the package, including E70 tires and Special Handling suspension.

Mach 1s were also blessed with the classic good looks you would expect from such a fine muscle car heritage. Buyers got a blacked-out hood with twin NASAstyle air scoops, a mean black spoiler and side striping, with Mach 1 decals. The package was completed with a honeycomb grille with driving lights, color-keyed mirrors and bumpers, black or 'argent'

colored lower bodysides. Inside, the buyer could upgrade the interior with high-backed bucket seats and a center console. The Mach 1 perfectly reflected a market that was now tending towards appearance, rather than performance concerns. But with the range of powerplants on offer, Mach 1 buyers could still specify a seriously hot car from the Mustang stable.

▶ The black spoiler can just be seen at the rear of this Mach 1.

1971 Mercury Cougar XR7 429

Mercury introduced its Cougar model in 1967. It was one of the handsomest cars of the year, and was an immediate marketing success for the division. The car successfully bridged the gap between the performance of the Mustang and the luxury of the Thunderbird. The two-door hardtop coupe was trimmed with a sports interior, and had the Cyclone V-8 engine. The model sold over 150,000 units in its first year.

Mercury produced an especially hot version of the Cougar in 1969 – the Cougar Eliminator. It was the Mercury version of Ford's Boss 302 and Mach 1.

The base engine offered was the 290 horsepower 351-cid, but the range of powerplants went right up to the 428 Cobra Jet. This produced 335 horsepower and could cover the quarter mile in just 14 seconds. With this engine, the Eliminator also came with an oil cooler, staggered shocks, tachometer, power front-disc brakes and heavy-duty suspension with various transmission choices.

The Eliminator was a limited production model of only around 500 examples.

The Eliminator made a second and final appearance in 1970, and could now be ordered with the Boss 302 and Boss 429 packages. The latter came with Ram Air induction. Styling changes were minimal, special striping, hood scoop and rear deck spoiler were the only signs to mark out the model as Cougar's performance special.

The Cougar was restyled more completely for 1971 and grew once more. It

Engine:	Super Cobra Jet V-8
Displacement:	429-cid
Horsepower:	370
Weight:	3314 lbs
Wheelbase:	112.1 inches
Base Price:	$3629
Number Produced:	25,416

was available as a two-door hardtop and two-door convertible. The concealed headlights had disappeared, and were now exposed and recessed. The protruding center grille had vertical bars and was framed in chrome. The rear bumper was integrated into the rear deck panel, which housed the large rectangular taillights. The sports interior included high-backed bucket seats, consolette with illuminated ashtray, glove box and Flow-Thru ventilation system.

Buyers also got full instrumentation with toggle switches, a cherrywood appliqué dash and leather seat facings. The Cougar XR7 was the most luxurious model in the line-up. When the 429-cid Ram Air cooled Super Cobra Jet was ordered for the car, a functional hoodscoop was fitted, joined to the air cleaner via a rubber seal around the rim. Thus equipped, the car could turn in a quarter mile time of 14.64 seconds. Lesser engines were also available – the 240 and 285 versions of the 351-cid V-8.

▲   This XR7 Cougar is equipped with chrome rocker panels, special badging and a unique vinyl-covered half-roof.

1971 Plymouth GTX 440+6

Plymouth people waited three years before finally following Pontiac's lead. That is, wrapping up one of their hotter big-block V-8s with a too-cool-for-school image to match. In 1964, anyone who was anyone recognized a GTO when they saw one.

While the same couldn't exactly be said in 1967 when Plymouth's GTX debuted, at least Chrysler's low-priced division had its face in Detroit's high-performance image race, and that was better than nothin'.

Not that Plymouth at the time didn't have enough more than muscle to offer the hot-to-trot crowd. Introduced for 1966, the 426 Hemi was as mean a mill as they came in those days. But Plymouth didn't do the Hemi any favors when it planted it between the flanks of Satellites and Belvederes, cars that didn't announce their presence in quite the same

Wheelbase:	115 inches
Weight:	4,022 pounds
Base Price (for standard GTX w/440 four-barrel):	$3,707
Engine:	440 cubic-inch V-8
Induction:	three Holley two-barrel carburetors
Compression:	10.5:1
Horsepower:	390 at 4,700 rpm
Torque:	490 at 3,200 rpm
Transmission:	four-speed manual
Suspension:	independent A-arms w/torsion bars in front; live axle with leaf springs in back
Brakes:	four-wheel drums, standard; power front discs, optional
Performance:	15.02 seconds at 96 mph for the quarter-mile, according to Motor Trend test of a similar 440+6 1971 Road Runner
Production:	135; 73 with automatic transmission, 62 with four-speed

sexy way, say, as an SS 396 Chevelle did. Whatta waste of machinery.

To help turn more heads, Plymouth designers took their trimmed-out, top-shelf Belvedere hardtop and altered its ego into the GTX street-prowler. Up front was a new hood featuring two scoops, both non-functional. On the left rear fender was a competition-type fuel filler, and bright exhaust tips ended

the standard dual exhaust system in back. Twin racing stripes were optional for the hood and rear deck, while bucket seats were included in the deal inside. Groovy red-line Goodyear tires were standard at the corners, as was a heavy-duty suspension underneath.

Beneath those two dummy scoops was a standard V-8 that then stood tall as the industry's largest displacement engine, the

440. Introduced the previous year for Chrysler's luxury liners, this RB-series big-block was created by boring out the 426 wedge-head V-8. In 1967, better-breathing heads, a warmer cam, and a free-flowing intake crowned by a single four-barrel carb transformed this lukewarm mammoth into Plymouth's Super Commando 440, a 375-horse monster that put the action behind the GTX's new image.

"It's exciting to look at and it's exciting to drive," wrote Hot Rod's Dick Scritchfield in

◀ Plymouth's first GTX appeared in 1967; its last came in 1971.

MILESTONE FACTS

- Total GTX production for 1971, foreign and domestic, was 2,942.

- Plymouth's Satellite was the base model for the 1971 GTX; earlier GTXs were based on the Belvedere, which was retired after 1970.

- Chrysler's triple-carb 440 V-8 debuted in 1969 as part of a special performance package based on mid-sized B-body models. Both Dodge's "440 Six Pack" Super Bee and Plymouth's "440 Six Barrel" Road Runner were stripped-down, race-ready rockets that put the "bare" in bare bones. Neither came with wheelcovers or even hood hinges—their lightweight fiberglass lids simply lifted off by hand after four pins were released at the corners.

- Plymouth's 440+6 V-8 was a $125 option for the 1971 GTX. It cost $262 beneath a '71 Road Runner's hood.

- The 426 Hemi was a $750 option for the '71 GTX. Only 30 were built.

honor of the 440-powered '67 GTX. "It's a model that has taken Plymouth out of the domestic snapshot album and put it right in the middle of the performance picture, and with a very sharp image I might add."

Only one optional engine was offered for the GTX, and its name was spelled H-E-M-I. But either way, with the base 440 or extra-cost 426, the '67 GTX was a real winner.

In 1968 the GTX was joined by its less-expensive Road Runner running mate, itself powered by a standard 383 Commando. Like the GTX, the Road Runner too could've been fitted with the optional Hemi, but then that

kinda defeated its budget-conscious purpose, didn't it?

A new power choice appeared for both Plymouths in 1970, the 440 "Six Barrel." This triple-carb big-block had first appeared the year before as part of a no-nonsense, race-ready package based on both the Road Runner and Dodge's Super Bee. The engine option alone was then extended to GTX (and Coronet R/T) buyers in 1970.

In Plymouth terms, the 440 Six Barrel V-8

▲ Radioactive paint, glaring graphics and an optional rear-deck spoiler made this 1971 GTX a real head-turner, even while standing still.

replaced the 440 Super Commando's single Carter four-barrel with three Holley two-barrels on an Edelbrock aluminum intake. Internal additions included stiffer hemi valve springs, beefed-up rocker arms and connecting rods, and flash-chromed valves. Output was advertised at 390 horses.

GTX customers could again chose between Plymouth's three big-blocks—the standard 440 four-barrel, the triple-carb 440 and the 426 Hemi—in 1971, but this time around they got to wrap all that Mopar muscle up in all-new sheetmetal. A truly fresh restyle for Plymouth's mid-size lineup produced softer lines and subtle contours, just what you'd expect from a Seventies muscle car. A wide choice of wilder than wild colors also added

▲ Once again Plymouth's trick Rally wheels were image enhancements.

▼ Optional instrumentation included a 7,000-rpm tach.

▼ Plymouth's "pistol-grip" shifter was just too cool.

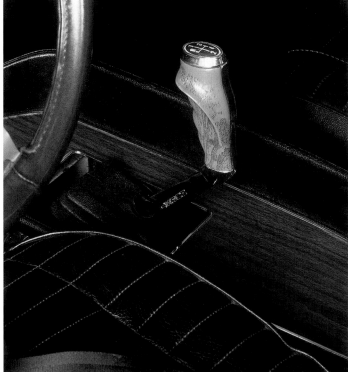

▼ Plymouth's entertaining "Air Grabber" hood (left) was a GTX option, as was the 390-horsepower 440+6 big-block V-8 (below).

to the attraction, as did optional spoilers and that zany "Air Grabber" hood with that crazy toothy grin painted onto the sides of the vacuum-operated flap that opened up at speed to let cooler, denser air into the carb below.

Or carbs. For 1971, the 390-horse 440 was officially named the "440+6" V-8, a tidy $125 option for the GTX. As in previous years, Plymouth's triple-carb big-block was offered with either the Torqueflite automatic or four-speed manual—no wimpy three-speeds here. Both choices were good, it all depended on how much you liked gear-jamming.

Plymouth customers who liked the 440+6 GTX didn't have much of a choice by the end

of 1971. The muscle car's days were all but through, and Chrysler's legendary Hemi and triple-carb 440 were both cancelled that year. Same for the subtly cool GTX, a big-block brute that may not have wowed the muscle car crowd like the GTO and others, yet still inspired a faithful following.

▲ That "+6" meant there were three two-barrel carburetors between these fenders.

353

1971 Plymouth Hemi 'Cuda

Chrysler Corporation initially didn't have a specific model able to compete directly with all those GTOs and SS 396s flooding from General Motors factories during the mid-Sixties. But Mopar men did have an engine more than capable of putting the muscle in muscle car—the fabled 426 Hemi.

Built in sparse numbers from 1966 to '71, the Hemi was rated the same each year: 425 horsepower. Actual output, however, was more like 500 horses, a plain fact that seat-of-the-pants responses supported with ease. Even when bolted into those rather mundane Dodge Coronets and Plymouth Satellites in 1966 and '67, the mean, nasty Hemi could still produce quarter-mile times in the high 13s—exciting performance indeed.

Various cooler mid-sized B-body Mopars were fitted with the rare Hemi option during its short, happy run from 1966 to '71, including Dodge's Charger and Super Bee and Plymouth's GTX and Road Runner. But in most minds, the best Hemi of 'em all came in a slightly smaller package. And that package debuted just before the muscle car class reached the end of its own short road.

New for 1970 in both Dodge and Plymouth ranks were two E-body ponycars. Dodge's was the fully fresh Challenger, while Plymouth's carried a familiar name: Barracuda. Introduced in 1964, Plymouth's first flying fish inspired an enthusiastic following even though it wasn't much more than a yeoman Valiant with fastback glass tacked on in back. It was treated to a revamped A-body platform and a new look all its own in 1967, and new that year as well was optional big-block power. Plymouth designers then introduced the hip "'Cuda" image in 1969.

Wheelbase:	108 inches
Weight:	3,800 pounds
Original price:	$4,300, approximate
Engine:	426 cubic-inch Hemi V-8
Compression:	10.25:1
Induction:	two Carter four-barrel carburetors
Horsepower:	425 at 5,000 rpm
Torque:	490 at 4,000 rpm
Transmission:	four-speed manual
Suspension:	independent A-arms w/torsion bars in front; live axle with leaf springs in back
Brakes:	heavy-duty four-wheel drums, standard (power front discs, optional)
Performance:	13.10 second in the quarter-mile, according to a Car Craft test of a 1970 model
Production (Hemi 'Cuda convertible w/four-speed):	2

▲ Hemi 'Cuda convertibles were as rare as they were fast—only seven of these 1971 models were built.

▼ What's shakin', baby? In 1970 and '71, it was Plymouth's groovy "Shaker" hood scoop, which attracted stares wherever it went.

Even groovier was the redesigned E-body Plymouth, which first appeared on drawing boards in Cliff Voss's Advanced Styling Studio in 1967. Voss's main goal was make more room up front for more engine. Squeezing a big-block between A-body flanks had not been easy, and extra underhood space for options like power steering, power brakes and air conditioning had been all but impossible to come by. Not so in the E-body's case.

Even the Hemi fit comfortably beneath an E-body hood in 1970. How did designers manage to seemingly stuff 10 pounds of stuff into a five-pound bag? By basing the E-body foundation on the bigger B-body's cowl structure, thus creating a much wider engine bay for Plymouth's new Barracuda. Spunky, rakish sheetmetal, credited mostly to stylist

▼ This fully loaded 1971 Hemi 'Cuda interior includes instrumentation, bucket seats and a console. Both four-speeds and automatics were installed behind the Hemi.

▲ Foglamps up front were standard too for Plymouth's 'Cuda line.

▼ Fender "gills" were new additions for the 1971 Barracuda.

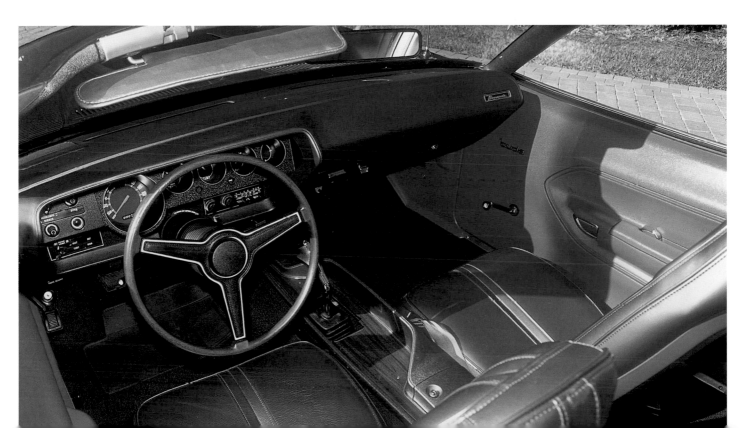

◄ The optional Shaker (1970 edition shown) was available atop other engines besides the Hemi.

▲ All 'Cuda models featured racing style hood pins.

John Herlitz, wrapped things up on top to give the third-generation predator-fish a truly distinctive appearance.

Accentuating sporty impressions even further was the latest 'Cuda rendition, which came standard with the 335-horse 383 big-block V-8 and was dressed up with front foglamps, hood pins, simulated hood scoops, a blacked-out rear panel, and "hockey stick" bodyside stripes that incorporated engine displacement identification at their tails. Three numbers could've been stuck on: 340, 383 or 440.

Those hockey sticks simply read "Hemi" when the optional 426 was specified. The 425-horse V-8 was only available for the 'Cuda, which then took on the "Hemi 'Cuda" name even though it wasn't officially an individual model.

All 'Cuda accoutrements were thus "mandated" when the Hemi engine option was chosen, and the new "Shaker" hood scoop was standard. Additional cast members included a 9-3/4-inch Dana rear end and a choice between a four-speed or the tough Torqueflite automatic.

Simply sticking right out through the hood, a Shaker scoop did just as its name implied whenever pedal met metal and a Hemi started rockin'. But looking cool wasn't its only function; it also allowed those twin Carter carbs below draw in cooler, denser outside air.

A heavy-duty radiator was of course also mandated for the Hemi 'Cuda, as were large 11-inch drum brakes all around and a beefed-up foundation. Ad called Hemi 'Cuda underpinnings "the ruggedest ponycar suspension in the industry." "The front suspension is the same extra-heavy-duty combination used on Hemi Road Runers and GTXs—the same torsion bars, shock

absorbers, anti-sway bar, spindles, ball joints, etc," continued that ad copy. "Ditto the rear suspension, which carries two extra half-leaves in the right rear spring, to prevent torque steer off the line."

Once off that line, the '70 Hemi 'Cuda produced some of the most frightening

▲ This immaculate 1971 Hemi 'Cuda has only 2,010 miles on the odometer.

▼ A front view of the 'Cuda shows the Shaker hood.

quarter-mile times ever published during the muscle car era. After a little tinkering, Car Craft's crew managed a startling 13.10-second quarter-mile pass. No wonder many

witnesses still call this Camaro-eating E-body the greatest of the Hemis—if not the greatest of all muscle cars.

Plymouth built Hemi 'Cudas again for 1971 before the end finally came for unbridled horsepower. Nonetheless, Chrysler's littlest Hemi still loomed large in the memories of

horsepower hounds for years to come, and still does today. Big time.

▲ A view of the Hemi 'Cuda's massive power plant, and the underside of the Shaker hood.

▼ This black two-door notchback Barracuda coupe looks like a sleek predator.

▲ Between 1970 and 1974 the 'Cuda was built on the same E-body platform as the Dodge Challenger.

▼ Design drawings for the 'Cuda.

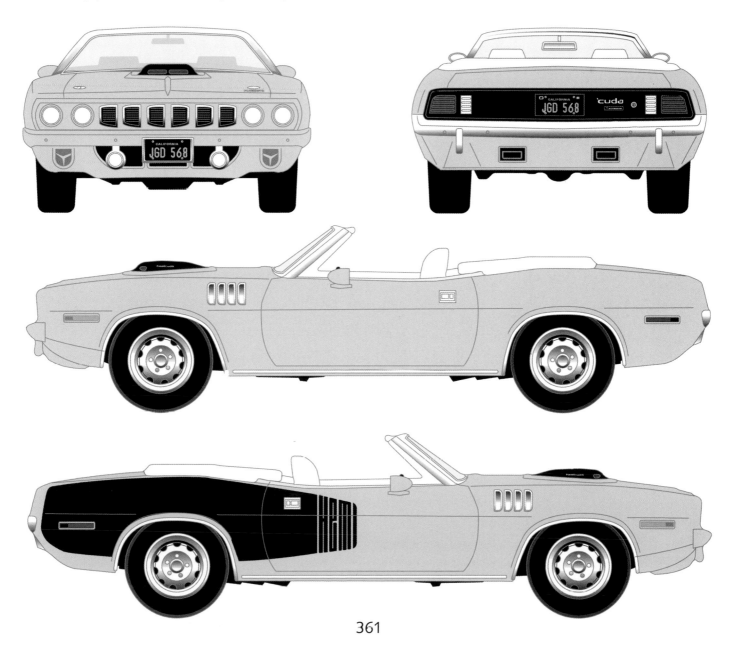

1972 Plymouth Duster 340

Dusters were members of Plymouth's entry level Valiant Group series, as were Scamp two-door hardtops and Valiant sedans. Interestingly, the mighty 'Cudas had also started out as Valiants back in '64, but by this time, the 'Cudas were configured on the larger 'E' Mopar body. The Dusters soon eclipsed the sales of the bigger car.

Dusters were engineered in 1969 for a 1970 launch. The name would ultimately outlast 'Valiant'. The 340 Duster achieved a great power-to-weight ratio that allowed the car to out-perform many larger cars fitted with more powerful engines. Car Life rated the 1970 model with a 0-60 mph time of just 6.2 seconds, and a quarter mile time of 14.7 seconds at an average 94 mph.

The 1971 Valiant models had set great sales levels, with a volume of 256,930 units in that year. Consequently, there was very little impetus to change this successful model. Only details of the model taillights and grille were changed.

The front side marker was also now slimmer and longer. The base Duster model for '72 shared this pattern of light revision, but the side market lamps were moved an inch or two higher above the lower feature line. Base Duster equipment included ventless side windows, a concealed spare tire and twospeed wipers. Outside, the car had a lower deck tape stripe, bodyside tape stripe, a unique grille, roof drip rail moldings and wide tires. Mechanically, the car was fitted with the 340-cid V-8 with dual exhaust, a three-speed manual floor shift, optional axle ratio, heavy-duty suspension and dual snorkel air cleaner. Duster interiors had been upgraded in 1971, and the car was equipped with an optional fold-down rear seat, optional electrically heated window defogger and had front and rear fender guards as standard. Lowback-style seats were a Duster option, and the car also had a locking glovebox.

Just as they had done with the Demon, Plymouth offered a mighty little compact in the shape of their 1972 Plymouth Duster 340. Like the earlier Demon, the car also made use of fun 'character' graphics to appeal to a young audience, and this 340 version had a wide tape strip running the full length of the car along the beltline with bold '340' lettering on the rear fender edge.

Effectively, the Duster was Plymouth's entry-level muscle car and came fully loaded with both plenty of performance goodies and a wallet-friendly price. The car continued to be a great success in '72, with almost identical sales to the 1971 model. Its fun image and targeted marketing was right on the money.

▼ Although the Duster 340 was the most expensive member of Plymouth's Valiant Group, it was still a great little muscle car for the money.

Engine:	V-8 overhead valve, cast iron block
Displacement:	340-cid
Transmission:	Three-speed manual
Compression Ratio:	8.5:1
Base Price:	$2728
Number Produced:	15,681

1972 Pontiac Trans Am

During the 1971 calendar year, Pontiac captured third place in the US auto producers' league for the tenth time in eleven years, but the image of the division was simultaneously losing interest from the buying public, and things were very difficult by 1972.

Pontiac had launched the Trans Am as a $725 Firebird option package in 1969. A 335 horsepower engine was offered as standard, with the option of a 345 horsepower Ram Air IV. Buyers got a limited slip differential and threespeed manual transmission. Despite its name and heritage, the Trans Am never actually raced in the eponymous series. Nevertheless, with 0-60 mph times of 6.5 seconds and quarter mile times of 14.3 seconds (averaging 101 mph), they were undoubtedly fully loaded in the performance department.

The Trans Am was heavily restyled in 1970, and the model was fitted with a new 'bull nose' front grille and streamlined fastback profile that made the car look longer, lower and wider. The 1972 Trans Am series reflected the same look, but was now fitted with the 300 horsepower 455-cid V-8 as standard.

The Trans Am interiors had the same standard features as the Firebirds, plus a Formula steering wheel, engine-turned dash trim, rally gauge cluster with clock and a tachometer. Outside, the cars were equipped with a front air dam, wheel flares front and back, full-width rear deck spoiler, shaker hood, 15-inch Rally II rims with trim rings and black-textured grille inserts.

Engine:	V-8
Displacement:	455-cid
Horsepower:	300 at 400 rpm
Compression Ratio:	8.4:1
Wheelbase:	108 inches
Base Price:	$4256
Number Produced:	1286

Sadly, a combination of circumstances almost resulted in Pontiac axing the car in 1972. Part of the problem was that buyers were deserting muscle car models in the fuel conscious seventies. But this wasn't the only problem Pontiac had to overcome in this year. The most damaging was a five-month long strike on the Firebird/Trans Am manufacturing line at the Norwood, Ohio plant. This resulted in the loss of thousands of cars, and millions of dollars. It very nearly caused the company to drop the model altogether. Further complications arose from the increased volume of Federal safety regulations.

These generally resulted in a lessening of performance, and this was certainly true for the Trans Am. Compression ratios were scaled back to cope with lower octane fuel and stricter emissions limits.

Despite all its problems, the Trans Am turned out to be a real survivor, and it was a best-selling model by 1974.

▲ Almost dropped from the GM range in '72, the Trans Am turned out to be a tough survivor.

1973 Plymouth Road Runner

Chrysler came to the muscle car arena rather late, but soon got into the swing of things. The fact that they had the Hemi and Max Wedge engines available to them was immediately helpful. By the late sixties, muscle cars were getting increasingly expensive, and moving away from their target audience because of this. Mopar now led the field with the first budget muscle cars, cars that Car and Driver Magazine dubbed 'econo-racers'. They evolved a simple but successful formula, take the lightest, cheapest, two-door body available to you, strip it of all the options and stick in the most powerful off-the-shelf V-8. The new Road Runner outdid even this brilliant idea, by adding all the desirable options back in, and then offering the whole package at a very attractive price.

Although the car didn't look anything like a typical muscle car, with an almost complete absence of chrome, bulges and hood scoops, it was an instant success, selling well over 40,000 cars in its first year. That made up one in five of the Plymouth intermediate sales. The car interiors were seriously basic, with rubber mats instead of carpet, a plain bench seat. Only the defining Road Runner badges hinted that there was a special kind of power under the hood, and a special kind of fun to be had from the car.

The standard power unit for the original Road Runners was a special 335 horsepower 383-cid V-8, but the Hemi was also available for $700. Road

Engine:	V-8, overhead valve, cast iron block
Displacement:	318-cid
Transmission:	Three-speed manual
Compression Ratio:	8.6:1
Body Style:	Two-door Hardtop Coupe
Weight:	3525 lbs
Wheelbase:	115 inches
Base Price:	$3115
Number Produced:	19056

Runner sales nearly doubled to 80,000 in 1969, and it was named as 'Car of the Year' by *Motor Trend Magazine*. Only a very few of these cars were Hemipowered, but this option was tested against five other econo-racers, and outpaced them all completely. It could get from 0-60 mph in 5.1 seconds. By 1971, however, only the GTX and the restyled Road Runner were equipped with the Hemi in a changing performance climate.

Styling was revised for the 1973 Road Runners, which were now part of the Satellite Group. The cars were now wider but not as long as the 1972 models.

They now had a combined Satellite/Sebring grille, the hood had a wide center power bulge and rectangular taillights were fitted.

▲ The performance era was drawing to a close in '73, but Road Runners were offered for several further years.

1973-74 Pontiac Trans Am 455 Super Duty

Detroit's original muscle car era came and went every bit as quickly as the mean machines themselves traveled from stoplight to stoplight. Pontiac's GTO officially kicked things off in 1964, and within 10 years it was all over save for the shouting.

But wouldn't you know it? It was Pontiac that again marked a high-performance milestone by giving us the last "great American muscle car." While rival engineers in Detroit were busy trading mph for mpg, Pontiac people continued building excitement in 1973 and '74, and they called this four-wheeled fun the 455 Super Duty Trans Am.

Arab oil embargoes and federal emissions standards notwithstanding, Pontiac engineers still somehow managed to unleash what may well have represented the company's best muscle car to date—and that, of course, was saying a lot. At the heart of this amazingly

1973-74 Pontiac Trans Am 455 Super Duty

Wheelbase:	108 inches
Weight:	3,760 pounds
Base Price:	$4,350
Engine:	455 cubic-inch LS2 "Super Duty" V-8
Horsepower:	290 at 4,000 rpm
Torque:	395 at 3,200 rpm
Induction:	single Rochester Quadra-Jet four-barrel carburetor

Transmission:	Turbo 400 automatic transmission (four-speed manual also available)
Suspension:	independent A-arms w/coil springs in front; live axle with leaf springs in back
Brakes:	power front discs, rear drums
Performance:	14.25 seconds in the quarter-mile in 1974; 13.8 seconds for the quarter-mile (310-horse model) in 1973
Production:	943 (another 57 Super Duty Formula Firebirds were also built in 1974)

emissions-legal beast was the LS2 455 V-8, a thoroughly modern big-block that, even with its hydraulic cam and relatively mild compression, still could've easily blown away most of Detroit's unfettered, atmosphere-choking supercar V-8s had it debuted five years earlier. Was it any wonder then that PMD officials felt this engine was worthy of a name that had made performance history a decade earlier? "Just when we had fast cars relegated to the museum section, Pontiac has surprised everyone and opened a whole new exhibit," claimed a 1973 Car and Driver report on the 455 Super Duty. Everything about the 455 SD V-8 was super-duper, from its new beefy block, to its burly nodular-iron

crank, to its bullet-proof forged-iron rods. A heavy-duty oil pump, 8.4:1 TRW forged-aluminum pistons, a Rochester Quadra-Jet four-barrel, and free-flowing cast-iron headers were also included. But the key to the whole works were the heads, which were tweaked within an inch of their lives by the horsepower-making gurus at Air Flow

MILESTONE FACTS

- Most witnesses agree that Pontiac created the muscle car in 1964; many also support the claim that the 455 Super Duty Trans Am was the last great muscle car.

- Pontiac's famous "Super Duty" moniker had been used first to identify the race-ready 389 and 421 V-8s that debuted in 1961 and '62, respectively.

- The 455 Super Duty V-8 went into 300 Firebirds in 1973: 252 Trans Ams and 48 Formulas. Another 1,000 were built the next year: 943 Trans Ams and 57 Formulas.

- The Trans Am's corporate cousin, Chevrolet's Z28 Camaro, was temporarily discontinued after 1974. But Pontiac's "screaming chicken" kept running right on through these troubled times and remained arguably America's only surviving muscle car until the Z/28 returned in 1977.

- Standard wheel size was 15x7. Two styles were offered in this size, the familiar Rally II or the polycast Honeycomb.

- Transmission breakdown for 1974 Super Duty Trans Am production was 731 automatics, 212 manuals.

- Transmission breakdown for 1973 Super Duty Trans Am production was 180 automatics, 72 manuals

- Styling updates in 1974 traded the '73 Firebird's round headlights for rectangular units.

- Reportedly the LS2 455 V-8 could rev safely to 6,000 rpm and run strongly on 91-octane fuel.

- Total Firebird production in 1974 was 73,729

- Total Trans Am production in 1974 was 10,255.

◄ Pontiac devotees were familiar with the Super Duty (SD) moniker, which first appeared during the early Sixties for a collection of factory race cars.

Research to flow better than anything Pontiac engineers had ever concocted. The end result was a low-compression big-block that made 310 real, net-rated horses while still remaining kind to the environment. Or was it?

Clever PMD engineers noticed that EPA engine testing only ran for about 50 seconds. They then accordingly developed a system that shut off the required exhaust gas recirculation valve after 53 seconds, allowing

the 455 Super Duty to breathe easier—and breathe out unacceptable emissions concentrations—after initially passing emission testing with supposed flying colors. Clean-air cops, however, smelled a rat. The ruse was quickly discovered, and Pontiac people were forced to remove their EGR inactivating system and retest the Super Duty by March 15, 1973. A less-aggressive cam was required to pass these tests. Advertised output then dropped to 290 horsepower. Even so, the 455 Super Duty remained a formidable force.

The 455 SD was originally introduced, in 310-horse form, to the press by Special Products Group chief Herb Adams on June 28, 1972, at GM's Milford Proving Grounds. Adams promised the Super Duty option would be available by that fall for the Grand Am, Grand Prix, LeMans and both Firebirds, Trans Am and Formula. Those testing hassles, however, delayed initial deliveries of the "detuned" 290-horse 455 SD until April 1973, and only then for the two Firebirds.

The 455 Super Duty F-body shocked the automotive press, most of whom were already convinced they'd already witnessed the muscle car's last stand. "The Last of the Fast Cars comes standard with the sort of acceleration that hasn't been seen in years," announced Car and Driver in a May 1973 road test of a pre-production 310-horse Super Duty Trans Am. "How it ever got past the

◀ A ducktail spoiler was again standard for the 1974 Trans Am, as it had been since 1970.

preview audience in GM's board room is a mystery, but here it is—the car that couldn't happen." Unfortunately it didn't stick around for long.

After building 300 Super Duty Firebirds for 1973, Pontiac sold only another 1,000 in 1974 before reality finally caught up this passionate Poncho. Although it did manage to slip by the smog police originally, the 455 Super Duty never would've been able to peacefully coexist with the catalytic converters to come. Its departure then for all signaled the end of the road for truly super supercar performance.

Was it a coincidence that the company that built the first great American muscle car also built the last? We think not.

▲ An 8,000-rpm tach was a bit optimistic.

▼ Fender-mounted air extractors became a Trans Am trademark in 1970 and remained standard until 1982.

▼ The 455 SD V-8 ran both clean and strong.

1994 Chevrolet Impala SS

Back in the sixties, the Impala was a car with classic muscle car potential, a prime candidate to be beefed up for the performance brigade. The car had been downsized in the early '60s, and the lowered weight meant greater performance potential. This had been a reaction to the compacts that hit the market at this time, including the Ford Falcon and Chevy's own Nova. Coupled with the size issue was the range of powerful Chevy V-8s available. For example, there was the meaty 348-cid Turbo Thrust available with either 340 or 360 horsepower, or the 409 Turbo-Fire that inspired the Beach Boys song. This could offer up to 409 horsepower, equipped with twin four-barrel carburetion.

An SS (Super Sports) handling package could also be fitted, complete with power steering and brakes, heavy-duty springs and shocks, sintered metal brake linings and a tachometer. But although the Impala could offer a truly hot package, and was a serious contender in the NASCARs of the early 1960s, only a moderate number of buyers were convinced.

Over the years, SS status was sometimes compromised, badges were affixed to cars with no performance equipment at all, but the legend persisted.

Chevrolet has often been inspired to resurrect old and evocative names from its rich and varied history. The Impala SS of 1994 came out of this impetus. The original SS had been capable of generating 400 horsepower, quarter mile times of around twelve seconds, and fierce admiration on the streets. Thirty years later, kids who had been too young to drive when the first cars were available had their dreams brought to life by Chevrolet. The new Impala SS was based on an ordinary Caprice Classic Sedan, but the engine was up-rated to the Law Enforcement 260 horsepower V-8 and suspension, complete with sequential fuel injection and all-wheel disc brakes. This propelled the car to fantastic performance. The Caprice was already a popular model, and its big smooth shape look really good when lowered. The all-black body of the SS, contrasted with polished aluminum wheels looked great straight from the factory. The

interior was slightly dull, in grey cloth, but performance was the inspiration

behind the car. The model was offered for only four years, but sold in excess of 40,000 units. It was living proof that the original muscle car concept of four-seater cars still had a loyal following.

▲ The Impala SS, a muscle car on the original four-seat template.

Engine:	LT1 Corvette V-8
Displacement:	350-cid
Horsepower:	260 at 5000 rpm
Compression Ratio:	10.5:1
Weight:	4218 lbs
Wheelbase:	115.9 inches
Base Price:	$22,920

1996 Chevy Camaro Z28 SS

Chevrolet's Super Sport legacy goes back a long way and has involved various models (including a few pickups in more recent years) over that span. Introduced for the 1961 Impala, the way-cool SS package then showed up on the compact Nova (1963), the mid-sized Chevelle (1964), the F-body Camaro (1967), the split-personality El Camino (1968), and

By the Seventies, though, the good ol' Super Sport ideal was no longer such a big deal. The original, the full-sized Impala SS, was last seen in 1969, and Chevrolet product planners last stuck an SS badge on the 1972 Camaro before finally ending the string entirely.... Case closed? Not at all.

With the rebirth of the great American muscle car in the Eighties came a new wave of nostalgia among car buyers, many of whom still remembered the Detroit's previous horsepower race. Automakers in turn then fanned these flames of desire by offering more and more muscle during the Nineties. In 1992, a typical hot American V-8 made about 205 horsepower. Within four years or so that bar had been raised to more the 300 horses. And along with the rise of those big ponies came the return of a familiar name.

In 1994 Chevrolet dusted off its Super Sport image

and applied it, peculiarly enough, to a four-door Caprice. Presto, instant Impala SS, a nicely performing family car that rolled on until 1996. That same a year, another SS model reappeared, only it wasn't exactly Chevrolet's idea, though it was sold directly through Chevy dealerships.

Checking off regular production option number R7T in 1996 put a driver behind the wheel of a new Camaro Z28 SS, which actually was created by an outside contractor,

Wheelbase:	101.1 inches
Weight:	4,365 pounds
Base price:	$24,500
Engine:	350 cubic-inch LT1 V-8 with iron block, aluminum heads
Induction:	electronic sequential-port fuel injection
Compression:	10.4:1
Horsepower:	310 at 5,500 rpm
Torque:	325 at 2,400 rpm
Transmission:	Borg-Warner T56 six-speed manual
Suspension:	independent A-arms w/coil springs in front; live axle with coil springs torque arms, trailing arms and tack bar in back
Brakes:	four-wheel vented discs
Performance:	13.5 seconds at 104.86 mph in quarter-mile, according to Hot Rod
Production:	2,410

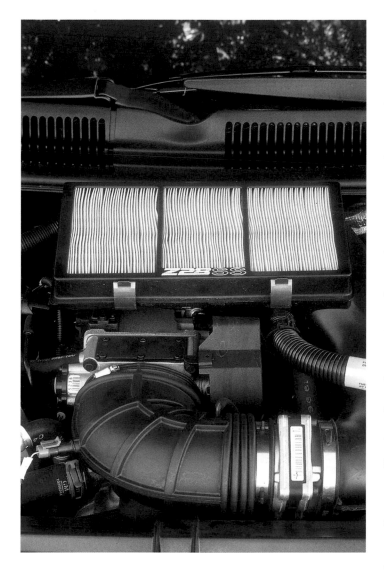

SLP Engineering, Inc., in Troy, Michigan. SLP was the same firm that had started doing similar conversion for Pontiac in 1992, with the end result being the hopped-up Firehawk Firebird. After the Firehawk took flight, SLP then became to General Motors what SVT (Special Vehicle Team, creators of the Mustang Cobra) is to Ford.

A '96 SS began life like any other Z28 Camaro at GM's F-body plant in St. Therese, Quebec. When the R7T option was ordered, Chevrolet sent a Z/28 from St. Therese to an SLP shop in nearby Boisbriand, where it was treated to the Street Legal touch, all the while remaining emissions legal to the strictest U.S. standards. Also met were General Motors' tough standards.

"Throughout the SS's development phase, our objective was to engineer the very highest

▲ SLP enhancements boosted the LT1 small-block V-8's output to 310 horsepower.

▼ The Camaro Z28 SS debuted just as Chevrolet's re-born Impala SS was retiring.

MILESTONE FACTS

• Prior to 1996, Chevrolet last built a Camaro SS in 1972.

• SLP Engineering offered its SS conversion for Camaro Z28 coupes and convertibles in 1996.

• The Camaro Z28 SS debuted just as Chevrolet was shutting down its Caprice-based Impala SS.

• The "SLP" in SLP Engineering originally stood for "Street Legal Performance."

• "Premium floor mats" wearing a "Z28 SS" logo were an SLP option for the 1996 Camaro SS.

• According to Hot Rod's Drew Hardin, "the upgraded SS suspension virtually glued the Camaro to the road."

quality vehicle," added SLP president Ed Hamburger in 1996. " In addition to offering world-class performance, another objective is to make the ownership process as easy as possible. For example, ordering a Z28 SS will be as simple as visiting your local Chevy dealer and asking for an order form". SLP's basic makeover began with a bulging forced-air hood that helped boost the Z28's LT1 small-block from 285 horsepower to 310. Underneath went thicker anti-sway bars front and rear and a Panhard bar in back, all with stiffened bushings for added precision. Corvette ZR-1 17x9 cast-aluminum wheels wearing Z-rated Goodrich Comp T/A rubber

▲ A numbered i.d. plate was standard inside,

▼ As were Corvette wheels at the corners.

◄ "SS" badging and a bold ram-air hood were trademarks of the SLP-tweaked Camaro.

◀ The 1996 Chevy Camaro Z/28 SS was a racing muscle car.

▼ A cutaway view of the 1996 Camaro Z/28 SS.

went on at the corners. "SS" fender tags, a slightly revised rear spoiler, and numbered i.d. plate on the console completed the deal, which added about four-grand to a Z28's base sticker.

Like its Firehawk Firebird cousin, the Camaro SS offered F-body buyers a chance at supreme F-body performance at a cost that wasn't all that tough to stomach, with its sure handling, souped-up LT1 power, and truly tough looks.

▼ A convertible Camaro from the 1999 model year.

1996 Dodge Viper GTS

The Corvette has long been known as "America's Sports Car," and probably always will be. Only one king can rule the road, and Chevrolet's 'glass-bodied two-seater has reigned supreme now for 50 years; its tenure alone guarantees a tough task for any car intending to unseat it. Sure, there have been pretenders to the thrown over the last half-century. But not one has actually dared to go toe-to-toe with the entrenched incumbent.

Ford's two-seat Thunderbirds from 1955-57? Though they were obvious knock-offs, they still represented a breed all their own, a species Dearborn officials like to call "personal luxury." More performance-oriented were the supercharged Studebakers of the Fifties, the blown Avanti (another Stude) in the Sixties, and American Motors' AMX, a two-seater that came in 1968 and went in '70. Nice tries all, but each was better off staying on its own familiar porch and letting Chevy's really big dog run wherever it wanted.

No so for Carroll Shelby's Ford-powered Cobras, built from 1962 to '68. Shelby American's crude 427 Cobra certainly could take a savage bite out of a big-block Corvette driver's lunch. Nonetheless, Sting Rays continued owning the American road during the Sixties, thanks to, if nothing else, sheer numbers. Twenty-thousand Corvettes a year easily overshadowed the couple hundred Cobras let loose during their entire run. Additionally, cost, convenience and class were all clearly in Chevrolet's favor.

Much the same still could be said three decades down the road when Dodge rolled out its vicious Viper in 1992. Like the Corvette in its infancy, the Viper came into this world with little more than the four wheels it rolled in on. In both cases, a sloppy soft-top and side curtains didn't quite cut it with spoiled Yankees. Forty-seven years ago Chevrolet designers rectified their situation by introducing a new Corvette body with real

Wheelbase:	96.2 inches
Weight:	3,445 pounds
Base Price:	$66,045
Engine:	8.0-liter (488 cubic-inches) V-10
Induction:	electronic sequential multi-port fuel injection
Compression:	9.6:1
Horsepower:	450 at 5,200 rpm
Torque:	490 at 3,700 rpm
Transmission:	six-speed manual
Suspension:	independent control arms w/coil springs in front; independent unequal-length control arms with toe-control link and coil springs in back, front and rear anti-roll bars
Brakes:	power-assisted four-wheel vented discs
Performance:	12.6 seconds at 113 mph in the quarter-mile, 0-60 in 4.0 seconds, both according to Car and Driver

▲ A sight to strike terror into your heart when this appears in your rear-view mirror.

▼ "Viper" brake caliper identification.

roll-up side glass and an optional removable hardtop. Then in 1963 the Sting Ray coupe was unveiled to the delight of toupee-wearing sports car enthusiasts everywhere.

Thirty years later, Viper drivers were roughing it and not liking it much at all. Complaints about the open-air cockpit were just the beginning. Many critics also felt the Viper's original shin-sizzling sidepipes weren't too cool. They not only made entry and exit a lot like jumping from the frying pan into the fire, they also didn't do much at all for the way the aluminum V10 announced its presence. According to AutoWeek's Matt DeLorenzo, the original Viper RT/10 roadster sounded like "a UPS truck at idle."

Although Dodge officials knew that they too were in no way intending to "out-Corvette" the Corvette, they did have ears and eyes; they could hear those complaints and they could see the obvious solution. In 1995 they introduced a closed version of their wild and wooly RT/10 roadster to hopefully help soothe the ruffled feelings (and follicles) of potential buyers who felt the original Viper was just too damned uncivilized. That this slippery roof also improved aerodynamics and thus raised top end was simply icing on the cake. Or was it the other way around?

Labeled a 1996 model, the Viper GTS coupe

▼ Full exhausts were extended to the 1996 GTS coupe's tail.

MILESTONE FACTS

- Dodge had a Viper prototype up and running in 1988. This red roadster then made its first public appearance on January 4, 1989.

- The Viper's V-10 engine came from Dodge's truck line.

- Dodge's Mitsubishi-based Stealth was initially chosen to pace the 1991 Indianapolis 500, but it was replaced by a pre-production Viper after a wave of complaints arose about a "Japanese car" pacing the All-American 500.

- Looking a lot like Shelby American's Dayton coupe was not necessarily a coincidence in the GTS's case. Carroll Shelby was one of the Viper's "founding four fathers. The other three were Bob Lutz, Francois Castaing and Tom Gale.

- Engineering goals for the GTS involved keeping weight at the same level as the RT/10 roadster. Adding the roof meant cutting pounds elsewhere—the GTS engine alone weighed 80 pounds less than its predecessor.

- The GTS coupe's V-10 used a lumpier cam, more compression (9.6:1, compared to 9:1), better-breathing heads, and revised exhausts to jump up from 415 horsepower all the way to 450.

▲ The Viper's 8.0-liter, 450-horsepower V10 engine was initially borrowed from Dodge's truck line.

adjustable foot pedals that could be mechanically moved four inches forward and backward. Dual airbags and better-located instruments were also included.

Both adding the roof and a revised floor pan resulted in a much more structurally sound body, and this newfound firmness was accented with a little-less-stout suspension, making the ride a little less rude. And while

▼ No-nonsense instrumentation was standard GTS fare.

represented the closest thing to a stab at sophistication for a car that already had made a name for itself as a brute-force beast. Along with its nicely styled-in hardtop, the GTS coupe also incorporated the breed's first real roll-up (electrically) windows, a more socially acceptable feature that then carried over into the Viper roadster's ranks. Although the already cramped passenger compartment was made even more foreboding with the low, fixed roof in place, at least designers managed to allow stature-challenged drivers a better fit behind the wheel. New for the GTS were

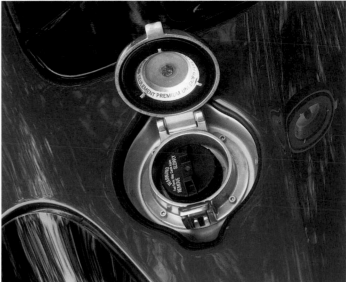

▲ ▶ Both above: fast-fill flip-up fuel cap avoids pit-lane delays. Looks good too!

the exhausts still traveled through the door sills—which still got hot and still wore a warning sticker saying so—they now led all the way back to the Kamm-back tail, where some critics say they released a note more

pleasing to the horsepower hound's ears. As for appearances, all GTS coupes were initially done only in blue with white racing stripes—a

▼ Sinister headlights.

combination copied directly from Shelby's victories Daytona coupes of 1964.

Don't kid yourself, however, the GTS coupe was no watered-down snake. Beneath that beautiful blue body went a lightened, pumped up version of the 8.0-liter V-10, which had been rated at 415 horsepower in previous roadster applications. Advertised output for the GTS was 450 horses, easily the most offered around Detroit in 1996.

More horsepower, more mph on top end, and more conveniences inside—could it get any

▲ A front angle view of a 2013 racing SRT Viper GTS. The car is the fifth generation of this iconic two-seat sportster from Dodge.

◥ The full-color instrument panel of the 2013 Viper GTS-R includes a full-time analog tachometer.

▶ The sumptuous interior of the 2013 SRT Viper GTS-R. The car is hand-built in Detroit.

better? Corvette customers might've thought so, but then maybe they had grown too soft. As far as sheer muscle was concerned, nothing beat a Viper GTS in 1996. At least nothing American.

1996 Dodge Viper GTS

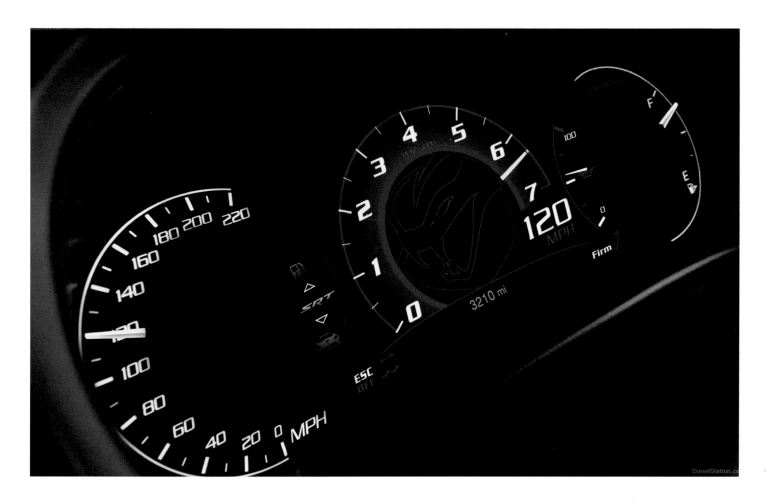

▼ The 2014 Viper SRT Viper TA (Time Attack) model has been designed for track enthusiasts.

▼ The rear view of the concept Viper GTS R.

▶ A convertible Dodge Viper from the 2010 model year.

▼ The interior of the 1998 Viper GTS-R. The car was engineered to develop 700 horsepower from the its 8 liter V10 engine.

◄ The 1997 Dodge Viper GTS Coupe.

1999 Pontiac Trans Am
30th Anniversary Edition

Most casual witnesses who witnessed Pontiac's 30th Anniversary Trans Am Firebird in 1999 couldn't have helped having an opinion. Gray area didn't exist; they either loved the car or not. Those residing down at the "nay" end of the scale, those who weren't tickled white and blue all over, had the same basic complaint: they simply couldn't stomach those wheels.

Indeed, from a Nineties perspective when ever-trendy monochromatic appeals dominated, those metallic blue rims did tend to stick out in stark contrast to that blinding white finish.

Ah, but therein awaited the rub. Call them garish if you will, but those wheels had to be there, they belonged on the car. Like the legendary "screaming chicken" that had been hanging around T/A hoods since 1973, those somewhat radioactive rims shouted out "Trans Am" in no uncertain terms. The color combo choice itself was obvious. All

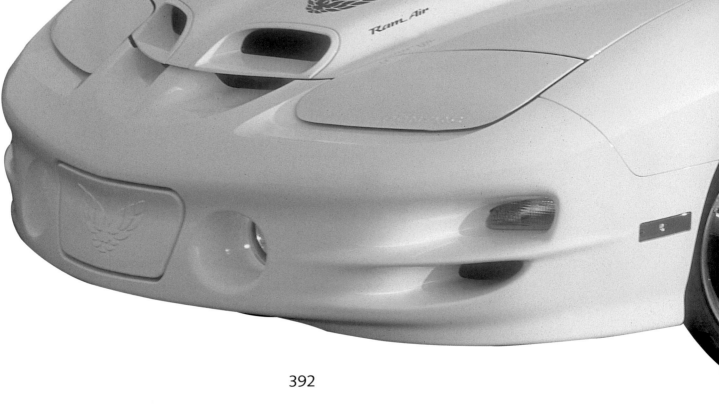

Wheelbase:	101.1 inches	Torque:	335 at 4,400 rpm
Weight:	3,474 pounds	Transmission:	four-speed automatic, standard; six-speed manual, optional
Base Price:	$35,495		
Engine:	5.7-liter (346 cubic inches) V-8 with aluminum block and heads	Suspension:	independent short/long arms w/coil springs in front; live axle with coil springs, torque arms and track bar in back.
Induction:	electronic-controlled sequential-port fuel injection with "WS6" Ram Air hood		
Compression:	10.5:1	Brakes:	power four-wheel discs
Horsepower:	320 at 5,200 rpm	Production:	1,600 in 1999; 1,065 coupes, 535 convertibles

of those first Trans Am Firebirds way back in 1969 were painted the same: Cameo White adorned by Lucerne Blue racing stripes. But commemorating the exclusive color treatment applied 30 years ago was one thing, carrying on in a rich, high-flying tradition of high-profile performance was another.

That the '99 30th Anniversary Trans Am stood out from the crowd so prominently even while at rest is exactly what Pontiac Motor Division's free-thinking builders of excitement had in mind—color-conscious critics be damned. Pontiac wanted to wake people up, something Trans Ams had been doing with little respect for teetotaler's tastes and

puritanical customs longer than any other American heavy-metal out there. Remember, Chevrolet's 50-year-old Corvette is made of plastic, not steel. Well, maybe there was a lot of plastic compound in the 1999 Trans Am, too, but you get the picture.

There also was a lot of purebred muscle in there thanks to the inclusion of a slightly detuned version of the C5 Corvette's 5.7-liter LS1 V-8. The LS1's 320 romping, stomping horses helped keep the 30th Anniversary Trans Am at the head of the modern muscle car pack, a familiar place for Pontiac's F-body bloodline. PMD people in 1999 were more than proud of the fact that the Trans Am was

- Until GM's recent cancellation of its F-body line, Pontiac's Firebird Trans Am was the only muscle car (save for America's Sports Car, the Corvette) to run uninterrupted from its birth in the Sixties into the new millennium.

- Special-edition anniversary Trans Am packages also appeared in 1979 (10th), 1984 (15th), 1989 (20th) and 1994 (25th).

- Production of 30th Anniversary Trans Ams, both coupes and convertibles, was limited to 1,600.

- Pontiac's 25th Anniversary Trans Am in 1994 also featured an exclusive blue-on-white finish. Its production was limited to 2,000.

- General Motors' recent cancellation of its F-body (Pontiac Firebird, Chevrolet Camaro) platform may well translate into soaring collector-car values for all of Pontiac's anniversary Trans Am models.

◀ Pontiac celebrated 30 uninterrupted years of Trans Ams in 1999 with a special-anniversary model (at the left). At the right is a 1969 T/A.

then the only muscle car (again remember, the Corvette is technically "America's Sports Car") able to lay claim to a continuous run dating back to the good ol' days of unbridled horsepower. While Chevrolet briefly gave up on the long-running F-body performance machine, the Z/28 Camaro, in the late-Seventies, Pontiac planners kept their hottest Firebird running even through the darkest days. Safety crusaders, clean-air cops, Arab oil sheiks—no one could stop the Trans Am.

Pontiac offered its 30th Anniversary Trans Am in both coupe and convertible form. Along with that exclusive paint scheme and those blue rims, all the 30th Anniversary models were also fitted with the warmly welcomed "WS6" Ram-Air hood, a feature that looked great and worked even greater to free a few extra ponies on the top end. Behind that free-breathing LS1 V-8 was a choice of either a four-speed automatic or six-speed manual transmission. As for those "medium-blue-tinted clearcoat" wheels, they were big 17x9 five-spokes fitted with P275/40ZR-17 rubber. Underneath was Pontiac's performance and handling package. Power-assisted four-wheel ABS disc brakes were standard, as was a special cooler for the power steering pump.

Inside, white leather buckets carried special "30th Anniversary" embroidery on their

▲ The 30th Anniversary Tran Am's standard bright blue wheels represented a love 'em or hate 'em proposition.

▶ A numbered console plaque also was included as part of the deal.

▼ Special identification carried over inside to the 30th Anniversary Tran Am's bucket seat headrests.

headrests, and anniversary identification also appeared on the floor mats and door panels. All cars also received an individually number plaque on the console. And convertibles were topped with an exclusive Medium Navy Blue cloth top.

Built with loyal collectors in mind, the 30th Anniversary followed in the limited-edition tracks of earlier commemorative Trans Ams. Save for the 10th Anniversary model of 1979 (7,500 built), no other birthday-marking Firebird sold more than 2,000 copies. Only 1,500 were sold in 1984, 1,555 in 1989 and the aforementioned two-grand in 1994. Only

1,600 1999 renditions were projected. As Firebird brand manager Tom Murray told Muscle Car Review magazine's Dan Burger in 1999, "we kept the production numbers small so the ones that are out there will be that much more valuable."

Now that the Firebird family itself is history, those values should be taking off soon. The Trans Am may be gone, but it never will be forgotten.

▶ At the time, the 1999 Trans Am was America's longest-running muscle car.

▼ Pontiac's WS6 ram-air equipment included an aggressive hood with twin scoops.

2001 Chevrolet Corvette Z06

Both critics and company officials alike couldn't say enough about the new "C5" (for 5th generation) Corvette after it hit the ground running in 1997. Practically no bolt had been left unturned by David Hill's engineering team when it had come time to reinvent America's Sports Car, resulting in a truly new Corvette from head to toe, from top to bottom.

The exciting LS1 V-8 up front. A unique transmission/transaxle in back. An innovative, more rigid frame (formed by water pressure) underneath. The list went on and on. Improved comfort and convenience combined with the best world-class Vette performance yet, and all this at a reasonable price as American as apple pie. Could it get any better?

Yes, at least from an enthusiastic road-warrior's perspective.

In the C5, Hill's gang had America's all-time best muscle car, the most well-rounded performer to ever roll down Mainstreet U.S.A. Viper fans could forget about it. Though their new Dodge GTS coupe certainly was hotter than hot, it simply couldn't compare to the C5 Corvette as far as real-world user-friendliness was concerned. On top of that its price

tag was more than 50 percent higher. Case closed.

But Hill knew that not all Corvette customers wanted the best of both worlds, performance and practicality. Some didn't mind riding on the wild side with the Viper clan, they didn't worry about making a compromise or two in the best interests of maximizing muscle. Thus came the 2001 Z06 hardtop, an even hotter Corvette that was, in Chevrolet's words, "aimed directly at diehard performance enthusiast at the upper end of the high-performance market." Added Corvette brand manager Jim Campbell, "The new Z06 will have great appeal for those who lust after something more—that indefinable thrill that comes from being able to drive competitively

Wheelbase:	104.5 inches
Weight:	3,115 pounds
Base Price:	$47,500
Engine:	5.7-liter (346 cubic inches) LS6 V-8 with aluminum block and heads
Induction:	electronic sequential fuel injection
Compression:	10.5:1
Horsepower:	385 at 6,000 rpm
Torque:	385 at 4,800 rpm
Transmission:	six-speed manual, located at rear wheels
Suspension:	independent double wishbone w/coil springs in front; independent with cast-aluminum upper control arms and transverse-mounted composite leaf spring
Brakes:	power-assisted four-wheel discs w/Bosch ABS
Performance:	12.6 seconds at 114 mph in the quarter-mile, 171-mph top speed (factory test)
Production:	5,773

at 10/10ths in a car purpose-built do to exactly that."

Once more, few bolts went untouched as engineers created the Z06 hardtop, which borrowed its name from another hot Corvette, this one created by Zora Arkus-Duntov in 1963. Duntov's original Z06 options package included the new Sting Ray's hottest V-8 working in concert with a beefed suspension and brakes to help make a trip from the showroom right to the racetrack possible. The plan was similar in 2001. Standard for the second-edition Z06 were wider wheels and tires, special brake-cooling ductwork front and rear, and the exclusive FE4 suspension, which featured a larger front stabilizer bar, a stiffer leaf spring in back, and revised camber settings at both ends. Weight was cut throughout

the Z06 by about 100 pounds overall compared to a 2001 Corvette sport coupe.

The Z06's exclusive wheels were 17x9.5 inchers in front, 18x10.5 in back—in both cases one inch wider than the standard C5 rims. Mounted on the Z06's widened rollers were Goodyear Eagle F1 SC tires, P265/40ZR-17 in front, P295/35ZR-18 in back. C5s in 2001 featured Eagle F1 GS rubber, P245/45ZR-17 at the nose, P275/40ZR-18 at the tail.

Beneath the new Z06's hood was another hot power source, this one created only for this application. And, like the car itself, this exclusive engine was named using a

◀ Chevrolet introduced its supreme Corvette, the Z06, in 2001.

legendary options code from Corvette days gone by. In 1971, the LS6 454 big-block was the hottest Corvette V-8 offered that year. Same for the 2001 LS6, which was based on the C5's existing LS1 small-block. A recast block, stronger pistons, raised compression (from 10.1 to 10.5:1), a lumpier cam, and bigger injectors were just a few of the dozens of LS 6 improvements. Output was 385 horsepower, 40 more than the LS1. Behind the LS6 was a new M12 six-speed manual transmission, the only gearbox available for the Z06.

These new parts and many others helped make the Z06, again in Chevrolet's words, "simply the quickest, best handling production Corvette ever." "We've enhanced Corvette's performance persona and broken new ground with the new Z06," added David Hill. "With 0-60 [times] of four seconds flat,

MILESTONE FACTS

• All C5 Corvettes in 1997 were targa-top sport coupes. A convertible joined the C5 line in 1998, and a fixed-roof hardtop followed in 1999.

• All Z06 Corvettes in 2001 were hardtop models. The LS6 V-8 was exclusive to the Z06, while all other Corvettes came standard with the LS1 engine.

• Production of Corvette sport coupes and convertibles in 2001 was 15,681 and 14,173, respectively.

• Z06 colors in 2001 were Quicksilver Metallic, Speedway White, black, Torch Red, and Millennium Yellow.

• Only two interior colors were offered for the 2001 Z06, black and black w/Torch Red accents.

• Z06 tachometers redlined at 6,500 rpm, compared to 6,000 on other Corvettes.

• Chevrolet's second-generation active handling package was standard on all 2001 Corvettes.

• The M12 six-speed manual transmission and FE4 suspension were both exclusive to the 2001 Z06.

▼ Powering the reborn Z06 in 2001 was the 385-horse LS6 V-8.

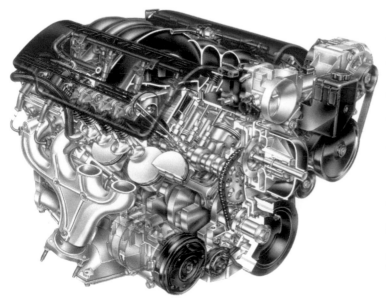

and more than 1g of cornering acceleration, the Z06 truly takes Corvette performance to the next level. In fact, the Corvette Team has begun referring to it as the C5.5, so marked are the improvements we've made and the optimization of the car in every dimension."

Chevrolet sold 5,773 Z06 Corvettes in 2001, followed by another 8,297 in 2002. Continued popularity in 2003 proved that David Hill wasn't just trying to ride Duntov's coattails when he reached back to 1963 for a suitable name for his latest, greatest C5.

Zora undoubtedly would be proud.

▲ Z06 nomenclature was first seen on Corvette order sheets in 1963.

▶ Comfort and convenience were enhanced inside the C5 Corvette, introduced for 1997.

2001 Chevrolet Corvette Z06

▲ The 2001-edition LS6 V-8 featured aluminum block and heads.

2003 Ford Mustang Mach 1

Unlike their counterparts at General Motors, Ford officials haven't been all that keen on nostalgic commemorations in recent years. Nary a balloon or birthday candle was seen when Dearborn's beloved ponycar turned 30, perhaps because Ford execs felt totally redesigning the 1994 Mustang was enough.

Not even a simple anniversary badge appeared. And when humble logos did appear on the 35th Mustang in 1999, that adornment paled in comparison to what Pontiac did to celebrate 30 years of Trans Am Firebirds that same year. Chevrolet's 30th Anniversary Camaro had been honored with equal enthusiasm two years before.

But apparently some of the Blue Oval boys (and girls) do have hearts, they can relate to fond memories of days gone by. Or perhaps someone at Ford simply decided to copy what Chevrolet had done in 2001 with its Z06 Corvette. Either way, the end result was a special-edition ponycar for 2003 that harked back to 1969, the year Ford designers unveiled what Car Life magazine editors called "the first great Mustang." That machine was the Mach 1, which—again in Car Life's words—offered "performance to match its looks, handling to send imported-car fans home mumbling to themselves, and an interior as elegant, and livable, as a gentleman's club."

Indeed, the idea behind the first Mach 1 was to combine a little class and a bit of prestige with a decent dose of performance, or at least a decent performance image. Base small-block Mach 1 fastbacks looked great in 1969, but weren't all that hot. On the contrary, the optional 428 Cobra Jet big-block V-8—fit with Ford's new "Shaker" ram-air hood scoop—instantly transformed the upscale Mustang into "the quickest standard passenger car though the quarter-mile we've ever tested," according to Car Life's critics, this after a stunning 13.86-second quarter-mile sprint.

It was this legacy of performance and pizzazz that Ford product planners tapped into 24 years later. They already had a decent all-around "hi-po" hauler in the Mustang GT, a nicely affordable thoroughly modern muscle car that offered even more comfort and convenience than that first Mach 1. Ford buyers in 2003 could also opt for the pricier SVT Cobra, back after

a one-year hiatus with 390 supercharged horses. Yet in between was a major gap. No problem. Those planners simply filled that hole with the 2003 Mach 1, a Mustang that looked an awful lot like a time machine.

First and foremost there was that familiar Shaker scoop protruding up through the '03 Mach 1's striped hood. Like its fully functional forerunner, this black baby could rock like Mick Jagger when the torque started twisting. "Let your mind go and it's the Sixties all over the place," wrote Hot Rod's Ro McGonegal about that new old-style scoop. Doing that twisting was a 2003 redo of the 2001 Cobra's 4.6-liter dual-overhead-cam, four-valve-per-cylinder V-8, a 305-horse screamer that made the latest, greatest Mach 1 even faster than its big-block ancestor. It also made the 2003 Mach 1 the first Mustang

Wheelbase:	101.3 inches
Weight:	3,465 pounds
Base Price:	$28,805
Engine:	4.6-liter dual-overhead-cam V-8 with four-valves per cylinder
Induction:	electronic sequential fuel injection with 57mm throttle body and functional "Shaker" hood scoop
Compression:	10.1:1
Horsepower:	305 at 5,800 rpm
Torque:	320 at 4,200 rpm
Transmission:	Tremec TR3650 five-speed manual (automatic optionals)
Suspension:	independent A-arms w/coil springs in front; live axle with coil springs in back
Brakes:	power four-wheel discs
Performance:	12.97 seconds at 103 mph in the quarter-mile, according to Mustang Monthly
Production:	9,652

outside of the SVT corral to offer DOHC V-8 power.

The new Mach 1 could out-handle its forefather, too, thanks to a special suspension package that featured stiffer springs (that lowered the car about a half inch), Tokico struts, and 17x8 wheels shod in Goodyear Eagle ZR45 rubber. Those aluminum five-spoke "Heritage" wheels were unique to the 2003 Mach 1 and fit the nostalgic image to a T, as did those blacked-out front rear spoilers and those old-fashioned rocker panel stripes. Fog lamps too were standard up front, per GT specs.

◀ Ford muscle car fans recognized the Mach 1's "Shaker" hood scoop, which fed cooler outside air to a 305-horse 4.6-liter V-8.

▼ The Shaker scoop and striping were all plainly reminiscent of Ford's first-generation Mach 1.

◀ Ford revived its revered Mach 1 moniker in 2003 to help mark the corporation's 100th anniversary.

Additional standard equipment included a Tremec five-speed manual transmission, power rack-and-pinion steering, power four-wheel Brembo disc brakes, stainless-steel dual exhausts, and a Trac-Lok 8.8-inch differential with 3.55:1 gears. A beefed-up 4R70W automatic transmission was optional.

Ordering the automatic required a few changes within the DOHV V-8. Crankshafts in auto-box engines were cast pieces, while their counterparts in stick-shift Mach 1s were forged steel. Output ratings remained the same, but redlines differed—5,800 revs in automatic cars versus a grand more in the manuals. Additional 4.6L DOHC updates in 2003 (in both cases) included revised cylinder heads with rerouted water passages, new cams (the intake valves were controlled by a bumpstick borrowed from Ford's 5.4L truck engine), and revamped exhaust manifolds that were port-matched to the heads.

▼ Nostalgic touches inside included "Bullitt" Mustang instruments, foot pedals and shifter knob.

Standard interior treatments also brought back memories as the Mach 1 was fitted with a bright aluminum shift "ball" and a "nostalgic instrument cluster," both features that had appeared previously on Ford's "Bullitt" Mustang. Indeed, it was the Sixties all over again when seated at a 2003 Mach 1's leather-wrapped wheel looking past those gauges over that black scoop that quivered with every bit as much as excitement as the driver.

All that was missing was an SS 396 Chevelle or Hemi Road Runner in the lane next door.

MILESTONE FACTS

- Ford's original Mach 1 Mustang debuted for 1969 as an upscale fastback.

- The original "Shaker" hood scoop option was offered atop various engines between Mustang flanks in 1969 and '70. It also peeked through the Torino Cobra hoods in 1970 and '71.

- Ford called its new Mach 1 Mustang a "modern interpretation of an American icon."

- Production breakdown by transmission choice for the 2003 Mach 1 was 7,709 manuals, 1,943 automatics. The 2003 Mach 1 was the first Mustang to mate Ford's 4.6-liter DOHC V-8 with an automatic transmission.

- Production breakdown by exterior color was 2,513 for Torch Red, 2,250 for Azure Blue, 1,611 for black, 1,595 for Dark Shadow Grey, 869 for Zinc Yellow, and 814 for Oxford White

- Two new Mach 1 colors were introduced for the 2004 model year, Screaming Yellow and Competition Orange. Commemorative identification, marking the Mustang's 40th anniversary, was also added.

2004 Pontiac GTO

It was only right that the same firm that ushered in the muscle car era in 1964 also ended things 10 years later. In nearly all opinions, Pontiac's GTO was America's first muscle machine, and many feel the division's 455 Super Duty Firebird, built in 1973 and '74, was the last. The last truly great one, that is.

From then on, it was Pontiac's Trans Am or nothing at all as far as most typical (translated: those who couldn't afford a Corvette) performance fans were concerned back in the horsepower-starved Seventies and Eighties. Though these "T/A" Firebirds basically represented mere shadows of their former selves, at least they stuck around every year, unlike their F-body cousin from Chevy, the Z28 Camaro. Then once real factory muscle started making its comeback some 20 years back, the long-running Trans Am was ready, willing and able to really start rolling again. Unfortunately GM's last F-body rolled into the sunset in 2002, leaving Pontiac without a traditional rear-driven V-8 muscle car for the first time since… well, since 1964.

No worries, mate. Built in Australia, Pontiac's newest pumped-up sport coupe

Wheelbase:	109.7 inches	Transmission:	six-speed manual or four-speed Hydra-Matic automatic
Weight:	3,821 pounds		
Base Price:	$33,000 (estimated)	Suspension:	independent A-arms w/coil spring struts in front; live axle with coils springs, trailing arms and adjustable toe-in link in back
Engine:	5.7-liter (346 cubic inches) LS1 pushrod V-8 with aluminum block and heads		
Induction:	electronic sequential-port fuel injection	Brakes:	four-wheel ventilated discs w/ABS
Compression:	10.1:1	Performance:	13.62 seconds at 104.78 mph in the quarter-mile, according to Motor Trend test of six-speed manual model
Horsepower:	340 at 5,200 rpm		
Torque:	360 at 4,000 rpm	Production (projected): 18,000	

picked up where the Trans Am left off and hit the ground running on the U.S. market in 2004 to rave reviews, both from contemporary critics with no "original" muscle car experience as well as those who lived it the first time around. The name alone was enough to stir the soul: GTO. Who cares that the car beneath that famous three-letter badge is a warmed-up version of General Motors' Aussie-marketed Holden Monaro, first seen at the Sydney motor show in 1998? It's a two-door coupe, it's suitably muscular, and it's certainly better than, say, nothing.

By then based on Pontiac's compact Ventura, the last original GTO had come and gone in 1974, looking more like a feeble farewell than a suitably honorable send-off for a legendary

▼ Buyers can choose between a six-speed manual or an automatic transmission

automobile. Rumors of a return began surfacing 20-odd years later, but these initially were nothing more than teases.

"We considered bringing the GTO back a number of times, but we never had the right product," explained Pontiac-GMC general manager Lynn Myers in January 2003. "We knew it had to be a V-8, rear-wheel drive and offer outstanding performance, but, until GM's leadership team looked at the Holden Monaro, nothing really fit."

Though looking to GM's affiliate Down Under might not have been the prime choice, Pontiac execs were undoubtedly pressured into a relatively painless plan of least resistance once word came down of the F-body's impending doom. Replacing the retiring Trans Am with a new GTO became that plan, but it had to be put in place fast, thus the use of the existing Holden platform. From first suggestion to production reality amazingly required only 17 months.

"The speed to market with the new GTO demonstrates GM's global product development capabilities and our renewed focus on customer enthusiasm," added Bob Lutz, GM vice chairman of product development and the former Chrysler man who had previously shepherded in Dodge's

▼   "GTO"-identified buckets are standard for the re-born "Goat."

Viper. "This car is a strong statement from both Pontiac and GM that we are determined to re-energize the car market with vehicles that command attention and excite the customer's senses."

The main source of the new GTO's excitement is its LS1 V-8, which has been the heart of the Corvette since the C5 debuted in 1997. Rated

at 350 horsepower, the 2004 GTO's LS1 is mated to a standard 4L60-E automatic transmission, which can be superseded by an optional close-ratio Tremec six-speed manual (the same gearbox used by the Z06 Corvette) for those who prefer to row their own way through the gears.

Additional standard hardware includes power-assisted four-wheel ventilated disc brakes (with a four-channel anti-lock system), four-wheel independent suspension, power

▲ Standard muscle for the 2004 GTO is supplied by the 5.7-liter LS1 V-8. Output is 340 horsepower.

MILESTONE FACTS

- Pontiac's original GTO was built from 1964 to 1974. Nearly 515,000 "Goats" hit the streets during that time.

- From 1964 to '68, GTO was America's best-selling muscle car.

- For 1974 only, the GTO was based on the compact Ventura platform. It had been a mid-sized model prior to that point.

- Pontiac got enthusiasts hopes up in 1999 with a GTO concept car, which was actually an inoperative foam model that, in the words of Car and Driver's Aaron Robinson, "was too ugly even for Hot Wheels to build."

- According to Car and Driver, the 2004 GTO represents "God-bless-America performance wrapped in a sleek and refined package at a price the rest of us can afford."

- Reportedly Pontiac's initial plans involve building about 18,000 GTOs a year for three years.

- Pontiac's 2004 GTO was introduced at the Detroit and Los Angeles auto shows in January 2003. Production began late that year.

old all-American Goat, the 2004 rendition's performance speaks for itself: 0-60 in 5.3 seconds, the quarter-mile in 13.62 clicks. Those numbers represent muscle enough for most drivers, and there's talk that Pontiac has an even hotter GTO in the works, a reborn "Judge" if you will. Offered from 1969 to '71, the original GTO Judge laid down the law in its day like few other factory hot rods. Will a similarly maxed-out GTO be back out in front again? At this point, the jury's still out.

In the meantime we do have yet another high-powered time machine, another new-wave muscle car that both revives fond memories and holds its own "in the now." Accord to Bob Lutz, "this latest GTO will carry on the proud tradition of a legendary line."

Hopefully it will also lead the way into a fast and furious future.

rack-and-pinion steering, and 17x8 cast aluminum wheels wearing BF Goodrich 245/45ZR-17 tires. Throw on some spoilers, appropriate "GTO" identification inside and out, and cool instrumentation and comfortable buckets within the cockpit and the deal's done. For about $33,000, a muscle-minded buyer can put himself (or herself) back behind the wheel of the car that started it all so many years ago.

Or at least something close to it. Though some critics early on have complained that the new Australian-born image fails to honor the

▲ Eye-catching instrumentation.

2005 Chrysler 300-C

Nothing is ever new under the sun and in 2005 Chrysler's original "beautiful brute" re-emerged once again fifty years after the first car in 1955. The new car displays styling hints of the original car , like the deep square sectioned grille.As the company was owned by Mercedes-Benz at the time, the Chrysler 300 used components derived from the E-Class, which included the rear suspension design, front seat frames, wiring harnesses, steering column, and the 5-speed automatic transmission.

The front suspension was a double wishbone system derived from the S-Class. The Chrysler 300-C was first shown at the 2003 New York Auto Show as a concept car. Sales in the U.S. began in the spring of 2004 as an early 2005 model year car. Designed by Ralph Gilles, the new 300-C was built in the same spirit as the original "letter car" as a high performance, full- size,sporty sedan. The car uses a 345 cu in Hemi V-8 in common with its ancestor. Using the Multidisplacement System (MDS), this engine can run on four cylinders when less power is needed in order to reduce total fuel consumption. When all 8 cylinders are needed, the 300-C can make 340 hp and 390 ft/lbs of torque. It uses a 5-speed automatic transmission and comes standard with 18 inch chrome-clad alloy wheels.

The Hemi engine features a pushrod induction tube, located on the side of the engine-block. This tube makes the 300-C more fuel efficient and quicker, because of the air being "pulled and pushed" into the engine's induction area. The engine uses a double rocker configuration, with a cam-in-block, overhead valve (OHV) pushrod design. There are two spark plugs per cylinder to effect a complete fuel/air mixture burn and to decrease emissions.

Chrysler also introduced the SRT-8 version of the car in 2004. This had a formidable 370-cubic-inch Hemi V-8 producing 425 hp allowing a 0-60 mph time in the low 5-second range and quarter-mile in the high 13-second range. It went on sale in February 2005 at the not inconsiderable sum of US$43,695. Additional features included leather SRT-8 performance-embossed seats and 20-inch forged, polished aluminum wheels, Brembo brakes, and a rear lip spoiler. The 2007–2008 SRT-8

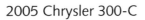

models had a rear spoiler molded into the body, which became standard throughout the entire 300 line-up. The 2007 models had a lower air dam at the front of the car which increased cooling to the engine by as much as 30%.

Engine:	Hemi V-8
Displacement:	345 cid
Horsepower:	340
Transmission:	5-speed automatic
Wheelbase:	120 inches
Length:	196.8 inches
Base Price:	$30,000 depending on options

▲ The latest Letter Car fulfills the promise of the original "beautiful brute."

2005 Ford Mustang GT

'**Mustang attracts two kinds of** drivers – those under 30 and those over 30. Really, that's its strength. America's most popular nameplate transcends demographics and socio-economic trends – because Mustang is really more than a car. It's an icon that's been woven into the fabric of America for 40 years and running.' (J. Mays, Group Vice President, Design, FoMoCo.)

The all-new, all-American 2005 Mustang is a bold, clean and contemporary version of possibly the most celebrated muscle car in the US. It is a purely American sports car. The new design is fresh and contemporary, but harks back to the venerable Mustangs of the past. Mustang was launched by Ford back in 1964 and just twelve months later it had broken auto manufacturing records by selling 419,000 cars in its first production year. By the end of its second year, 1,000,000 Mustangs were out on the roads of America. Somehow, Ford had managed to tap into a reservoir of un-catered for demand. Young, performance orientated, fun-loving, glamorous, the car reflected many buyer's view of themselves for the first time. It was the start of a love affair that would continue to the present. Through over 300 film appearances, including 'Bullit' and 'Gone in 60 Seconds' the image of the Mustang is entwined in American pop culture and continues to have resonance to this day – a bad-boy car, hip, smooth and definitely trouble.

The new car has undergone some fundamental development. The front wheel has been moved forward, significantly reducing the front overhang. The wheelbase has also been lengthened by six inches, pushing all the wheels further out to the corners. This has also increased the cabin size.

Ford has tripled its investment in the car's interior, in order to offer the buyer an almost limitless customising opportunity.

So far as the exterior appearance is concerned, the shark-like nose reminds us of the 1967 model, while the jewelled round headlamps in trapezoidal housings look startlingly modern. The GT also has circular fog lamps in the black grille, and an upright lower fascia with an 'air dam' performance look. The body profile of the GT is low and aggressive looking, due to it

body-color lower rocker panel. But power is at the heart of every Mustang. The new car will be equipped with an impressive 4.6-liter V-8 delivering 300 horsepower, which used to be the exclusive territory of the racing stock – the likes of Mach 1, Cobra and Boss Mustangs. This will make the car the most affordable 300 horsepower machine in the US. A SOHC V-6 will also be available, producing 202 horsepower.

Engine:	V-8
Displacement:	281-cid
Horsepower:	300
Transmission:	Close-Ratio 5R55S Automatic
Induction:	Electronic Throttle Control
Body Style:	Two-door Sports Coupe
Number of Seats:	4

▲ The 2005 Mustang GT will be the most affordable 300 horsepower car in the US, priced at under $20,000.

2008 Dodge Challenger SRT 8

When Barry Newman (as Kowalski) heads into oblivion in his 1970 Dodge Challenger, a legend was born. A legend that would re-emerge in 2008. The original concept of the model was as a "pony car competitor" for the Ford Mustang. The Mustang had its day of fame in the movie Bullitt (1968), the Challenger had its three years later in Vanishing Point. Both films achieved cult status. Vanishing Point was re-launched in 1998 as a not-so-successful TV film. But the Challenger was to fare better with its metamorphosis in 2008.

The new version of the car is a two-door coupe. It shares common design elements with the first generation Challenger, despite being significantly longer and taller. The chassis was a modified version of the LX platform (with a shortened wheelbase) that underpins the 2006 to the current Dodge Charger, the 2005-2008 Dodge Magnum, and the 2005-Current Chrysler 300. The LX platform was adapted from the Mercedes E Class, reflecting Mercedes-Benz's ownership of Chrysler at the time. All (7119) 2008 models were SRT8s, equipped with the 370 cu in Hemi and a 5-speed AutoStick automatic transmission. The entire 2008 US run of 6,400 cars was pre-sold.

The 2009 SRT8, while still equipped with the 370 cu in Hemi V-8, was virtually identical to its 2008 counterpart. The main difference was the choice of either a 5-speed automatic or a 6-speed manual transmission. Standard features included Brembo brakes, a sport suspension, bi-xenon headlamps, heated leather sport seats, keyless ignition, Sirius satellite radio, and 20-inch forged aluminum wheels.

The extras were in addition to the amenities already offered on the R/T and SE models, such as air conditioning and cruise control. In addition, the 2009 had a proper "limited slip" differential. A "Spring Special" SRT8 Challenger was offered in B5 Blue, but due to rolling plant shutdowns, only 250 Spring Special Challengers were built before the end of the 2009 model year.

For 2010, SRT8 models added Detonator Yellow to the range of available colors (at extra cost), and only as an optional "Special Edition Group" car.

Yellow Challengers would only be built for a limited time (October/December 2009) for the 2010 model year. Another retro color, Plum Crazy Purple, was also available during the Spring 2010 production, this was offered exclusively in the "Spring Special" package. Another retro color, Furious Fuchsia (similar to the Panther Pink of the 1970s) was limited to a single production day at Chrysler's Brampton, Ontario plant.

Engine: Hemi V-8

Displacement: 345 cid

Horsepower: 425

Trans: 5-speed automatic/6-speed manual

Wheelbase: 116 inches

Length: 197.7 inches

Base Price: $40,095

▲ The exciting new Challenger SRT lives up to its heritage.

2010 Chevy Camaro

Chevrolet are keeping retro styling cues high on their agenda with this the fifth generation Camaro. The car happily just misses the complete retro look, combining retro styling cues with modern functionality by using the very latest technology and modern components. It seems that most informed reviewers are hard-pressed to discover anything disappointing with the exterior appearance of the car, and early customer response has been really good.

However, while the exterior has been universally praised the interior has received some slightly critical reviews as it is felt to be "rather more vintage than retro" with its high-mounted gauges and center stack that look cool, but prove to be "ergonomically challenging" in operation. With the car's high belt line and low roof, coupled with its dark upholstery, there have been comments about the interior being gloomy.

This Coupe, based on the GM Zeta platform, comes in five different trims: the LS and LT versions are powered by a 217 cubic inch V-6 producing a very respectable 304 hp. The SS versions use two different V-8s. The SS, with 6-speed manual transmission, is powered by a GM LS3 unit of 376 cubic inches putting out 426 hp at 5900 rpm. Presumably, this version is aimed at all-out performance freaks with little concern for economy. By contrast, the auto version uses a GML99 V-8. This develops 400 horsepower, and features an Active Fuel Management system which allows the engine to run on just four cylinders during light-load driving conditions (such as highway cruising) to improve fuel economy.

Other features of the model range include a fully independent four-wheel suspension system, variable-rate power steering, four-wheel disc brakes standard on all models (four-piston Brembo calipers on SS models), a StabiliTrak electronic stability/traction control system, Competitive/Sport modes for the stability system offered on SS models, launch control on SS models equipped with the six-speed manual transmission, and six standard air bags that include head curtain side-impact air bags and front seat-mounted thorax side air bags. An RS appearance package is available on LT and SS trim levels, which includes HID headlamps with integrated halo

rings, a spoiler, and RS-specific tail lamps and wheels. Rally and hockey stripe packages are also available in several colors.

Importantly, despite its modern sophistication the sporty element of the original car is not lost in this fifth generation Camaro.

Automobile Magazine says that, "out among traffic, the Camaro sticks out," and not simply because of its unmistakably loud exhaust note.

Engine: (SS) GM LS3 V-8	
Displacement: 376 cid	
Horsepower: 426	
Wheelbase: 112.3 inches	
Length: 190.4 inches	
Weight: 3750 lbs	

▲ The new Camaro's exterior styling is a happy combination of retro and ultra modern lines.

2012 Dodge Charger SRT8

The 2005 SRT8 was equipped with a voracious 6.1 liter Hemi V-8, but the 2011 Charger weighed in with an even larger 6.4 liter hemi V-8. The newly styled 2012 car squeezed even more and far greater fuel efficiency from the same powertrain. The twenty-five percent fuel economy over that of the 2011 model was due to the engine's new cylinder-deactivation system. The hemi's aggressive engine power was channeled through a five-speed automatic. Despite the car's full-sedan size and rear-wheel drive, the SRT8 was not only super quick in a straight line but, thanks to its fully hydraulic steering assembly, the car was highly maneuverable in bends and corners. Even at high speed, the car maintained complete stability, and thanks to its slippery aerodynamics and faster windshield angle, produced very little wind noise. The majority of the 2012 Challenger's suspension components had been modified by SRT and the car rode a half-inch lower when compared to the 2011 car. These modifications also made the ride far smoother than that of the car's predecessor. The new SRT8 also had improved stopping power due to its beefed up braking system, with Brembo calipers, and more precise steering.

SRT CEO Ralph Gilles dubbed the 2012 SRT8 "the outspoken one." The car's revised muscle car styling was also comprehensively revised, inside and out. The car now sported side skirts, a rear spoiler, a diffuser-style rear

Wheelbase:	120.2 inches
Weight:	4,360 pounds
Base price:	$47,425
Engine: 16-valve V-8	6.4 liter 470 horsepower OHV
Transmission:	Five-speed automatic
Brakes:	Antilock Brembo brakes with vented and slotted front and rear discs
Performance:	0-60 in 4.5 seconds, quarter mile in 12.8 seconds at 115.5 mph

bumper, fat chrome exhaust tips, and a hood equipped with functional vents at its leading edge. Inside, the car now featured a revised leather-covered dash, complete with an 8.4-inch touch screen display with a Performance Pages function.

The result of all of these changes was a blast from the muscle car past with a touch of modern refinement, a refined four-door sedan equipped with incredible performance. The car could be enjoyed as both a weekday commuter and weekend thrill machine that would surpass many German high-performance cars. The 2012 SRT8 brought the muscle car era up-to-date with a blend of heritage and innovation.

▼ The 2012 Dodge Charger SRT8 is a fully loaded muscle car sedan with a beautiful body and advanced technology.

◀ The superfine interior of the 2012 Charger SRT8. The leather and perforated suede seats are both heated and ventilated, and have the SRT logo embossed in their seatbacks. The dash is also wrapped in leather, while the Harmon Kardon audio system is equipped with nineteen speakers.

▼ The design of the 2012 Dodge Charger is dominated by the aggressive matte black honeycomb grille which incorporates upper and lower air intakes in a single blacked-out frame. Its only decoration is the SRT badge.

◀ The SRT can achieve 0 to 60 miles per hour in the upper 4-second range, with a quarter mile time in the upper 12-second range. The car has a top speed of 175mph.

▲ The 2012 Charger SRT8 Super Bee was a more basic car designed for the core performance enthusiast. Prices for this model option started at $42,625.

▲ The thick-rimmed leather-wrapped performance steering wheel is heated, and equipped with paddle shifters.

▼ The 2012 Dodge Charger Super Bee. The car shared the same top speed as the SRT8.

▲ Prices for the 2012 Charger SRT8 started at $47,425.

▼ The SRT8's split five-spoke twenty-inch forged aluminum wheels are equipped with Brembo four-piston Red calipers and vented and slotted rotors. The wheels are fitted with TP245/45R20 all-season performance tires.

▼ The 2011 and 2012 SRT8s. Both cars developed 470 horsepower from their 6.4 liter hemi V-8s.

◀ Several United States police forces have harnessed the super chasing power of the SRT8.

▲ The SRT8 is equipped with a 6.4 liter hemi V-8 engine. Equipped with Fuel Saver Technology, the challenger powertrain can develop 470 horsepower and 470 pounds-per-feet of torque.

▶ The SRT8's illuminated rev counter.

Index

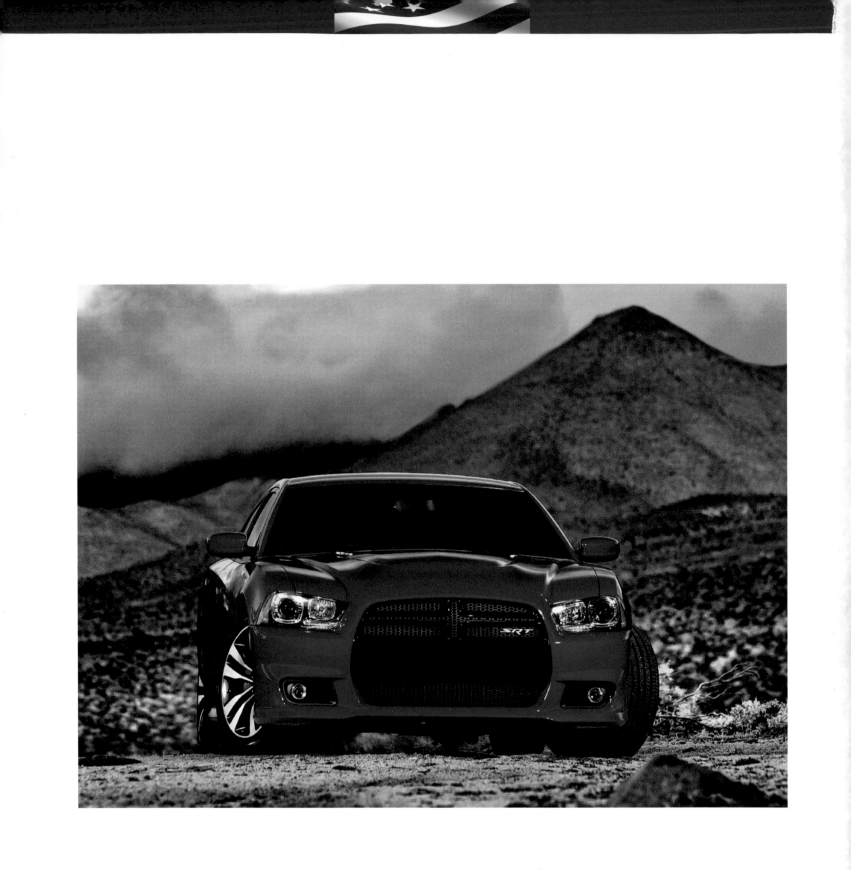